Increasing Learning & Development's Impact through Accreditation

William J. Rothwell · Sandra L. Williams · Aileen G. Zaballero

Increasing Learning & Development's Impact through Accreditation

How to drive-up training quality, employee satisfaction, and ROI

palgrave
macmillan

William J. Rothwell
The Pennsylvania State University
University Park, PA, USA

Sandra L. Williams
Northeastern Illinois University
Chicago, IL, USA

Aileen G. Zaballero
Rothwell & Associates, LLC
State College, PA, USA

ISBN 978-3-030-14003-8 ISBN 978-3-030-14004-5 (eBook)
https://doi.org/10.1007/978-3-030-14004-5

Cover design by Fatima Jamadar

This Palgrave Macmillan imprint is published by the registered company Springer Nature Switzerland AG
The registered company address is: Gewerbestrasse 11, 6330 Cham, Switzerland

William J. Rothwell *dedicates this book to his wife,* **Marcelina V. Rothwell**.
She is the wind beneath his wings.

Sandra L. Williams *dedicates this book in memory of her father,*
Robert C. Williams—*always a supporter of learning & development*
and a strong proponent for continued education.

Aileen G. Zaballero *dedicates this book to her mother,* **Aleli**,
and in loving memory of her father, **Alfredo**, *for their continuous*
support and encouragement.

Foreword

I first met Dr. William J. Rothwell in 2010 when I attended the American Society for Training and Development (now the Association for Talent Development) International Conference and Exposition in Chicago. Dr. Rothwell was there as a speaker and I as an attendee. I made it a point to be in the front row of his session. I wanted the chance to meet one of the most significant people to have such a tremendous impact on my career through his writing, although he did not know it or me. Through his written wisdom and guidance, I was able to successfully secure the accreditation of a comprehensive corporate training program in one try.

When I became Manager of Learning & Organization Development at Rotary International in 2007, I committed to the organization's CEO that I would get Rotary's professional development program accredited to issue Continuing Education Units (CEU). That promise ultimately led me to the International Association for Continuing Education and Training (IACET), the successor organization to the US Department of Education task force that initially developed the CEU. Upon review of IACET's accreditation standard, it became clear that accreditation was going to require some work to thoroughly demonstrate and ensure that the processes for which Rotary conducted needs assessments, designed and developed curriculum, secured highly qualified instructors, delivered instruction, and measured and evaluated results—and the environmental conditions in which all of that occurred—were sound and consistent with best practices.

In preparation for accreditation, I worked with our learning team to establish a number of policies and procedures to govern our learning function. To do so, we consulted with a plethora of resources, including several textbooks that we had used in our graduate programs in learning and development, many of which were authored by Dr. Rothwell. That is how I came to know of him. Most of what I know about learning and development, I learned through his work.

In 2009, a year before my meeting Dr. Rothwell, Rotary's Learning & Organization Development function was fully accredited by IACET, and we have been reaccredited twice since. That remains one of my proudest professional accomplishments.

That accomplishment took a lot of work and a lot of hours of combing through numerous books. This book would have been a godsend for us had it been published back then. It is an excellent compilation of the material we had to seek out separately and is a comprehensive resource that is sure to prove helpful for any learning function seeking accreditation.

Dr. Rothwell, Dr. Sandra Williams (with whom I have the great pleasure of teaching alongside in the Human Resource Development graduate program at Northeastern Illinois University), and Dr. Aileen "Leen" Zaballero did an outstanding job assembling the information needed to not only secure accreditation but also run a world-class learning function. While this book is intended to assist those desiring to seek and prepare for accreditation, I highly recommend it to anyone who is responsible for managing the learning function.

Kristopher J. Newbauer Ed.M, MHRM,
SPHR, SHRM-SCP, CPLP, CPT
Head of Global People & Talent
Rotary International
Chicago, IL, USA

Preface

A few years ago, the authors of this book worked together to conduct research on the status of instructional design in organizations. Many organizations of different kinds and from different locations participated. As the authors carried out the study, they realized that employers were looking for a way to make organization-sponsored training and continuing education more appealing to workers. One way to do that is to pursue accreditation, which may qualify some training initiatives for college credit, as well as ensure that the learning meets the highest standards of quality.

Why Will This Book Be Helpful to You?

When organizational leaders begin to think about pursuing accreditation for their training and continuing education efforts, they inevitably think of many questions that must be addressed early in the process. This book seeks to answer as many of those questions as possible.

What Do We Mean by Training, Learning & Development (L&D), or Workplace Learning and Performance (WLP)?

Training, learning & development (L&D), or workplace learning are terms that are often interchanged, but it is important to understand the distinctions between training, human resource development (HRD), and workplace learning and performance (WLP). Training and development is rooted in the origins of education. However, the field of adult education emerged from the recognition that the learning needs of adults are different from children in that adults are influenced and motivated by their immediate needs and interests. Furthermore, the drive to learn is focused on actual problems that need to be solved (Knowles 1990; Merriam et al. 2007). "Learning is embedded in everything workers do to achieve results on their jobs ... investigating problems, finding solutions, serving customers, and performing work on a daily basis" (see p. 2 in Rothwell 2008). Rothwell further differentiated training to be "something done to others" where knowledge and skills are imposed on them. Training is an episodic "push" strategy aimed at improving job performance and increasing production with a "problem-centered" approach. Learning on the other hand is "something that individuals do on their own" where knowledge and skills are drawn from others. Learning is a "pull" strategy aimed at improving the learner holistically with a "person-centered" approach (see p. 3 in Rothwell 2008). The notion of development is future focused and emphasizes growth opportunities and potential performance. Career development, human resource development (HRD), and organization development emerged to improve individuals, groups, and organizations. Instructional system design (ISD) models evolved to adapt the changing working conditions. "Although training remains the word that most people in the field identify with, the term workplace learning and performance reflects the ways that WLP professionals are trying to contribute more to their organizations by encompassing technology, applying business acumen, demonstrating bottom-line value, and managing talent in organizations" (see p. 31 in Estep 2008).

What We Mean by Terms Used in This Book

The learning and training field uses many different terms, such as 'continuing education of employees', and those terms tend to differ depending upon the background and focus of authors about training. In this text, we use terms most frequently encountered in today's employee education climate, referring to the education of adults within organization settings as *Learning and Development*, rather than *Training*. We also take a practical approach to the terms used in order to focus primarily upon topics of interest to a manager, and where a manager has influence. Clearly, a learning and development manager will have influence over the training activities and creative pursuits within the learning and development department. A line manager, or operations manager, will have influence over the activities of persons on the job and the day-to-day performance of the work that needs to be accomplished for the organization. An executive leader will have influence over the direction of training, the philosophy of employee education held by the organization, and the emphasis placed by the organization on the continuous development of its employees. All learning and development (or training) that occurs is intended to positively influence the actions of workers—those doing the work of the organization—across many levels and throughout the enterprise.

Below, we define certain concepts that apply across jobs and levels of education, and we describe the expectations associated with key training terms as used in this book.

- **Client Outcome**: the resulting impact of an internal change upon the external client experience. The client outcome tends toward greater satisfaction, increased loyalty, fewer returned purchases, etc. These types of client outcomes are increasingly considered true measures of business results and are sometime distinguished from "performance outcomes." Client outcomes differ markedly from training outcomes or training results.
- **Goal**: a measurable expected change, usually carrying a time deadline for achievement. For most organizations, a goal sets a target level for a new result.
- **Instructional Objective**: a planned change in worker/learner behavior at the end of a training session, or upon completion of a training course. The instructional objective will focus upon a change in knowledge, skill or attitude (or all three), and it will be specific in describing the change expected (per individual) at the end of training. The worker/learner behavior change takes place as a result of learning within the training session(s) and is not a result of experience or practice on the job.
- **Learners**: adult individuals actively engaged in personal knowledge, skill, or attitude improvement. Learners in this text generally refer to employees or workers within the organization.
- **Learning and Development Department**: the structured unit within an organization charged with improving worker performance and increasing the organization's talent effectiveness.
- **Learning and Development**: determining and meeting the needs of adult workers within an organization to enhance employee performance, and actively pursuing the development of talent throughout the organization to achieve strategic goals.
- **Performance Objective**: a planned change in worker behavior when he/she returns to the job and performs work in a different manner. This

performance is a result of the person doing the job differently after experiencing training. The individual worker's (or trainee's) ability to actually apply what was learned in training to the job is not entirely due to the training experienced. Line managers have great influence upon a person's ability to achieve performance objectives because line managers have control over the environment of the workplace, the resources available to the worker, and the structure of the work unit. Clear performance objectives can lead to improved work output, but only if the expected new worker performance is made clear to the individual and supported by positive influence from the manager.

- **Performance Outcome or Business Outcome**: the business result of work being conducted differently. This is a measured change in overall productivity of a group of workers, or of a business unit. The performance outcome or business outcome is usually the result of many people doing their jobs more effectively or efficiently after experiencing training. For example, overall yield may be increased, output volumes may be increased, or mistakes may be reduced across the business unit's output.

At the onset of a pursuit of accreditation, or an investigation of the accreditation process, the above terms need first to be clearly defined and described by your learning and development organization. You must be able to distinguish terms used at each step of the learning and development process in order to assure your organization's clarity of purpose, achieve organizational objectives, and ensure effective communication.

What Is Meant by Accreditation in This Book?

There is a long-term trend globally for individuals to pursue certification and for organizations to pursue accreditation. *Certification* means that individuals meet research-based standards that are aligned with competence. *Accreditation* means that the learning and development program meets research-based standards, which is aligned with quality.

Why We Wrote This Book

By writing this book, we wish to inspire people to pursue greater professionalization within the learning and development field. Just as medical doctors go through intensive training to ensure they are qualified and then pursue rigorous licensure requirements, hospitals must also meet rigorous quality standards to ensure they provide the environment for physicians to apply their skills. We believe that learning and development deserves well-qualified practitioners who manage accredited training programs that are aligned with rigorous quality standards.

We also hope this book will serve as a catalyst for the crucial conversations within organizations and between organizations about accrediting learning programs. Do learning programs really meet rigorous standards of quality as identified by best practices from well-researched sources? Do organizations' learning programs match up to learning best practices? We urge you to address these and related questions as you read this book.

How Is This Book Organized?

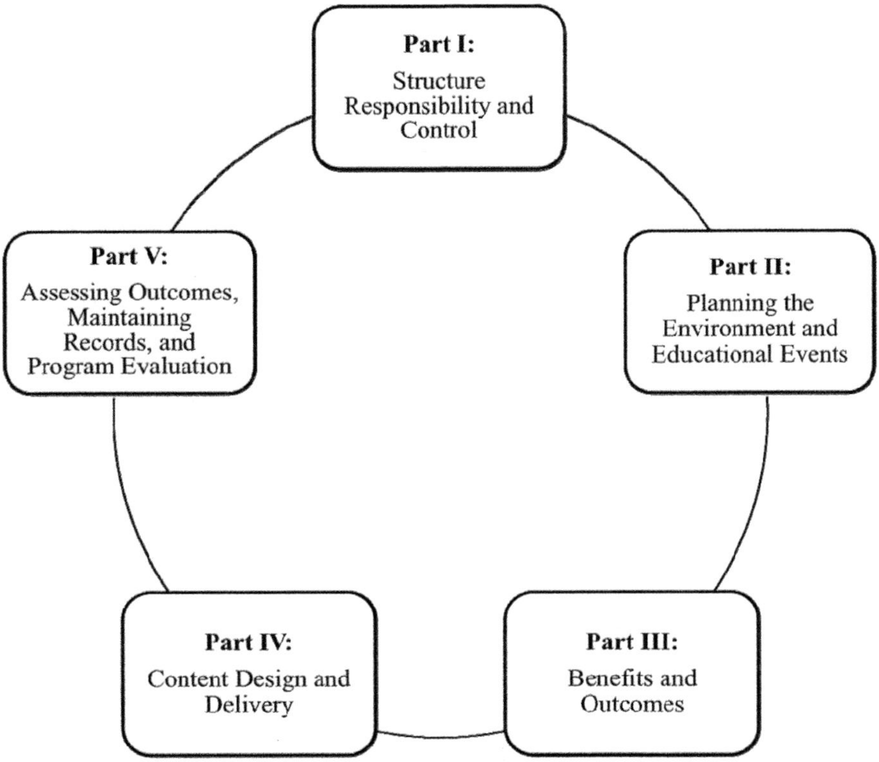

Book Organizer

The **Preface** explains what prompted the authors to write this book and offers a short explanation of terms. Chapter 1, ***Introduction***, provides the rationale for accreditation. The value proposition from practitioners and educators is shared, with a strong emphasis for building a business case for learning and development programs to become accredited. Chapter 1 Supplement includes **The Advance Organizer**, intended to help managers zero-in on learning and development topics so that it is possible to identify only those chapters of primary interest to busy readers.

Part I: ***Structure, Responsibility, and Control*** includes the following chapters. Chapter 2 is entitled ***Align Learning and Development with Organization Mission and Values***. It describes how to link learning to the essential business needs of a sponsoring organization. Chapter 3 is ***Structure for Accountability***. It examines how an organization should structure a learning and development department to meet business needs. Chapter 4 is entitled ***Establish the Learning Environment***. It promotes unique perspectives needed for managing the learning and development function within different organizational settings.

Part II: ***Planning the Environment and Educational Events*** includes the following chapters. Chapter 5 is called ***Plan for Quality and Strategic Learning***. It explains the Learning Blueprint that links learning and development's products to the organization's core knowledge needs. Chapter 6 is entitled ***Is Training the Answer? Assessing Learning Needs***. It describes how to assess the need for learning and development and communicate that need to leaders, thus helping to ensure that the training produced meets organizational strategic goals.

Part III: ***Benefits and Outcomes*** includes three chapters. Chapter 7 examines the ***Intended Learning Outcomes*** of learning and development, distinguishing training program goals and performance objectives. Chapter 8 is ***Who Should Be Involved in Instruction?*** which addresses different roles and skills of persons involved in delivering learning and development effectively. Chapter 9 encourages managers to ***Conduct Learning Events Professionally*** and describes professional integrity, competence, and certifications for learning and development staff.

Part IV: ***Content Design and Delivery*** includes two chapters. Chapter 10 looks at ***Deciding What to Include*** in learning products, or how to write instructional objectives and design learning sessions. Chapter 11 reviews ***Methods to Achieve Consistency*** in learning and development products.

Part V: ***Assessing Outcomes, Maintaining Records, and Program Evaluation*** includes the following chapters. Chapter 12, called ***Learner Feedback and Job Application***, looks at on-the-job application and examines what employees learn. Chapter 13 reviews learning and development ***Program Evaluation and Records***, outlining a process for critical examination of the full learning and development program. And finally, Chapter 14, ***Accreditation Sources***, reviews accreditation bodies and sources of accreditation for learning and development programs.

State College, PA, USA — William J. Rothwell
Chicago, IL, USA — Sandra L. Williams
Atlanta, GA, USA — Aileen G. Zaballero
2019

References

Biech, E., & American Society for Training and Development. (2008). *ASTD handbook for workplace learning professionals*. Alexandria, VA: ASTD Press.

Estep, T. (2008). The evolution of the training profession. In E. Biech (Ed.), *ASTD hand book for workplace learning professionals* (pp. 9–32). Alexandria, VA: ASTD Press.

Knowles, M. (1990). *The adult learner* (4th ed.). Houston, TX: Gulf Publishing.

Merriam, S. B., Caffarella, R. S., & Baumgartner, L. M. (2007). *Learning in adulthood: A comprehensive guide* (3rd ed.). Hoboken, NJ: Wiley.

Rothwell, W. (2008). *Adult learning basics*. Alexandria, VA: ASTD.

Acknowledgements

Completion of a book such as this one requires collaboration and the combined efforts of many parties at several stages of the work. At the conceptualization of this book in 2016, Kris Newbauer proved both inspirational and encouraging of the need for an accreditation-focused guide for managers of learning and development programs. The authors thank him for his encouragement, for his support of the book progress throughout 2017 and 2018, and for his contribution in writing the book's foreword.

Appreciation goes to the many people who participated in interviews about learning and development quality and accreditation. These persons came from various backgrounds, professions, and educations. Collectively, they represent several areas of expertise within the field of talent development and accreditation. Their quotes are used throughout the book as the "business case for accreditation." These contributions add a qualitative depth of expression for our reader, enabling readers to understand the significance of accreditation in learning and development efforts from a practical perspective. Interviewed contributors included: Reg Bonfoco; Jessica Burnett; Scott Critchfield; Peter Finn; Dr. Arthur Holder; Dr. Maureen C. Jones; Laureen Kaczmarek; Dr. Karen LaMarsh; Dr. J. Kevin Perry; Clyde Seepersad; Dr. Kyle Schiefelbein-Guerrero; and two anonymous contributors.

We are also sincerely grateful to those who served as reviewers of the manuscript pre-publication: Peter Finn, Mark Hurley, Kris Newbauer, and Joe McClary. Insights provided from these four reviewers helped the book to focus on managers as readers and to offer examples useful to managers of learning and development programs.

Contents

About the Authors

William J. Rothwell, Ph.D., SPHR, SHRM-SCP, CPLP Fellow is President of Rothwell & Associates, Inc. and Rothwell & Associates, LLC (see www.rothwellandassociates.com). He is also a Professor of the Workforce Education and Development program, Department of Learning and Performance Systems, at the Pennsylvania State University, University Park campus. He has authored, co-authored, edited, or co-edited 300 books, book chapters, and articles—including 111 books.

Before arriving at Penn State in 1993, he had 20 years of work experience as a Director of Training, HR and Organization Development in government and in business. He has also worked as a consultant for numerous multinational corporations—including Motorola China, General Motors, Ford, and many others. In 2012, he earned ASTD's prestigious Distinguished Contribution to Workplace Learning and Performance Award, and in 2013, ASTD honored him by naming him as a Certified Professional in Learning and Performance (CPLP) Fellow. In 2014, he was given the Asia-Pacific International Personality Brand Laureate Award (see www.thebrandlaureate.com/awards/ibp_bpa.php). He was the first US citizen named a Certified Training and Development Professional (CTDP) by the Canadian Society for Training and Development in 2004.

His recent books include *Innovation Leadership* (Routledge, 2018), *Improving Human Performance, 3rd ed.* (Routledge, 2018), *Evaluating Organization Development: How to Ensure and Sustain the Successful Transformation* (CRC Press, 2017), *Marketing Organization Development Consulting: A How-To Guide for OD Consultants* (CRC Press, 2017), *Assessment and Diagnosis for Organization Development: Powerful Tools and Perspectives for the OD practitioner*

(CRC Press, 2017), *Community College Leaders on Workforce Development* (Rowman & Littlefield, 2017), *Organization Development in Practice* (ODNETWORK, 2016), *Mastering the Instructional Design Process, 5th ed.* (Wiley, 2016), *Effective Succession Planning, 5th ed.* (Amacom, 2015), *Practicing Organization Development, 4th ed.* (Wiley, 2015), *The Leader's Daily Role in Talent Management* (McGraw-Hill, 2015), *Beyond Training and Development, 3rd ed.* (HRD Press, 2015), *Career Planning and Succession Management, 2nd ed.* (Praeger, 2015), *Organization Development Fundamentals: Managing Strategic Change* (ATD Press, 2015), *The Competency Toolkit, 2 vols, 2nd ed.* (HRD Press, 2015), *Creating Engaged Employees: It's Worth the Investment* (ATD Press, 2014), *Optimizing Talent in the Federal Workforce* (Management Concepts, 2014), *Performance Consulting* (Wiley, 2014), the *ASTD Competency Study: The Training and Development Profession Redefined* (ASTD, 2013), *Becoming An Effective Mentoring Leader: Proven Strategies for Building Excellence in Your Organization* (McGraw-Hill, 2013), *Talent Management: A Step-by-Step Action-Oriented Approach Based on Best Practice* (HRD Press, 2012), the edited three-volume *Encyclopedia of Human Resource Management* (Wiley/Pfeiffer, 2012), *Lean But Agile: Rethink Workforce Planning and Gain a True Competitive Advantage* (Amacom, 2012), *Invaluable Knowledge: Securing Your Company's Technical Expertise-Recruiting and Retaining Top Talent, Transferring Technical Knowledge, Engaging High Performers* (Amacom, 2011), *Competency-Based Training Basics* (ASTD Press, 2010), *Effective Succession Planning: Ensuring Leadership Continuity and Building Talent from Within, 4th ed.* (Amacom, 2010), *Practicing Organization Development, 3rd ed.* (Pfeiffer, 2009), *Basics of Adult Learning* (ASTD, 2009), *HR Transformation* (Davies-Black, 2008), *Working Longer: New Strategies for Managing, Training, and Retaining Older Employees* (Amacom, 2008), and *Cases in Government Succession Planning: Action-Oriented Strategies for Public-Sector Human Capital Management, Workforce Planning, Succession Planning, and Talent Management* (HRD Press, 2008). To learn more about William Rotwhell, visit the following wiki site www.wikipedia.org/wiki/William_J._Rothwell. He can be reached by email at WJRothwell@yahoo.com and by phone at 814-863-2581. He is at 647 Berkshire Drive, State College, PA 16803.

Sandra L. Williams, M.B.A., Ph.D. is Associate Professor and Program Coordinator of the Human Resource Development Program, Department of Literacy, Leadership and Development, at Northeastern Illinois University, Chicago, IL, where she also serves as the Graduate Student Advisor in Human Resource Development. Her work is a unique blend of business consulting, training program development, and current research in the human resource development field.

Before moving into academia, Dr. Williams gained practical experience in management and training through 20 years as a Senior Vice President, Managing Director, and Training Manager in the banking and finance industry, holding positions at Continental Illinois National Bank and Trust Company of Illinois and Bank of America. She also operated her own business within the talent development field as a partner in Sharedecisions, LLC.

Dr. Williams creates and delivers training programs that offer practical tools in leadership, mentoring, and corporate responsibility. Topics include Ethics for Leaders, Trust Building in Higher Education, Trust in the Workplace, Leading with Integrity, and Strategic Responsibility. As a consultant, she designs and facilitates customized training programs for businesses, service organizations, and higher education institutions. She is the creator of several values-based ethics training programs offered to commercial organizations by the Better Business Bureau of Chicago called: Ethics for Business Success. Former clients include Bank of America, True Value Corporation, Deloitte and Touche, the Illinois CPA Society, Integritas Institute, the Society of Corporate Compliance and Ethics, Northeastern Illinois Foundation, and the Union League Club of Chicago.

Dr. Williams' written work focuses on e-mentoring, trust in the workplace, and case studies in HRD consulting and assessment. She has published over 30 articles and proceedings, written 16 training guides and workbooks for managers, and has made over 60 presentations to executives, administrators, and researchers. Her written work has been published in research journals, management magazines, and practitioner blog sites, including the *Journal of Organizational Excellence*, the *International Journal of Evidence Based Coaching and Mentoring*, *Business Horizons Journal*, *Human Resource Development International*, *New Horizons in Adult Education and Human Resource Development*, *Corporate Responsibility Officer*, *Human Resource Management Perspectives*, and the *Association for Talent Development* Web site.

As an educator, Dr. Williams teaches courses in HRD and the Organization, Business Writing in HRD, Instructional Design, Instructional Techniques and Technologies, and Consulting in Human Resource Development. She also mentors students in Internships and Practicums in the Human Resource Development program at Northeastern Illinois University. As program coordinator, she is responsible for the undergraduate and graduate curricula in HRD as well as the faculty and teaching professionals within the program, which consists of 275–300 students and 12 faculty members.

Dr. Williams is also a farmer and was awarded the Farm Credit 100 Fresh Perspectives Honoree Award for sustainability in natural resources by First Farm Credit Services in 2016. She can be reached at s-williams24@neiu.edu or 773.442.5378. She is located at #3017 Goodwin College of Education, Northeastern Illinois University, 5500 N. St. Louis Avenue, Chicago, IL 60625-4699.

Aileen G. Zaballero, Ph.D., CPLP is a senior partner of Rothwell & Associates with a dual-title Ph.D. in Workforce Education and Comparative International Education from The Pennsylvania State University. She is a Certified Professional in Learning and Performance (CPLP) with more than 20 years of experience in the learning and development field.

Aileen was part of the R&A research team with Dr. Angela Stopper and led by Dr. William J. Rothwell that explored talent development from a global perspective. Partnered with ATD, 31 industry thought-leaders from around the world were interviewed and 1500 talent development professionals from Asia, Europe, Latin America, Middle East, and United States were surveyed. The purpose of this research was to describe the components of talent development that organizations can use to build their own individualized talent development structures. An outcome of the research is ATD's Talent Development Framework. This framework is a guide that allows organizations to rearrange, remove, and add functions to fit their needs.

Aileen was also part of the Penn State research team that developed a competency model and career map for the Advanced Commercial Building Workforce, utilizing the US Department of Labor's competency model framework and aligning it with the Department of Energy's Better Buildings Workforce Guidelines. The goal of this project was to produce an easy-to-understand representation of specified job titles and its associated credentials that will support targeted and effective investments in education and training in response to the demand for a skilled and qualified workforce. The outcome of this research is the *Energy: Advanced Commercial Buildings Competency Model* published on the US DOL's Competency Model Clearinghouse.

Aileen's additional works include training the DACUM process for facilitators at the National Occupational Competency Testing Institute; examining the competencies and challenges of instructional designers; and supporting Curacao's Ministry of Education to shift to a competency-based education. Aileen co-authored a book chapter titled, *The Participation of Women as Leaders in South and Southeast Asia: A Comparative Analysis in India, Malaysia, and Philippines* (2015, Information Age Publishing,

Inc.); co-edited and co-authored *Optimizing Talent in the Federal Workforce* (2014, Management Concepts); and co-authored a chapter in *Organization Development Fundamentals: Managing Strategic Change* (2014, ASTD Press); authored and co-authored chapters in *Performance Consulting-Applying Performance Improvement* (2013, John Wiley & Sons); and co-edited *The Encyclopedia of Human Resource Management Volume 2: HR Forms & Job Aids* (2012, John Wiley & Sons). She can be reached at agz@rothwellandassociates.com or 702-296-7556. She is at 19 Colonnade Way Ste 124 State College, PA 16803.

List of Figures

List of Tables

1

Introduction

The demographic changes in today's workforce are forcing organizations to focus on knowledge transfer, rather than training for job performance. Not only is the knowledge of matured workers leaving the workplace rapidly, but newer and younger workers are also demanding immediate access to information. Products and services are sold electronically, installed technologically, and serviced virtually—with all the work conducted by multiple generations dispersed around the world. The global nature of customer access is increasing the need for cross-cultural and cross-functional skills within organizations. The competitive business environment today can be defined as a digital economy that is driven by a volatile, uncertain, complex, and ambiguous (VUCA) world. "In response to disruption, organizations are increasingly pioneering new models, frameworks, methods, structures and processes to engage with the customer" (see pp. 1–2 in Cousins 2018), which creates a need to build a "learning agile and future ready-workplace" (see p. 20 in Raghuramapatruni and Kosuri 2017).

Organizations are responding with learning interventions which are worker-driven, where employees are encouraged to create a portfolio of skills. Because individuals now have many different jobs and many different employers, organizations are no longer promising lifelong employment security, but are promoting lifelong learning. Workers of all generations are seeking rapid information and portable skills, not long-term experiences or organizational support. This shift in the relationship between the employer and the worker "emphasizes the need for workers to build

W. J. Rothwell et al., *Increasing Learning & Development's Impact through Accreditation*,
https://doi.org/10.1007/978-3-030-14004-5_1

and document their skills and special knowledge as a basis for continued employability" (see p. 69 in Shaffer and Zalewski 2011).

All of these factors put considerable pressure on employee learning and development (L&D). Programs must be accurate, content sustainable, and technologically flexible. Additionally, the training programs must take responsibility to meet both current worker and strategic organizational expectations while delivering practical, adaptable, and transferable learning outcomes that update skills and specialized knowledge.

Within this melee of expectations, how can a L&D program assure its relevance to a business, institution, government, or professional association? How can it meet strategic objectives? How can training management assure quality both in knowledge transfer and in content relevancy? What process or authority can guarantee the quality, financial return, and customer service benefits?

1.1 Rationale for Accreditation

One answer lies in accreditation. Accreditation is a process of independent attestation to the adherence of standards that meet the requirements of a profession. Accreditation demonstrates "an effective form of professional control that can have a positive impact on values and organizational culture" (Pomey 2002; Pomey et al. 2004; see p. 147 in Segouin 1998 as cited by Paccioni et al. 2008). Accreditation is a planning and control process that ensures quality, professional competence, and accountability.

Unfortunately, adult education—which extends past formal schooling—has been haphazard in its design and implementation. Furthermore, workplace training has lacked rigor in its standards of program planning, production, and assessment. While organizations worldwide spend billions of dollars on workforce education, there remain few measures of quality consistency within the training world. However, accreditation can ensure quality control. In addition to quality, accreditation is valuable for several reasons, as summarized in Table 1.1.

Accreditation is a needed element within the L&D profession. There is a vast array of offerings and training products in the marketplace, many of which are indistinguishable from a quality standpoint. Accreditation helps to make that quality distinction possible. Completing the accreditation process is not mandatory for L&D departments. However, accreditation does present a strong value proposition. Building a business case for accreditation informs and educates

Table 1.1 Value of accreditation—quotes from practitioners and educators

Key value	Quote	Practitioner/educator	Organization/position
Accountability, Continuous improvement, Structure, Efficiencies, Reflective process	*Accreditation provides accountability for our programs. Being vetted by another organization in a very rigorous way to confirm we met the standards was really a huge value for us. It added value to our membership and with our corporate partners and university partners, which added an external value. From a more intrinsic value, it forced us to be much more consistent in the way we were developing programs and required a certain amount of uniformity. It created a lot of efficiencies and a continuous improvement structure that included a process of reflection. It fits into our overall strategic plan of being the gold standard in terms of leadership programs, diversity and inclusion programs for our engineers.*	**Peter Finn**	Society of Women Engineers (SWE) Deputy Executive Director and Chief Learning Officer
Accountability	*Among my colleagues, within my inner circle at (Engineering Firm) we all pretty much agreed that having a third party review our program ensures accountability, and is very valuable.*	Anonymous	Corporate Learning and Development/ CEU Program Lead
Accountability	*The fundamental value of accreditation means that students have a reason to trust you. They know you've got a stamp of approval. It also provides external accountability. When you have an accreditation review, you've got to explain why you're doing it that way. You've got to be prepared to justify it.*	**Dr. Arthur Holder**	Graduate Theological Union Accreditation Liaison Officer (ALO)

(continued)

Table 1.1 (continued)

Key value	Quote	Practitioner/educator	Organization/ position
Credibility	*Accreditation provides credibility in the marketplace and internally. Once we achieved our accreditation, we had a leg up in the market place among our competitors and certainly had a more appealing story to tell our customers or prospective customers. It also elevated our credibility internally with our leadership in that we're now recognized by a major accrediting body.*	**Dr. J. Kevin Perry**	Society of Automotive Engineers (SAE) International Director, Professional Development
Competitive advantage	*Having your organization accredited by international organization truly does give that organization a competitive advantage when it comes to training. Employees know that when they are going to be learning something that is beneficial and will help them in their careers. What I find is a lot of organizations who don't go through the accreditation process often just throw things together, and their programs often have no real impact.*	**Reg Bonfoco**	Canadian Financial Securities Company Continuing Education Specialist
CEU designation	*Having the CEU designations sets you apart from those that could just be obtained online. The value of continuing education is so critical and is essential to stay current on how your industry or segment has changed.*	**Scott A. Critchfield, CFP**	Coach Learning Professional

(continued)

Table 1.1 (continued)

Key value	Quote	Practitioner/educator	Organization/ position
CEU designation, Legitimacy	*A course accredited by a legitimate organization only provides, what I like to refer to as, 'teeth to the program' that is being delivered. Having something accredited through an organization is really to promote the fact that the programs that are developed and delivered do meet the international standard for learning. So, what that does is it actually helps in promoting the course that people are going to be taking and also lets them know that it has met very rigorous standards in order to qualify for the CEU.*	**Reg Bonfoco**	Canadian Financial Securities Company Continuing Education Specialist
Framework/ guideline	*Accreditation was helpful because it provided a framework as we moved forward to a comprehensive distance education and provided a guideline for developing learning communities. I tend to go back to the standard sometimes when I'm looking for language around (digital learning) ... and the accreditation standards certainly provides the language to use.*	**Dr. Kyle Schiefelbein-Guerrero**	Graduate Theological Union Director of Digital Learning
Guidelines/ roadmap	*Accreditation provided a set of rules by which we operate our program. It removed all of the debate of 'maybe we should do this'/ 'maybe we should do it that way'. It allowed us to say or refer to the standard, and the standard is the roadmap ... the guiding light that makes it much clearer to the team about how to conduct the program.*	**Dr. J. Kevin Perry**	Society of Automotive Engineers (SAE) International Director, Professional Development

(continued)

Table 1.1 (continued)

Key value	Quote	Practitioner/educator	Organization/ position
Integrity, Impactful, Optimal outcomes	*Our certifications are globally accepted certifications and are our core business, so it was critical for us to ensure global integrity and that the training, to prepare candidates for our certifications aligned to the value of the certifications globally. We really wanted to make sure that our training solutions are impactful and have optimal outcomes.*	**Jessica Burnett**	ISACA Senior Product Manager
Marketability	*The value of accreditation from a marketing perspective—helped us really distill our marketing message of why you should care that we're accredited because it really allowed us to speak to the fact that you know: we really understand the needs analysis; we really think about learning styles; we really think about appropriate ways to evaluate skills; we think about the breadth of a quiz relative to the content.*	**Clyde Seepersad**	Linux Foundation General Manager, Training and Certification
Quality	*We were really focused on achieving a consistent quality product in the market.*	**Laureen Kaczmarek**	ISACA Senior Director, Product Development and Content Strategy
Quality improvement	*The philosophy of the accreditation process is all about improvement, specifically quality improvement.*	**Dr. Maureen C. Jones**	The Pennsylvania State University Senior Instructor and Teaching Assistant Professor for the Master of Health Administration and Accreditation Coordinator for the MHA Programs
Qualified trainers	*We felt that by going through and requiring accreditation for trainers ensures that: 1] they truly were subject matter experts in the content, and; 2] that they were skilled in the actual facilitating of training courses.*	**Laureen Kaczmarek**	ISACA Senior Director, Product Development and Content Strategy

decision-makers, and it starts with asking yourself: "*What's in accreditation for me?*" and more importantly, "*What's in it for my organization?*" and "*How does accreditation contribute to my organization?*" Without establishing a sound business case, key decision-makers cannot advocate for its value. Buy-in will be minimal and resources, specifically financial resources, will be allocated elsewhere, as illustrated below.

> *We followed standards for accreditation and began the initial application … but we stopped when the biggest check was due. Because it actually was not clear for our audience what the business value is for having our programs accredited. My assumption was … potential customers prefer an accredited provider to a non-accredited provider. But it turns out that in this case, they don't prefer accreditation … because they don't know, they don't understand what the implications are. They've never seen an accredited provider. They have never seen the accreditation process … the business value was not clear. We have to spend more time educating different industry sectors about why they should care about accreditation.*
>
> –**Clyde Seepersad**
> *Linux Foundation*
> *General Manager,*
> *Training & Certification*

1.2 Business Case

> *Business case is huge because without it … you're not going to have a chance.*
>
> –**Peter Finn**
> *Society of Women Engineers*
> *Deputy Executive Director and Chief Learning Officer*

Organizations of many types and sizes face tremendous risks to continuity and sustainability. The longevity of a business life is not guaranteed. Organizations often endure extreme conditions to bring quality product or services to members, clients, customers, or other stakeholders. Risks are faced and a return is sought in order to continue to produce that product or provide that service. Accredited internal learning helps the business production case because it provides a rationale and an effective way of allocating limited resources. The business case provides the means of determining which learning initiatives should be pursued—and for how long. The business case for achieving accreditation of the L&D program involves the following combination of benefits:

- Today's current risk is reduced.
- Tomorrow's risks can be avoided.
- Adaptation to change is enhanced.
- People cost is reduced.
- Innovation becomes a constant.
- A return on investment (ROI) can be calculated.

1.2.1 Today's Risk Reduced

Organizations with operations that serve customers with quality, manufacture a product, or offer consulting guidance are all at risk today from errors, misjudgments, and mistakes. This risk of business operation is reduced through accredited L&D efforts. Safety can be improved, accidents mitigated, and disasters avoided through training aligned with industry regulations and standards of practice. Teaching employees to identify risks, operate safely, and properly mitigate critical incidents is a significant risk reduction to the operation. Reducing that risk literally enables the organization to stay in business.

1.2.2 Tomorrow's Risk Avoided

As organizations serve customers and benefit communities, expectations for consistency and applicability rise. Thus, in order to meet client and community expectations, an organization must continually improve the product it makes or enhance the services it offers. Accreditation forces L&D efforts to focus on knowledge enhancement, ensure skill improvement, or consider attitude changes of various stakeholders. Accredited training teaches employees to meet future marketplace needs through the talents they develop by setting learning goals for their performance. The "generic education" approach to training is inadequate and should be avoided. Rather—via accreditation—specific job-related skills are developed in employees to anticipate demand and meet client and community expectations.

1.2.3 Adapt to External Pressures to Change and Re-size

Organizations face pressure from the outside—external drivers of information, technology, logistics, and globalization. Firms must not only react to those drivers but also must anticipate and prepare for the changes which those drivers initiate. Readying an organization to make change continually is far-sighted, and it requires a workforce that is flexible and adaptable.

Accredited training provides the organization with a constant "heads up" attitude and an ability to see further faster. Accreditation sponsors strategic skills in your people—employees capable of seeing change on the horizon, readying the enterprise for a re-scaling, and managing the change as it arises. Accreditation accomplishes this because it forces an examination throughout the enterprise—a scoping of the need for a higher order of thinking, visioning, and combining. Organizations that have consistent quality training and robust learning processes are naturally more scalable than organizations that do not. These organizations have testified that achieving accreditation has made size and scale change within their organizations easier and more productive.

1.2.4 Reduce Direct People Costs

Leaders know that the few resources to manage any operation are time, money, and people. Economics tells us that if any one of those resources can be reduced, costs decrease, and profits improve. A higher return is earned from the revenue stream. In the people resource area, any improvement in efficiency or effectiveness reduces the cost of labor or personnel performance. Thus, from an economic standpoint, reducing the cost of labor by increasing the productive capacity of your internal talent decreases the total cost of making your product or providing service. Therefore, the return to the firm becomes greater. Accreditation causes a greater return to the organization, which can be calibrated through carefully defined evaluation standards.

1.2.5 Always Innovate

The benefit and reduced cost resulting from accreditation arises simply from always innovating, always producing more effectively, or always providing service more efficiently. Accreditation brings the organization its own sense of "always"—a constancy of betterment and innovation. This constancy of betterment comes from accredited L&D being grounded in continual improvement.

Just like continually re-calibrating a factory machine, or Web site, to produce goods or information more accurately, accreditation forces a constant recalibration and fine-tuning of the people aspect of your enterprise. Employees can think more productively or process information more astutely because L&D programs are always challenging them to do so. This is fine-tuning the "people machine" within your workplace. Accreditation does this by causing learning within your organization to be systematic. Learning becomes the "norm" of the organization—not a factor dependent upon the sponsorship of one executive leader. Learning causes innovation throughout the organization by driving new ideas, and new ways to do things—and this drives bottom-line results.

1.2.6 Attract Workers You Want

Accreditation assures employees that new skills or knowledge gained is verified and portable. This is a benefit to employees in their lifelong learning—something that is especially attractive to today's millennial workers who like personal attention. Today's employees want to enhance their work skills through continued education. They also want that continued education to have up-scaling benefits. As a provider of quality training guaranteed through accreditation, your organization becomes the attractive employer of choice because the learning protocols have definable and lifelong benefits.

Accreditation is an investment that presents the value proposition for the participants (learners), the organization, and the customers. Without adequate consideration for the value of accreditation, key problems could arise—specifically the allocation of resources to retain skilled workers.

> *At first, leadership did not necessarily see the need for accreditation of our in-house L&D organization. To demonstrate the business case, I researched the number of certified employees and their associated certification requirements for annual continuing education units (CEUs), then calculated the costs for these employees to take an external course versus an internal course. We have a large professional population across a number of disciplines with a variety of certifications, such as Professional Engineer, Certified Safety Professional and Certified Industrial Hygienist. These certifications all require annual CEUs to maintain certification. Although we provide in-house training on proprietary processes, procedures, equipment, methodologies, and scientific research findings used in our business; our employees had to go outside of the company to get additional training just to receive their CEUs. Now, with accreditation, we can support our professional employees by providing CEUs through in-house training, precluding the need for them to take additional external courses, thus containing training dollars inside the company.*
>
> ***–Anonymous***
> *Multi-National Energy Corporation*
> *Technical Learning & Development Manager*

1.3 Conclusion

Grounded in methods for continuous improvement, accreditation improves the overall quality of learning to optimize the potential talents of your organization. Employees can identify and reduce risks more effectively, can produce more efficiently, which increases returns, and can adapt to organizational scale changes. Further, workers will see your organization as an employer of choice because of the quality of ongoing individual learning (which accreditation guarantees). Workers will seek you out as an employer and remain longer with your firm, because of the lifelong learning you provide.

This book covers two purposes: promote accreditation as a proof of training value and offer principles for quality learning program structure, delivery, and improvement, such that accreditation can be achieved. The accreditation topic will be approached from a value perspective, with an emphasis on the quality of learning and development programs, staff professionalism, and learner impact.

Manager Tips

Below are suggested value propositions for accreditation. These can be used, as applicable, to defend your efforts for accreditation, and to promote the benefits of accreditation to executives and key decision-makers.

A. Accreditation will reduce people costs by increasing the productive capacity of your existing talent—thus improving your bottom line.
B. Accreditation ensures a continuous learning model that is grounded in best practices, an attractive offering to millennial workers.
C. Accreditation promotes innovation and verifies a strong commitment to continuous improvement in both product and service.
D. Accreditation validates the claim of qualified and competent personnel within your organization.
E. Accreditation ensures a consistent approach to instructional design and training delivery—and the learner experience. Learning is not haphazard.

F. Accreditation demonstrates that all your learning and development programs meet standardized quality requirements and protocols.
G. Accreditation signifies to learners that they are receiving high quality, reputable training that has undergone a rigorous design process by skilled learning and development professionals.
H. Without accreditation, the learning and development program risks continued plodding down a path of ignorance, talent depletion, and economic drain.

Supplement

Before you dive right into the main chapters, take a moment to assess your learning and development program. Complete *Supplement Tool 1A—The Advanced Organizer*. Use it as a diagnostic tool to help you assess what you most want to know about accreditation for learning programs—and where you can find it in this book—fast.

Supplement Tool 1A: *The Advanced Organizer*

Directions: Read each item in the Organizer below. Circle a *True (T)*, a *Not Applicable (N/A)*, or *False (F)* in the left column opposite each item. Spend about 10 minutes on the Organizer. Be honest! Think of learning and development in your organization as you would like it to be—not what some expert says it is, or what you think your organization is presently doing. When you finish, score and interpret the results using the instructions appearing at the end of the Organizer. Then be prepared to share your responses with others you know to help you think about what you most want to learn about accreditation for the training and continuing education experiences offered by your organization. If you would like to learn more about one topic below, refer to the number in the right column to find the chapter in this book in which the subject is discussed.

Questions:

Circle your response for each item below	My learning and development organization takes steps to...	Chapter which covers the topic
T N/A F	Align learning and development with the organization's mission and values	2
T N/A F	Structure learning and development in the organization to ensure accountability	3
T N/A F	Manage the learning and development function effectively	4
T N/A F	Have a strategic plan for learning and development	5
T N/A F	Assess the needs of the learners to determine the best solution	6
T N/A F	Clarify the desired outcomes for learning and development programs	7
T N/A F	Clarify who is qualified to be involved in delivering learning interventions	8
T N/A F	Establish standards for effective instructional delivery	9
T N/A F	Decide what is essential to address in learning and development programs	10

Circle your response for each item below	My learning and development organization takes steps to…	Chapter which covers the topic
T N/A F	Ensure consistency across learning and development programs so that learners in one program receive treatment comparable to learners in other, similar programs	11
T N/A F	Take steps to ensure that learning transfers effectively back to the job and improves job performance	12
T N/A F	Have complete and required records and ways to ensure effective program evaluation	13
T N/A F	Reference resources to become accredited	14

____________________ **Total**

***Interpretation of Results*:**
Give yourself *1 point for each T* and a *0 for each F or N/A* listed above. Total the points from the *T* column and place the sum in the line opposite to the word **Total** above. Then interpret your score as follows:

13–10 points	*Congratulations! Give your organization grade of A* Your organization is ready to pursue training accreditation
9–8 points	*Give your organization a grade of B* Your organization is ahead of most organizations in preparing to pursue training accreditation
7–6 points	*Give your organization a grade of C* Your organization is about average, and that means your organization should take steps to improve its training efforts if there is desire to pursue accreditation for training
5–3 points	*Give your organization a grade of D* Your organization is below average. That means you need to play catch up if your organization is to pursue accreditation for training
2–0 points	*Give your organization a failing grade* Take immediate steps to improve how well your organization manages training if there is a desire to seek accreditation for the organization's training

References and Additional Resources

Cousins, B. (2018). Design thinking: Organiza tional learning in VUCA environments. *Academy of Strategic Management Journal, 17*(2), 1–18.

Paccioni, A., Sicotte, C., & Champagne, F. (2008). Accreditation: A cultural control strategy. *International Journal of Health Care Quality Assurance, 21*(2), 146–158.

Pomey, M.-P. (2002). *Preparing for accreditation: A tool for organizational change?* Ph.D. Thesis, Department of Health Administration, University of Montreal, Montreal.

Pomey, M.-P., Contandriopoulos, A. P., François, P., & Bertrand, D. (2004). Accreditation: A tool for organizational change in hospitals? *International Journal of Quality Health Care Assurance, 17*(3), 113–124.

Raghuramapatruni, R., & Kosuri, S. R. (2017). The straits of success in a VUCA world. *IOSR Journal of Business and Management (IOSR-JBM)*. e-ISSN 2278-487X, p-ISSN 2319-7668, 16–22.

Segouin, C. (1998). *Accreditation of health facilities: From international experience to French application*. Paris: Doin Publishers.

Shaffer, L. S., & Zalewski, J. M. (2011). Career advising in a VUCA environment. *NACADA Journal, 31*(1), 64–74.

Part I

Structure Responsibility and Control

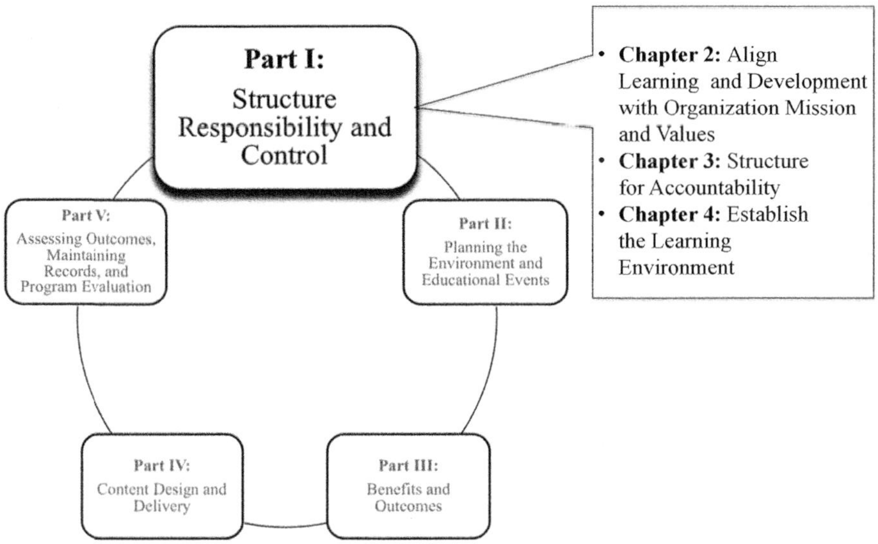

Fig. 1 Chapter organizer

Accreditation benefits organizations, training managers, and learning and development (L&D) efforts because it registers measured improvement in the skills and talents of employees. Leaders can be assured that employee training aligns with the strategic goals of the organization, thereby helping the organization to challenge its competitors and succeed in its mission. Accreditation also distinguishes the organization as "unique" in its field and differentiates it among its challengers and customers. For the learning and development manager, accreditation assures adult learning quality—identifying the program content as deep within its field and establishing the program as the "standard-bearer" for the respective profession. This quality assurance, achieved and sustained through accreditation, provides credibility to learners and elevates the program above the external workforce. Finally, accreditation assures the employee of commitment to his/her continued development and knowledge creation. Accredited training is transferable education, which is highly valued by the mobile, global worker of today. Thus, accreditation aids the organization, training management, and employees. This comprehensive view of the learning profession provides training practitioners with authority to both alter and sustain the worker's learning today and to enable talent growth for tomorrow. The chapters in Part I will focus on: aligning training programs with an organization's strategy, mission, and values to assure direction and focus in the employee's education (Chapter 2, "Align Learning and Development with Organization Mission and Values"); developing a results-driven training unit or department within the organization (Chapter 3, "Structure for Accountability"); and managing training programs to support talent development throughout all business units (Chapter 4, "Establish the Learning Environment").

2

Align Learning and Development with Organization Mission and Values

A learning and development program's mission and values are its grounding message. Together, the mission and values form the foundation upon which employee learning resides. Mission and values are based upon vision and interwoven into strategy, but each also needs to stand alone as distinct messages, because they make the training unique. In practice, a Mission and Values Statement is one document that contains both messages.

2.1 Vision, Mission, and Values as Strategy

Organizations operating as corporations, family-owned businesses, nonprofit endeavors, municipalities, or associations hold mental images of the very long-term service of the organization and its benefit to society. This is called the organization's Vision. The vision for the enterprise may or may not be written down on paper, but it represents an ideal for what the organization strives to become—twenty or more years in the future. Visions are long-term idealizations of future benefits to others, which are hoped to be sustainable. Visions include such ideals as, secure living, grounded faith, a wholesome animal kingdom, safe transportation, physical health for all humans, and many more. Visions set the very long-term picture of the organization's endeavor. The following is an example of a vision statement.

W. J. Rothwell et al., *Increasing Learning & Development's Impact through Accreditation*,
https://doi.org/10.1007/978-3-030-14004-5_2

Rotary International's Global People & Talent team's vision statement

"Leading the way to an extraordinary employee experience"

Source: *Kristopher J. Newbauer, Ed.M, MHRM, SPHR, SHRM-SCP, CPLP, CPT Head of Global People & Talent of Rotary International.*

The mission of the organization is a statement which sets forth the enterprise's practical purpose for today and tomorrow. The mission creates the intermediate focus and purpose of the organization—leading to what it will be like in the future. The mission is a simple statement of why the organization exists (to produce goods or provide services) and what external need it serves in the marketplace today (whom it provides products or services for). The mission is a concrete statement that can be understood by many and sets forth the direction of the organization based upon its current and expected environment.

Rotary International's Global People & Talent team's mission statement

Our passion is people: Helping employees gives us our greatest satisfaction. That is why we support, empower, and develop them to their fullest potential so that they may make positive and lasting contributions to Rotary and its Secretariat.

Source: *Kristopher J. Newbauer, Ed.M, MHRM, SPHR, SHRM-SCP, CPLP, CPT Head of Global People & Talent of Rotary International.*

When written down and communicated, both the vision and the mission of the organization are rallying points for workers and provide a stimulus for employee actions. Ideally, the Mission Statement excites enthusiasm and motivates people within the organization to make the future, the envisioned state, become a reality. Decision-makers ponder which actions to undertake in the current and intermediate-term, and which are aligned with the mission, to ensure the vision becomes a reality for the whole organization.

> *Your mission provides you milestones. Accreditation asks: what do we need to do in learning to get various parts to keep our mission pushing forward?*
>
> **–Dr. Kyle Schiefelbein-Guerrero**
> *Graduate Theological Union*
> *Director of Digital Learning*

Values for the organization are descriptions of expected behaviors to be applied at work by members inside the organization. Values depict how we should behave toward one another at work (Meglino & Ravlin, 1998). Values for each organization are intrinsic nuances to its culture and help to describe behaviors to be taken by members when executing the mission. Values are natural human conditions which exist in every culture and which we collectively create inside an organization in order to rely upon one another. At work, values depict the expected behaviors of all members—executives, managers, supervisors, associates, and line employees. A few key values in every organization describe the behaviors that everyone relies upon, and which help to guide members with integrity in their actions (Palazzo, 2007). Values integrate the purpose of the organization with the behavior of its employees in achieving its mission.

Rotary International's Global People & Talent team's values

- We are passionate about helping others. This means we are:
  - Eager to assist others
  - Enjoy working with people
  - Joyful when working with people
  - Energized by making a difference
  - Service-oriented
  - Proactive; anticipate others' needs
- We are optimistic and positive. This means we:
  - See good in everyone/thing
  - Assume good intentions
  - Welcome constructive feedback
  - Are forward-looking
  - Approach problems as opportunities
- We are professional. This means we:
  - Are respectful & treat others w/dignity
  - Deliver polished presentation skills
  - Demonstrate confidence and are knowledgeable
  - Acknowledge and apologize for mistakes
  - Engage constructively in conflict
  - Seek out new knowledge & skills
  - Commit to doing our best work
  - Protect and preserve confidentiality
  - Act honestly and ethically
  - Model behaviors we expect
- We are good teammates. This means we:
  - Put the interests of the team above our own interests
  - Offer to help/seek help from others

- Supplement & complement each other with our varied knowledge, skills, and abilities
- Are reliable and trustworthy
- Address conflict directly
- Hold each other accountable

Source: *Kristopher J. Newbauer, Ed.M, MHRM, SPHR, SHRM-SCP, CPLP, CPT Head of Global People & Talent of Rotary International.*

Operationally, nearly every organization operates under a business strategy, usually written down in a strategic plan. That strategic plan consists, in part, of the organization's vision, mission, and values. The strategic plan articulates the organization's vision (its long-term ideal), defines its mission (intermediate purpose), including broad goals for areas where actions are to be taken, and describes the values held by the organization (behaviors through which the goals will be pursued). In short, the vision idealizes a new state of affairs for the future, the mission depicts where the organization is going in the intermediate-term, and its values describe how members will behave to help the organization get to its future place. The strategic plan articulates and communicates all three parts.

2.2 Alignment Benefits Accreditation

The key for accreditation is to create a direct alignment of learning and training to the organization's mission and values. Alignment means the unit responsible for learning and development has its own documented learning and development department's Mission and Values Statement, which is linked to the organization's overall vision, mission, and values.

The mission and values articulation can be two separate documents defining each aspect separately, or it can be one Mission and Values Statement for the learning & development department. Importantly, both mission and values not only provide direction, but they also unify people and claim authority for the learning to be conducted within the organization. Learning and training plans that are aligned with the organization's overall business plan guide managers and staff to design training that benefits all members.

SAE's values include enhancing the customer experience and focusing on customer satisfaction. Our accreditation standard includes several learner-centric requirements which align with our company's customer-centric focus.

–Dr. J. Kevin Perry
Society of Automotive Engineers (SAE)
International Director, Professional Development

One very critical piece to alignment is the underlying philosophy, or perspective, on employee education held by the larger organization, and a learning director or learning & development manager must be keenly aware of that underlying philosophy. An aligned Mission and Values Statement provides direction to the training path; unifies the roles and responsibilities among the training team; and claims authority at the L&D unit level for the development of learning events across the organization.

2.2.1 Philosophy on Employee Education

Professional development, learning development is central to our overall strategy, and it's something that really impacts a lot of what we do. When they made me Deputy Executive Director and Chief Learning Officer, it shows that they placed a big value on our learning programs.

–Peter Finn
Society of Women Engineers
Deputy Executive Director and Chief Learning Officer

Some organizations view training as a necessary effort, which must be included in the operation for compliance or employee safety reasons. Perhaps government regulators periodically review the organization's processes or functions for compliance with government regulations—such as EPA standards or OSHA regulations. In these cases, training may be mandatory and expected to exist by government requirement. Training employees, therefore, is viewed as an educational exercise which must be conducted in order to be compliant. This is a compliance philosophy of employee education and learning—training is done because it is required.

Other organizations view training, or learning and development, as an opportunity to enhance and share the knowledge and talents inherent in the people presently employed in the business. Some are even re-naming the training effort as talent development. In these cases, employee education is conducted to improve the overall knowledge base of all employees and to elevate that knowledge as a competitive advantage carried by the organization. Here, learning is viewed as a key asset for the organization—a needed effort to enable the organization to excel in its endeavors. By continuing to invest in employee learning and by aiding further employee education and development, the organization grows its internal talent to accomplish larger goals and objectives. Employees are viewed as full persons, whose talents are valued, so training efforts are undertaken to maintain and develop those talents. This is a talent development philosophy of employee education and training.

Most organization's philosophy of employee education lies along a continuum anchored by these two philosophies: a compliance perspective and a full person talent development perspective. It is extremely important for managers of training to have a clear understanding of the organization's philosophy about employee education and to understand where on the continuum the organization resides. The key point is that learning and development does both. It can help a worker meet current performance requirements, continue to meet requirements as work conditions change, and prepare for higher levels of responsibility to meet requirements in the future. Learning and development (L&D) efforts can also help the organization comply with existing legal provisions and help individuals meet professional continuing education requirements. The organization's education philosophy controls time, resources, and quality efforts; and learning & development will be controlled by the organization's employee education philosophy. As a learning and development manager, you need to understand and embody that philosophy because resources and support for training programs will only be considered through that viewpoint.

2.2.2 Provides Direction

> *I went to the accreditation workshop, and it was very apparent that I had my work cut out for me in terms of what we need to do. Our programs were not really formalized. We were riding the bike as we built it. There were a lot of things that we needed to get in place. The accreditation process kind of forced us to get things in place. So, our organization saw the value in this and it is now a core part of our strategy. Professional Excellence or Professional Development is one of the core components of our strategic plan.*
>
> ***–Peter Finn***
> *Society of Women Engineers*
> *Deputy Executive Director and Chief Learning Officer*

Alignment with the organization's mission guides the learning and development effort to focus upon skills, competencies, knowledge, and attitudes needed in pursuit of today's purpose. Alignment also guides the learning and development department to create new educational programs that build skills to guide the next generation of employees in pursuit of tomorrow's possibilities (the vision).

The Mission and Values Statement clarifies the intention of the learning & development department because it broadly defines what the department does and what it does not do. As a guide, a good Mission Statement is a blend of realism and optimism—two terms that are generally at odds with one another. However, through its optimism, the learning & development department's Mission and Values Statement offers hope to members regarding what can be accomplished through learning. A realistic Mission and Values Statement doesn't promise nirvana for members—it states what will be developed and offered as training in pursuit of the overall long-term vision and mission of the organization.

2.2.3 Unifies the Team

Planning for employee learning and development centers upon the roles and responsibilities of all those involved in the learning effort. The learning & development department's Mission and Values Statement unifies the training staff. All of the training staff—training managers, designers, facilitators, technicians, and writers—are unified under the plan as set forth in the Mission and Values Statement of the learning & development department. Also, parties can understand the purpose of learning as a functioning department within the organization and recognize how the education provided supports the growth and direction of the organization and its members. Further, roles and responsibilities of training personnel can be clarified, grouped, or teamed in accordance with the central mission of the learning & development department because everyone involved in training works toward one overarching purpose.

2.2.4 Claims Authority

The Mission and Values Statement should claim the authority for learning within the entire enterprise. The authority for learning needs to reside within one, dedicated unit, so the functions and tasks are specific and contained. This expressly benefits accreditation because the learning unit becomes the locus of education. Training cannot be done haphazardly, or piecemeal if it is to be of high quality. For accreditation, both responsibility and authority need to be clear and distinct. The Mission and Values

Statement sets the foundational authority for learning within one learning & development department or unit. Training is not reactive to the wishes or desires of a few but is undertaken for the benefit of all members broadly. Thus, through the articulation of a learning & development department's Mission and Values Statement, the learning and development function itself has a purpose and a reason for existence. Claims of authority also reinforce responsibility. When the mission and values of the learning & development department are linked to the organization's mission and values, that authority becomes embedded, and the unit becomes responsible for training quality. Thus, the learning & development department is credible internally, which benefits the programs that are developed and offered.

> *Everything we do has a direct linkage to our mission and vision - from language through a course set up. If a request is rendered for a course to be developed, we review everything and make sure that it lines up to our mission and vision. If it doesn't meet the mission and vision, it simply does not get published.*
>
> **–Reg Bonfoco**
> *Canadian Financial Securities*
> *Continuing Education Specialist*

2.3 The Steps to Writing a Mission and Values Statement

Writing an effective Mission and Values Statement for the learning effort is a multiple-step process that expresses the fundamental reason for educating employees in your workplace. The recommended steps are illustrated in Fig. 2.1.

A clearly written and readable Mission and Values Statement is intentioned to clarify the focus of your training effort because it clearly defines not only what the learning and development department will do, but it also defines what the learning & development department will not do. In actuality, writing a Mission and Values Statement for an organization's learning & development department takes a lot more time in thinking and deliberating than the number of words on paper would suggest. The steps to writing a Mission and Values Statement, as illustrated in Fig. 2.2 will take time and quite a bit of hard thinking to create a meaningful directive. Chapter 2 Supplement: 2A-Tool for Managers to Write a Mission and Values Statement (at the end of this chapter) provides a more detailed explanation of each step.

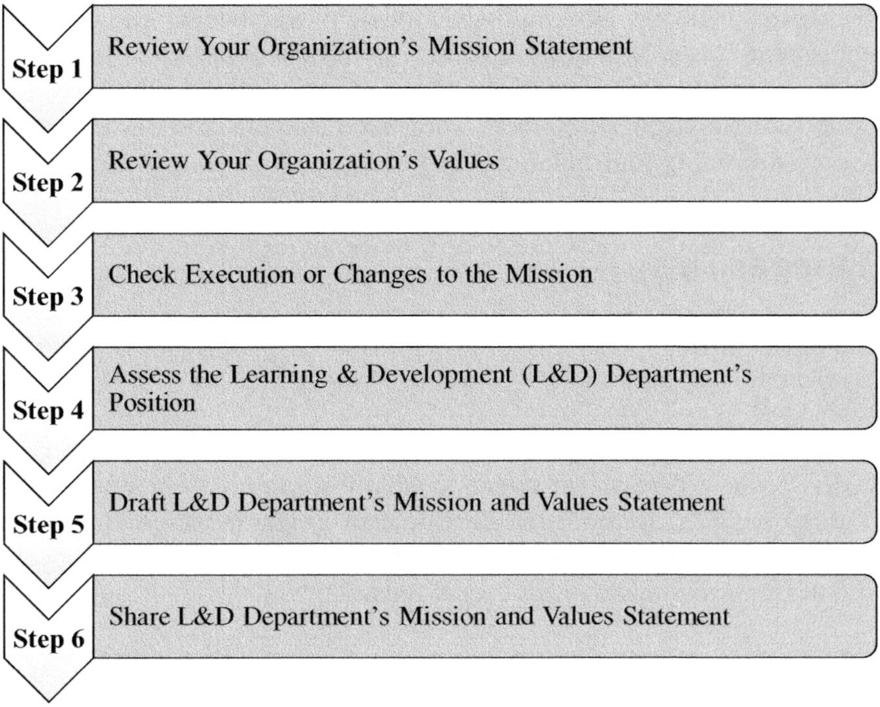

Fig. 2.1 The Steps to Writing a Mission and Value Statement

2.4 Conclusion

In a competitive marketplace, it benefits an organization to align its learning programs with its overall mission and values to assure direction and focus in all the employee education efforts. Learning programs which are accredited purposefully align the learning and development efforts with mission pursuit, and support of the organization's core values. Ultimately, this alignment helps to accomplish the organization's strategy, which involves all of the organization's product, processes, technology, and people initiatives. In pursuit of strategy, the training offerings provide the compass for employees to be ready for tomorrow's jobs and to envision a new future. By aligning the learning & development department's mission and values with the organization's overall mission and values, employees are grounded in the foundational principles and expected behaviors of the organization. Based upon that foundation, learning efforts can then provide employees with the skills to create tomorrow's products, the abilities to utilize tomorrow's technologies, and the adaptability to move in new directions. Thus, workers are prepared, through training, with a capacity for change. The Chapter 2 Supplement—*Steps to Writing a Mission and Values Statement*—provides a step-by-step tool for aligning the mission and values of your employee learning and development efforts with your organization's mission and values, thereby embedding your training purpose.

Manager Tips

A. Keep it short. Less is better. Use a process of shrink, shrink, shrink the original ideas down to a few succinct statements. One or two sentences are ideal.

B. Include the two components described above—what the learning & development department does and what it supports. Write one sentence about what the learning and development program does. Write another sentence that describes how the learning effort supports the organization's long-term purpose, its overall mission.

> ***Example***
>
> The training department's mission is to provide individual learning/education in marketing, operations, and quality (what it does) across the enterprise (claims the authority of the training department). The department is committed to supporting continued growth and performance (the organizational purpose that is supported) of [XXXX] through the development of people.

C. Be simple and specific in your values. Use only a few words here, as well. Simply state what each core value means in the training workplace, for the people involved in the delivery of education, and for the output of training. Be sure to describe each value the organization includes in its larger Values Statement. Don't skip any.

> ***Example***
>
> Throughout the programs offered, training encourages both transparency and forthrightness in our associates. We strive to be a reliable team of professionals, concerned for the continued development of employees and the inclusion of all.

D. Communicate your learning & development department's Mission and Values Statement. Use it at business meetings. Communicate to all staff members within the learning & development department, and confirm with staff that the values will be upheld. Then, spread the word throughout your organization of what the learning and development effort stands for, and how others can depend upon your training rigor and quality. Use the company Web site or other communication vehicles to broadcast your learning and development purpose for all employees.

Supplement

Supplement Tool 2A: *The Steps to Writing a Mission and Value Statement*

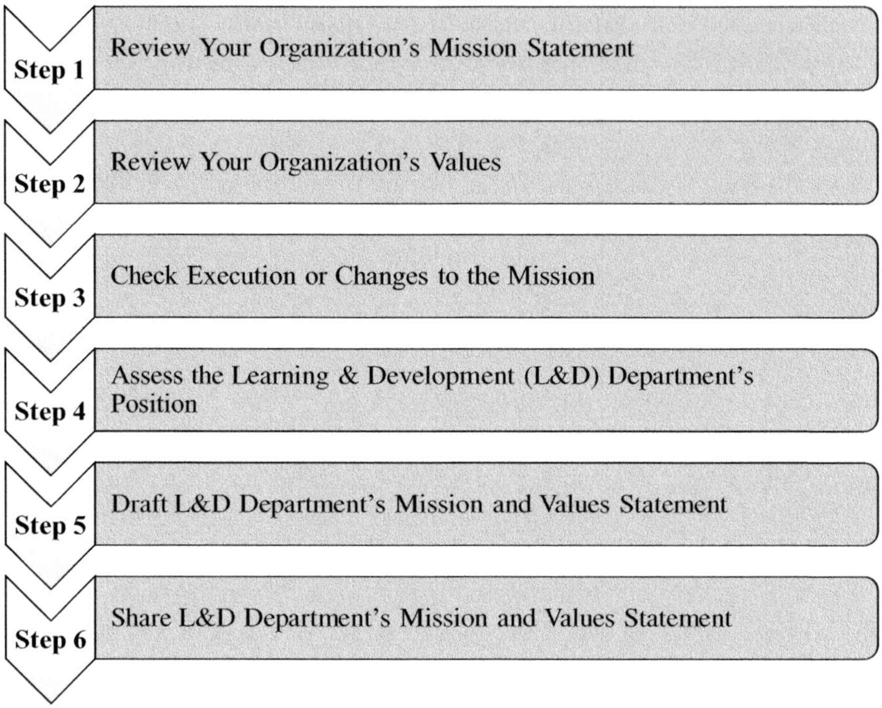

Fig. 2.2 Supplement—The Steps to Writing a Mission and Value Statement

Step 1: Review Your Organization's Mission Statement
Review your organization's larger Mission Statement. Look for the overall direction of the enterprise. What is your organization trying to accomplish? Is the organization primarily a manufacturer of a product? A provider of services? An agency for the interests of a public, or an agent for a group of common interests? A keeper of protocols or regulations? How does your organization describe its purpose and its aims for the future?

Make a short list of common themes that arise continually from the information put forth by the organization, or merely the statement(s) frequently made by the owners/founders/leaders. How are the organization's vision and mission described or talked about? What are the organization's wishes for its future? How is the organization's purpose emphasized?

Does the organization seem to emphasize the quality of its products? Performance of the whole? Growth of the enterprise? Does it emphasize culture? Quality of life for its employees? This is the first place to start thinking about a Mission Statement that would have a similar focus.

Step 2: Review Your Organization's Values

Review your organization's values. As mentioned previously, values are manifested in expected behaviors. Now, you want to look at the specific values your organization espouses that point toward expected employee behavior. Your organization will likely address three to four core values such as honesty, fairness, concern for others, and achievement. These values might be on the company Web site, or in an employee handbook. The organization will likely describe its values in a distinct vernacular, using each described value as a behavior guide for reaching tomorrow's vision. Below is a general description of each of the four core values found at most organizations.

- **Honesty**: Being honest is telling the truth in an open and forthright manner. Honesty means being willing to share information and sharing it freely, not holding anything back. Honesty involves speaking truthfully and revealing all the important information. The information that is provided is accurate and complete; it's not just part of the story or only a few facts. Honesty is telling the whole truth consistently, while not embellishing or distorting. It is an intention not to mislead or misinform.
- **Fairness**: Fairness means being impartial and doing what is right. It also means displaying consistent actions and decisions across different situations and between different persons. Fairness involves being dependable and reliable; someone who can be counted upon to consider all of the parties impacted.
- **Concern for Others**: Concern for others means caring about the well-being of other people and helping them out. Being concerned for the general well-being of others includes assisting them in their achievements and their pursuit of happiness. Concern for others means not being opportunistic, not taking advantage of other people, and not being self-serving. Concern for others is an attitude of taking action to benefit other individuals in the workplace—action to assist, substitute, or help out. It involves behavior which protects the interests of others, for the benefit of all.
- **Achievement**: Achievement, or accomplishment, involves being competent and maintaining a certain skill level to do the tasks at hand. Achievement is a desire to get things done, and it involves pursuing hard work to accomplish goals. The concept represents a commitment to complete the tasks at

hand. Achievement can include prioritizing different demands to succeed in accomplishing personal objectives effectively, and it can involve meeting expectations of a work nature because one is being relied upon.

Your organization may include terms other than the ones above as additional values, such as diversity, integrity, or teamwork. If so, look at each key value and determine how your organization emphasizes these concepts. How does your organization describe these expectations? What does your organization mean by its values? How do the values guide the behaviors of members within your organization? Look, too, for values, which are idiosyncratic to your organization, or expected behaviors, which the organization has adopted as values. Idiosyncratic behavior expectations arise in words such as speed, ignite, or big.

Make a short list of the core values at your organization. Look at how your organization expresses each one. Examine the words used to describe each value, and review which ones seem to be more important, or emphasized most often. Use these words as starting places for the words needed to express your learning & development department values.

Step 3: Check Execution or Changes to the Mission

Check for any changes to how your organization executes its mission. Have there been any new strategic initiatives announced recently? What is being worked on now that is being done for long-term effect? What is being worked on now for a change in the future? There might be a new product initiative, a new product development, or a product upgrade. Your organization may have had to recall a product for deficiencies, or it may be adding new products to its manufacturing base. There might be a new service initiative, such as a relationship emphasis, or a customer service mandate. Has your organization undergone a big structural change, merger, or divestiture? Have there been any significant changes to processes or policies? Look for technology improvements or adoptions that are driving changes in the workflow at your organization or driving changes in how people task out their work.

All of these are key business changes that will alter both the intermediate and long-term effort of the organization. Any long-term effort will eventually have an effect on the organization's Mission Statement. Check with other key managers within your organization. Discuss any large initiatives or change efforts that everyone is aware of, or which everyone is anticipating. Determine how strongly those new ideas are being absorbed across the enterprise.

Step 4: Assess the Learning & Development Department's Position
Assess the learning & development department's position as it matches both the original mission and values, and the identified changes. What does your learning & development department do in its educational and skill-building efforts that are also related to product, service, creativity, process, or agency? What does your learning & development department create, foster, and promote in its educational efforts? How does the learning & development department support the products, service, creativity, and agency of the organization as a whole? How does the learning & development department presently support any major strategic efforts underway?

Take a re-look at your learning & development department's mission, or what you wrote above. Does your training mission need to be updated because of an update to the organization's mission? You may want to include specific initiatives, or ideas about those initiatives, in your learning & development department's written Mission Statement.

Step 5: Create Learning & Development Department's Mission and Values Statement
Write down the learning & development department's Mission and Values Statement, specific to the learning and education effort within your organization today. You can split this into a mission segment, and a values segment, if preferred.

Mission Segment
Your learning & development department's Mission and Values Statement is one brief document that reflects the unit's authority for the education of all members and the responsibility for administering all training programs. The learning & development department's Mission and Values Statement specifically depicts the development of learning programs for a long-term purpose, and that purpose must be linked to (support of) the organization's purpose. It needs to be a statement, which supports the continued development of educational content for employees in pursuit of the mission of the larger organization. You want to write your long-term training pathway. You will want to cover two key aspects of your learning & development department's Mission Statement. Those two aspects are:

1. What the learning & development department does for the employees of the organization.
2. How that effort supports the mission of the organization overall.

These two aspects can be a simple two sentences and in that manner can actually comprise the whole of your Mission Statement. However, it's hard to be succinct and still be complete. Here are two examples:

Sample Training Mission Statements

- The training department of ABC Bank focuses upon comprehensive financial education in individual, corporate, and trust-related finances and is established to assist ABC Bank in its mission as a financial enterprise serving both individual clients and commercial businesses.
- The professional Training and Development Community focuses on working with agency leaders to predict and develop strategies/approaches that continue to improve a workforce capable of accomplishing NPS strategic goals. (National Park Service, U.S. Department of the Interior, retrieved March 2, 2018)

Values Segment

The values segment included in the statement needs to confirm the behaviors expected within the organization and describe those behaviors with a learning/educational meaning. Your learning values need to link to the values of the organization as a whole and address each of the organization's core values as expected learning behaviors. Below are some helpful hints to what you might consider regarding core values for a learning effort.

- Honesty in Learning—What does honesty mean for instructional designers, facilitators, training planners, and all the training employees? Does it mean open in content? Does honesty in training mean complete and comprehensive in content? What does it mean for content to contain all the needed components in your programs? Is the training effort comprehensive or focused? Are all the skills necessary to the enterprise addressed in the learning & development department?
- Fairness in Learning—How is learning offered to the members? Is learning available to all employees? Can individuals request training on their own, or do they need to be sponsored by a superior? How is learning assessed? Are programs evaluated for their educational contribution to the organization? Are programs assessed on their monetary, or ROI, contribution? Are programs continually improved, or benchmarked for quality? How are programs compared when offered across different units within the organization?

- Concern for Others in Learning—How does the learning & development department assist others in developing new knowledge and skills? What concerns about the employees are considered in training designs? How does training assist employees in developing new attitudes, or in developing interpersonal and managerial skills? How does it educate individuals so they can best utilize the benefits, services, and personnel offerings of the organization? How are conflicts managed or conflict issues addressed? How do the training efforts support team unity or group productivity?
- Achievement in Learning—How does the learning & development department measure its own success? How does it know it is meeting the educational needs of the members? How does learning enhance employee accomplishments? How does the learning & development department accomplish its designed programs? What descriptors or words define the culture of accomplishment for a training professional? What does the learning & development department cultivate or promote regarding professional development?
- Diversity in Learning—What does diversity mean in a learning and educational environment? What values are promoted that drive diversity and inclusion? How does the learning & development department encourage inclusionary practices or protect individuals from discrimination and harassment? How is diversity approached in management practices and in outreach initaitives?
- Quality of Work-life—How does the learning & development department support individuality? How does it respect differences, yet promote team effort? Is interpersonal trust promoted or developed among members? What does involvement in one's own learning and development mean for training?

Step 6: Share the Learning & Development Department's Mission and Values Statement

Write your Mission and Values Statement in a simple document that contains two segments: one for your mission and one for your values. Use your learning staff to collaborate and affirm the statement. Share your Mission and Values Statement with all members of the learning team and with other executives and organization managers. Place the mission and values document on your organization's Web site, or on the learning & development department's Web site. Make sure it is accessible to all employees. Spread the word throughout your organization of what the learning effort stands for, and how others can depend upon your training rigor and quality.

References and Additional Resources

Cuilla, J. B. (1999). The importance of leadership in shaping business values. *Long Range Planning, 32*(2), 166–172.

Darling, J., & Scharfer, C. (1997). Spirituality in the workplace. *Lapis*, 63–67.

Fisman, R., & Khanna, T. (1999, January). Is trust an historical residue? *Journal of Economic Behavior & Organization, 38*(1), 79–92.

Meglino, B. M., & Ravlin, E. C. (1998). Individual values in organization: Concepts, controversies, and research. *Journal of Management, 24*(3), 351–389.

Palazzo, G. (2007). Organizational integrity—Understanding the dimensions of ethical and unethical behavior in corporations. In W. C. Zimmeli, M. Holzinger, & K. Richter (Eds.), *Corporate ethics and corporate governance*. Berlin: Springer. https://doi.org/10.1007/978-3-540-70818-6_9.

3

Structure for Accountability

The success of any learning organization relies on having a structured learning and development department that is accountable—one that trains its employees with authority, and which is analytical in its approach to the training effort. This chapter focuses upon developing a results-driven learning and development function within the organization, one which has a defined structure, establishes an appropriate responsibility and control system for assuring quality education delivery, and awards training credits fairly.

> *Whenever you're developing a new program or you're thinking about changing or developing some new policies or revising things … go back and look at the standards to see what it is that we're going to be held accountable for, and keep that in mind all the way through.*
>
> **–Dr. Arthur Holder**
> *Graduate Theological Union*
> *Accreditation Liaison Officer (ALO)*

3.1 Models for Structure

The learning and development function should be housed within a distinct and identifiable unit within the organization. That unit should be unique and purposed exclusively as a learning, training, or continuing education operation. It should be separate and distinct from other operations within the organization and should not be subsumed within a collective department of "other administration" or "other shared functions."

W. J. Rothwell et al., *Increasing Learning & Development's Impact through Accreditation*,
https://doi.org/10.1007/978-3-030-14004-5_3

The learning and development function might be a part of the overall HR organization—often as a separate unit within the broader structure for human resources. Alternatively, the learning and development function can be a completely separate responsibility or operate as a fully independent department, reporting to a Chief Learning Officer (CLO) or Learning Executive.

The precise organizational plan for the learning and development function will depend upon the mission and values of the organization and its philosophy on employee education (described in Chapter 2, "Align Learning and Development with Organization Mission and Values"). The organization's philosophy on employee education will guide its strategic intent for enhancing employee growth. It will also guide where the learning and development function is located within the organization structure, and how training is positioned. A long-standing debate has existed about whether to place the learning and development function within HR, within an operating division, or as a stand-alone separate unit. The placement of learning and development within the organization sends a clear message to all members. This organizational placement will signal the intent for employee development—be it as one of compliance and cost control (training placed within an operations or finance unit), as an added benefit to workers internally (training placed within the HR unit), or as a strategic learning effort to help the organization excel in its endeavors (training established as a stand-alone learning unit). The placement of the learning and development function as its own operating unit can be an indication of the leadership and management's view that employee learning has a strategic value, and a sense that direct "ownership" of the training effort is present.

> *From the first touch point with the customer, all the way through creating content, fulfillment and ongoing quality assurance, we had to make some internal changes, including new teams of people, business development managers and creative workflows - like a complete system integration. We had to align people internally to assure we were meeting the requirements of the program itself.*
>
> ***–Jessica Burnett***
> *Senior Product Manager, ISACA*

There are three basic models to conisder for structuring the learning and development function. These include: a centralized training organization; a decentralized training organization; embedded training organization; and a federated training organization.

3.1.1 Centralized Training Organization

A centralized training organization operates as one unit where all programs, resources, and professionals are housed, and where management decisions about training curriculum, programs, and delivery methods are made. All processes related to employee learning are directed within this single unit, which usually reports to one senior executive, perhaps a Chief Learning Officer (CLO). The primary advantage of this model is the consistency it provides across the organization. The centralized model helps to drive alignment with business strategy because it allows for the development of a common set of metrics or scorecards to measure and report training quality. A centralized learning approach also supports the culture and values of the enterprise because corporate values can be communicated and reinforced through the training content. A few disadvantages to this organizational structure is the tendency to create predetermined course topics that are implemented across regions and geographies producing a static supply of training products, and the propensity for learning professionals to design and deliver training for skills according to traditional enterprise topics (such as sales, finance, logistics, and accounting).

3.1.2 Decentralized Training Organization

A decentralized training organization is one in which the learning and development function is housed within different operating units throughout the organization. In this design, each business function, such as marketing, IT, finance, or manufacturing, would control training related to its specific area of operational behaviors. As an example, training within the finance operation would focus upon topics such as comparative analytics, or risk/return trade-offs. Training within the marketing operation would focus upon topics such as pricing, customer relations, or selling skills. Each decentralized learning unit has its own training lead or training team that develops customized content for the business unit(s) it supports. This model can be preferred by larger organizations where learning can be distributed across multiple lines of business, addressing unique products, or differentiated geographic areas.

3.1.3 Business Embedded Model

The business embedded model is characterized by the strategic alignment of learning with the organization overall, with some training processes centralized and others decentralized. The business embedded model relies on a clearly articulated mission and strategy for the overall organization, to which the learning and development function aligns its core programs and values, while also meeting specific needs of business functions for operation-specific content or training innovation. In the business embedded model, courses have limited life cycles, topics are customized to current performance needs, and programs are developed quickly using benchmarked designs and mixed delivery vehicles (including outsourced vendors). Each business unit is supported by learning consultants who analyze and respond to the unit's topical training needs, with the consultants also serving on an overarching learning team or council. The learning consultant reports to the central training organization, ensuring that similar needs across business units can benefit from the designs of skilled learning and development professionals.

> *Our Education Program Developer team is able to be responsive to business opportunities because each developer is assigned to a particular set of technology and market categories. That team, over time, develops deep expertise and a robust network of industry relationships in these assigned market areas.*
>
> **–Dr. J. Kevin Perry**
> *Society of Automotive Engineers (SAE) International Director, Professional Development*

The business embedded model has the advantage of versatility at the business unit level, while maintaining the organization's mission and values across the broader distributed organization. It requires more acceptance of versatility in learning and allowance for differentiated responsibility and performance outcomes. It is usually not possible to evaluate or measure the overall impact of training throughout the organization. Furthermore, assessments of the varying performance needs within the organization are conducted on a segregated basis.

3.1.4 Corporate Universities and the Emerging Federated Model

Because of the increased recognition of training's critical role in contributing to the strategy of many organizations, there is an increasing trend in large companies, which have separate business units, to organize the learning and development function as a blend of the business embedded model with the centralized training model (Gosh 2018), an example of this trend are corporate universities. The resources for a corporate university are extensive, and corporate universities are usually found in large global organizations with multiple product lines with differentiated service regions or customer groups. However, even without the resources required for a corporate university, the combined centralized and embedded models are used frequently and referred to as the federated model.

The federated model is a blended approach which allows the organization to gain the benefits of centralized management and accountability, while at the same time ensuring that specific training programs, content, and delivery meet the timing and topical needs of specific lines of business. The centralized administration of learning management brings efficiencies of scale to the learning and development function, while the decentralized embedded function enables quick and customized content creation and delivery. The federated model notably has emerged with the development of electronic technologies for adult learning, which enable organizations to offer organization-wide learning through employee Web sites and other electronic platforms. The centralized platforms needed by such e-learning environments are managed efficiently from a centralized electronic learning system, referred to as a learning management system (LMS) and supported by a learning technologies team. Concurrently, specific departments and functions remain free to develop topical content to meet specific business needs and talent expertise. This helps to further specialize detailed topics for delivery to specific employee audiences.

3.2 Responsibility and Accountability for Learning

The accreditation process requires accountability through assessment: to be assessed you have to be much more explicit internally about things that were implicit knowledge… things in people's head about the way we did things… and so we learned a lot by just being required to go through the process of writing things down. How do we do it? Who does what? When does it happen? Because I was actually surprised about how much of it was previously uncaptured knowledge. It was sitting in the heads of individual folks.

–Clyde Seepersad
Linux Foundation
General Manager, Training & Certification

Regardless of the organizational structure of the learning and development function, the unit must operate under a single prescribed authority established by the organization. That authority ensures that both responsibility and control of the learning function rest within an identified unit or department. Positions and/or offices to whom the learning and development function is responsible, and which place the L&D function resides, must be determined and established. A responsible functionary position, such as a learning director, training manager, learning executive, or learning officer, should be created, documented, and authorized by the organization.

3.2.1 The Senior Learning Executive

The senior learning executive position is responsible for both training education and outcome results. One of the important roles of the senior learning executive position is to promote the value of continued education to employees, encouraging their development of competencies to meet both current job demands and the future requirements of their profession. Another important role is to link employee education and learning to organizational performance, so the organization is assured that employees have the skills for strategic competitiveness and sustainability. Overall, the role of the learning executive has become more visible as organizations move to more global structures with flexible workforces. The key sustainability role of the learning executive is to help define the link between skill-building through the education of employees, also called continued talent development, to the overall company performance and success.

3.2.2 Senior Learning Executive Responsibilities

Responsibilities specifically outlined for the senior learning officer or learning executive position should include oversight of four important aspects: learning processes; learning administration; learning maintenance; and training audit.

3.2.3 Learning Processes

Learning processes include performance and needs assessment, GAP definition and description, analyses of both employee skills and job content, instructional design activities, materials/media development, program implementation, and program evaluation. Details of each of these processes are described in later chapters. Important at this stage is the establishment of specific roles within the organization for learning and development professionals to perform the distinct duties related to each of the learning processes. Learning professionals must be capable of addressing the distinct learning processes of assessment, design, delivery, implementation, and evaluation. Individual roles related to these processes might include organization change agent, assessor, learning and development advisor, instructional designer, instructor/facilitator, graphic designer, media manager, researcher, or performance consultant—to name just a few. It is critical that the processes associated with training and learning be executed by competent learning and development professionals, each with specific assigned roles and carrying out defined duties within the learning organization.

3.2.4 Learning Administration

Administration involves establishing policies for authority, policies for guidance, and policies for performance appraisals of the training personnel. Policies for authority determine which training jobs hold approval authority for expenditures, budgets, allocation of company resources, and the awarding of Continuing Education Units (CEUs). Policies for guidance determine the plan for execution of the learning and development department's structure (be it centralized, decentralized, embedded, or federated), as well as which content must be centrally provided, or which might be uniquely designed.

Persons within the learning and development function who carry out the duties of training might need to be certified in specific tasks, media skills, or connected with specific academic communities. Leading practitioner organizations within the training and talent development field, such as the Association for Talent Development (ATD), offer credentialing programs for learning and development professionals to gain the practical competencies needed to perform specific training roles. Learning administration for the organization must assure that each member of the training staff is reviewed for performance on a regular basis, and that individuals are appraised on performance relative to the company standards of best practices in education and learning.

3.2.5 Learning Maintenance

Maintenance is needed for consistent application of the policies and standards for training, as established in the learning processes (as discussed in 3.2.3 Learning Processes). Maintenance includes retaining and updating policies, executing established procedures, responsibly enacting protocols, and assuring that training standards are upheld for quality. The key to maintenance is a separate process to audit or internally review the effectiveness of the learning organization in its overall execution of the learning design processes, learning administration, and learning maintenance. At a minimum, the organization should have a periodic internal review of its courses to ensure that the quality of the learning events is sustained, that trends in past learner/participant feedback and other evaluation findings are incorporated, and to assure that the defined protocols used in learning and development activities are applied consistently.

3.2.6 Training Audit

Accreditation process is like having a mirror held up to you and saying, 'here's what's working well' and 'here's what seems not to be working so well'.

–Dr. Arthur Holder
Graduate Theological Union
Accreditation Liaison Officer (ALO)

For accreditation, a learning and development review process, or training audit, must operate under a prescribed authority established by the organization. That authority first ensures that both responsibility and control of the learning and development function rest within the formalized learning and development unit or department. Second, that authority assures that the audit or review process rests with persons separate from those you create the training, but who are responsible for compliance with best practices or quality learning standards. A standard of practice for training and/or learning must be selected and complied with. That standard might be offered through an accreditation program for a specific industry or through a broader standard bearing organization for the training profession, such as the International Association for Continuing Education and Training (IACET) or the American National Standards Institute (ANSI). Both IACET and ANSI have developed prescribed standards for adult education and training practices which organizations are encouraged to follow for accreditation (see Chapter 14, "Accreditation Sources").

A learning and development effort, structured with delineated responsibilities and an internal audit, must follow a structured approach to assessment, design, production, execution, and evaluation. Established authority for structure, processes, and systematic monitoring assures internal responsibility, creates high-quality learning and development products, and ensures a quality improvement learning process with continuity.

3.3 Accountability for Continuing Education Units (CEUs)

High-quality training organizations offer Continuing Education Unites (CEUs) as evidence of learning achievement. CEUs serve to quantify non-academic education credits. CEUs are calculated for learning events as time spent by learners in training. Currently there is a growing trend toward competency-based training, which would require a demonstration as evidence of knowledge or the "ability to perform" instead of "completed time in training".

3.3.1 Purpose of CEU

To further the accountability and authority for learning and development, today's organizations must accurately calculate the number of CEUs awarded for each training event offered. CEUs provide evidence to outsiders, and to an organization itself, of the ongoing learning accomplished by each employee. The accumulation of CEUs is verification of current knowledge and proof of updated skill-sets within the workforce. Furthermore, individual employees are rewarded for learning by the earning of CEU credits, which serve as evidence to validate the individual's overall expertise and build their portfolio of skills, knowledge and abilities.

> *Having the CEU designation sets your training apart from those programs that could just be obtained online…from any other available offering.*
>
> **–Scott A. Critchfield, CFP**
> *Coach, Learning Professional*

3.3.2 Calculating the CEU

The individuals within the organization who are responsible for calculating the CEU must be trained in the calculating formula and understand what types of activities during a session are allowable as bona fide training time. The organization should calculate contact time for each course and ensure that a process is in place for consistent measurement of the CEU. The calculation method utilized by the organization should be consistent and systematically applied. Changes to portions of programs, to content, to program duration, or to mode will require the recalculation of the CEU awarded for a specific learning event or program. The learning and development department should have a documented process for calculations within its standard operating procedures. It should record the number of CEUs awarded for each training event and for each participant or learner (see Chapter 13, "Program Evaluation and Records").

> *We cannot give a certificate with CEUs at the end of a classroom course unless we are confident that the learner attended the entire course. Even though the learner may be able to pass a course test, we still require that the learners attend the entire course. We do the same thing with our on-demand courses. We had to build in that functionality for accreditation.*
>
> **–Dr. J. Kevin Perry**
> *Society of Automotive Engineers (SAE) International Director, Professional Development*

When a training event changes delivery mode (i.e., from face-to-face facilitated instruction to online self-paced learning), a recalculation of the number of CEUs awarded based upon the new delivery mode should be determined. Suggested is a time tracker procedure for each training event as it is being developed, and a review process for training event-time measurement as the training is delivered.

CEU Formula : 1 Continuing Education Unit = 10 Contact/Instructional Hours

Contact hours are hours of participation in an organization-based educational program conducted under responsible sponsorship, capable direction, and qualified instruction. Contact hours can include classroom time, self-paced instruction time, pre-post assignments, or homework time as part of the training event. Contact hours generally mean the time spent by participants in direct learning activities. Time spent at orientation, welcoming events, pre-training events, breaks, meals, and celebration is not considered learning time. Thus, attendance hours are subtracted by time spent on breaks,

Table 3.1 Formula to calculate CEU

Face-to-Face or classroom Mode	Example A	Online or self-paced Mode	Example B
Sum of all instructor-led contact minutes	420 mins. All day event	Sum of minutes spent for all students. (times ranging from 45 minutes to 240 minutes)	Sum = 1130 mins.
Less: not-allowed minutes (breaks, lunch, welcome, introduction and conclusion modules)	breaks, lunch and welcome: 120 mins	Divide by number of students (9), for Average Contact Minutes	Average= 125.5 mins
Allowable Contact Minutes	300 mins	Divide Average Contact minutes by 60	= 2.09 hours
Divide minutes by 60 = Allowable Contact Hours	5.0 hours	Divide Contact hours by 10	0.209
Divide Contact Hours by 10	0.5	Write CEU in tenths	0.209
Total CEU's	0.5 CEUs	Eliminate fractions of hours, round down for Total CEU.	0.2 CEUs

arrival, welcome announcements, closure, or celebration events to calculate contact hours. Only contact hours form the basis for calculating the CEU. The basic calculation requires a recording of contact minutes in training, which is then converted to hours of training and converted again into CEU. This is a fairly basic summation for classroom or face-to-face training events. For self-paced or distanced learning/online events, the calculation is based upon the average minutes spent by all independent learners, not including outliers.

The formula for both face-to-face (classroom) training and online or self-paced (individual or distanced) training is offered in the following examples (Table 3.1).

As shown above (Example A), in a classroom setting where learning is face-to-face, a total of 5.0 hours of content equates to 0.5 CEUs. In an online or distance learning situation (Example B), where the learners averaged 125.5 minutes to complete the training event, the content equates to 0.209 CEUs, which is then rounded down to .2 CEUs. A worksheet for calculating the actual CEU for use by managers is included at the end of this chapter.

3.3.3 Recording CEUs

Smart management of the learning and development effort will keep documented records of each individual trained and the CEU awarded to each individual upon completion of training. Management may need to enforce training hours completed versus hours of attendance in order to award CEUs accurately. Whatever process is utilized, the persons responsible for the learning provider's accreditation must be sure that there is a fair and just method for the allocations of CEU credits per individual. Keep a recording for individuals to track their own progress and to export CEUs if employees are externally transferred, retire, or otherwise depart the organization.

3.4 Conclusion

The success of any organization relies on having a structured learning and development department that is accountable—one that trains its internal and external learners with authority, and which is analytical in its approach to the training effort. This chapter focused on developing a results-driven training unit or learning and development department within the organization—one that sets the standard and establishes an appropriate responsibility and control system for assuring quality education outcomes. For accreditation, this learning and development unit operates under a prescribed authority established by the organization. That authority ensures that both responsibility and control of the training function rest within a formalized learning and development department or unit. A learning effort, structured with delineated responsibilities, then encourages an analytic approach to training assessment, GAP identification, production responsibility, and learning event execution. Accreditation for structure and authority, accompanied by an analytical approach, assures internal functional responsibility to establish, monitor, and improve the learning process.

Manager Tips

A training effort structured in a delineated manner, which establishes both responsibility and control of the learning and development function can be effectively utilized to further the business purpose of the organization. Training efforts, established with a formal learning and development structure, containing authority for learning processes, learning administration and learning maintenance, then encourage an analytic approach to the work of learning as a human resource achievement. A formalized training unit or learning and development department can effectively approach needs assessment, GAP identification, program development, production responsibility, and event execution with authority. This establishment of structure and authority, accompanied by an analytical approach to development and maintenance of training programs, assures a process to realistically improve learning across the workforce and accomplish learning goals.

A. Structure your learning and development organization according to your business' size and purpose. If you have a small, regional, or mid-sized business, a centralized training structure is likely to be appropriate.
B. Work with other business managers to create a learning and development structure that meets the timing and topic needs of line managers and employees.
C. Negotiate proactively with your senior executive to determine an appropriate structure for your learning and development unit to be responsive to the organization's needs, agile in delivery, and able to consistently reinforce the organization's values and mission.
D. Identify the position(s) within your learning and development organization, which are responsible for learning creation, learning delivery, and learning maintenance.
E. Outline staff responsibilities in specific jobs and roles within your learning and development structure. Write responsibilities for training and learning activities into formal job descriptions for your staff.
F. Establish a process to measure the effectiveness of the development, administration, delivery, and support of the education/training programs provided.
G. Create and maintain a periodic internal review process that ensures adherence to standards for continuing education and training, either generic educational standards such as those offered by IACET or standards for accreditation provided by your industry.
H. Designate persons responsible for the calculations of CEUs and the maintenance of CEU records. Assure that calculations are established and allocated differently for both face-to-face and online, self-paced training events.
I. Allocate the CEU to both learning events and to individuals.

Supplement

***Supplement Tool 3A**: CEU WORKSHEET (Face-To-Face Event)*

Session/Segment Name: ______________________________

Morning Schedule	Segment	Mins Allowed	Mins Non-Allowed
X:00 – X:30 am	Welcome and ___________		30 - 60
X:30 – X:XX	MODULE	____ mins	
X:XX – X:XX	MODULE	____ mins	
X:00 - X:15	Break		15
X:XX – X:XX	MODULE	____ mins	
X:XX – X:XX	MODULE	____ mins	
X:XX – X:45	Lunch		45 - 90

Afternoon Schedule	Segment	Mins Allowed	Mins Non-Allowed
X:00 – X:15 pm	Logistics or Reminders		____ mins
X:30 – X:XX	MODULE	____ mins	
X:XX – X:XX	MODULE	____ mins	
X:00 - X:15	Break		15
X:XX – X:XX	MODULE	____ mins	
X:XX – X:XX	MODULE	____ mins	
X:XX – X:45	Group Picture and Graduation		____ mins

Non- Allowed Minutes ________ Mins.

Allowable Contact Minutes ________ Mins.

Allowed CONTACT HOURS = ________ (Allowable Contact Minutes/60)

TOTAL CEU = ________ (Allowed Contact Hours/10)

***Supplement Tool 3B**: CEU WORKSHEET: Online/Self-Paced or Homework Learning Event*

Session/Segment Name: ______________________________

Learners	Minutes Recorded	Included in Average? Y/N
Participant A:	_____ Minutes	
Participant B:	_____ Minutes	
Participant C:	_____ Minutes	
Participant D:	__0__ Minutes	N
Participant E:	_____ Minutes	
Participant F:	No Information	N
Participant G:	_____ Minutes	
TOTAL # of Learners: _____		

Total Contact Minutes – ALL ______ Mins.

Allowable Contact Minutes ______(Total Contact Minutes / # of Learners)

Allowed CONTACT HOURS = ______(Allowable Contact Minutes/60)

References

Gosh, P. (2018, May 15). What are the structures of HRD systems in organizations? *Navigation*.

Hassell, B. (2016, June 20). Where should the learning department go? *CLO Media*.

4

Establish the Learning Environment

A learning and development program's management is the designated authority that establishes and directs the full education process. Management establishes the learning environment, be it physical or electronic, and directs supporting resources to the learning programs. Support resources further include registration methods, signs, seating, visual aids, tools and equipment, refreshments when appropriate, evaluation methods, and follow-up. This chapter will cover the essential functions to establish the learning and development environment—including assessing the learning conditions and providing learning support.

> *Our interpretation of the standard led us to require that our E-Learners experience the entire online course. In other words, the full runtime of the course before they take the final learning assessment. So, we programmed in a functionality where they have to experience every slide before they advance to the next one.*
>
> ***–Dr. J. Kevin Perry***
>
> *Society of Automotive Engineers (SAE) International Director, Professional Development*

W. J. Rothwell et al., *Increasing Learning & Development's Impact through Accreditation*,
https://doi.org/10.1007/978-3-030-14004-5_4

4.1 Learning Environment and Resources

The learning environment is everything that surrounds learners and instructors—supporting them as they engage in their respective efforts to learn or to train. A physical learning environment includes the people engaged in learning and training, the physical facilities (such as classrooms, furniture, materials), and the overall climate (temperature, sounds, lighting, and colors). In an electronic environment, the surroundings include e-entry, access, e-design, and interaction technology. Every organization has an obligation to establish a learning environment that is able to support learners and instructors. Literally, hundreds of variables can affect the learning environment. For that reason, it is difficult to list them in exhaustive detail. But one thing is clear, when something is amiss, people will notice. For instance, suppose the classroom seats 500 people but only 10 people are enrolled. That huge classroom will be noticeable to learners. As another example, suppose training is offered in an electronic environment that requires specific software for tool use. Inability to manipulate all the learning software tools will be noticeable to learners. One way to tell if the environment is conducive to learning is to ask learners and instructors if the conditions are sufficient to support their activities.

Research on the learning environment revealed that twenty-six (26) factors may positively or negatively influence the ability of people to learn and apply what they learned in the workplace (Rothwell 2002). When these factors encourage learning, learners are more likely to be willing to learn; when the factors discourage learning, learners are less likely to be willing to learn. For example, one consideration is the role of the learner's immediate supervisor and whether he or she supports the learning. (See the instrument at the end of this chapter.)

4.2 Assessing the Learning Environment

Assessing the learning environment means measuring what the learning and development department has established as a physically and psychologically comfortable environment for the implementation of courses and programs. This can be done formally by polling learners and instructors about the environment. It can also be done informally by casually asking learners and instructors if conditions support and encourage their learning activities or if any conditions hinder their learning and require correction.

Identifying which environment individuals prefer for their learning is much like assessing learning styles, as each person may differ. Some people prefer one sense over others—such as learning tied to the sense of sight, sense of hearing, sense of touch, sense of taste, or sense of smell. Today, there are definite differences in preferences between electronically based environments, such as those offered in online learning, and residential environments, such as those experienced at conferences and in classrooms. Even within an e-environment, some people prefer certain types of navigation arrangements such as toolbars, links, or expansion columns. These preferred senses or arrangements reflect a preferred environment and may favor a preferred mode of learning.

Learning style can also affect the teaching style of instructors. Both designers and facilitators who have one dominant learning style will often favor that style in their training delivery, despite whether the instruction takes place in a physical or an electronic environment.

I make the analogy to the Peanuts characters of the Charles Schulz comic strip… look at the different personalities of Charlie Brown, Lucy, Linus and Peppermint Patty. One of those characters, or all those characters are probably in your office right now, and one teaching style won't work on all of them.

–Scott A. Critchfield, CFP
Coach, Learning Professional

It is possible to measure the preferred learning environment of your employees and then use the resulting information from both instructors and learners to modify the environment to support learners and instructors more effectively. (See, e.g., the instrument found here: www.usm.maine.edu/sites/default/files/Office%20of%20Academic%20Assessment/assess-res_lep.pdf.) However, it is unlikely that one learning environment will fully, and comprehensively, meet the needs of all learners and all instructors within your organization, due to individual differences. Increasingly, training is offered in a combination of environments or mixed delivery environments, which can consist of both physical surroundings and online surroundings blended together. To the extent that learning can be made adaptive and customized to the needs of individuals particular to your organization, the more successful the training is likely to be (Rothwell, Benscoter, King & King 2016).

4.3 Providing Support Services

Support services include anything that helps instructors and learners carry out their respective roles in teaching and learning. It is the organization's responsibility to create an environment that is conducive to both training delivery and learning, and structured support services help to do that. Structured support services include, but are not limited to: registration methods to help learners enroll in planned learning events; signs or links that direct learners and instructors where to go and when to go there; software tutorials that provide instruction on technology use and access; seating arrangements in classroom venues; equipment to support learning (such as audiovisual devices or Internet devices); refreshments; and, evaluation of learning events. Managers of the learning and development function must assure that support services for the training effort are indeed structured, that they are consistently provided to both instructors and learners, and that they are continually available.

It is also important to make accommodations for learners with disabilities. Learners may need help with accessibility. That can include the senses of sight, hearing, physical issues, and so forth. Consider a few useful tips for making learning more accessible to all:

- Make the learning expectations clear prior to the learning event (such as due dates and attendance requirements),
- Provide an overview at the opening of each lesson,
- Write down technical jargon and provide definitions,
- Make assignments available both orally and in writing,
- Give participants the option to record what is said by instructors,
- Encourage questions and answers,
- Make exams available in multiple formats,
- Provide a written script for all videos and make copies of slides available,
- Ask learners if they have other needs.

4.3.1 Registration Methods

Make registration as user-friendly as possible. Consider:

- Do learners know how to sign-up or enroll themselves in planned learning events?

- How easily has the organization made it for learners to find notifications of planned learning or to access online offerings?
- How easy has the organization made it for learners to obtain approval from their managers to attend training and to get budgetary approval for related expenses such as cyber seats costs, travel, lodging, and needed hard copy materials?

Remember, too, that registration done online may have special challenges if learners are expected to work from their desks or from home. For instance, some organizations provide learners with signs that say "Quiet, please. I am currently busy in an online professional development program. Please come back in a few minutes." Issues associated with those special challenges should be addressed in the instructions for the learning experience.

4.3.2 Notifications and Access

Be sure that signs, invitations, and notifications make it easy to find physical facilities and e-learning environments and that links work for online registrations and access. Consider:

- Can learners and instructors find events?
- Is the electronic learning environment accessible through an employee portal or Web site?
- Can learners access electronic offerings from remote locations, or must they be at a specific computer lab or workstation?
- If events are held physically in hotels or conference venues, have notifications and logistical reminders been sent out to learners and instructors?
- Is it clear who is confirmed to attend, where the event will be held, when the event will begin, and what the schedule (start time, end time, and break and lunch times) will be?
- Do signs/notifications need to be in multiple languages, and does online content need translation to be accessible to all learners globally?
- Do signs need to be made available in braille?
- Has reasonable accommodation been made for learners with disabilities?

4.3.3 Seating Arrangements

Seating affects how people interact both face-to-face and electronically (see www.ctl.yale.edu/ClassroomSeatingArrangements). If learners are organized in a classroom with a traditional seating arrangement where chairs face the front of the room, then learners are directed to pay more attention to the instructor than to each other. In these environments, learners are directed to learn primarily as receivers of information. If learners are organized to sit at round tables, they are positioned to focus on each other and to interact in small group activities. In interactive environments, learners are encouraged to learn from each other, rather than from the facilitator. Even in electronic environments, seating options can enhance learning. If online learners can break out into small group spaces within the electronic host site and return later to the larger group, interaction can be improved. The point is that the seating arrangement should be constructed in ways that create an environment supportive to interactions and exchange. When in doubt, instructors can ask learners if they feel the seating arrangements are appropriate for the communication in which they engage and the interactions they experience while participating.

4.3.4 Equipment to Support Learning

Facilitators of training require much physical equipment to support what they do during training delivery. Physical support may include:

- A podium at the front of a classroom,
- A computer to support PowerPoint and other software presentations,
- A projector,
- Microphones,
- Remote controls,
- Speakers,
- Whiteboards,
- Flipcharts,
- Translation services,
- Closed captioning.

Within electronic environments, the technology used—both hardware and software—must support instructors as well. Further, the technology established must be useable by the facilitators. Technology resources and needs will change depending upon the level of interaction needed for quality learning. Some electronic environments are completely passive, with no same-time communication possible between learners and instructors. Other electronic environments are real-time interactive, offering multiple communication modes to support simultaneous interaction among learners and between learners and instructors. Learners may also require individualized equipment—such as computers or tablets and interactive devices; this is true for both physical environments and electronic environments.

4.3.5 Refreshments

In the classroom and other physical places, some refreshment is usually expected. That may include a minimum of water and coffee in morning, lunch at noon, and snacks in the afternoon. Within an online environment, breaks are often planned for learners to excuse themselves from Internet devices and obtain food or other refreshment individually. What refreshment or break time is provided, and how many resources are allocated to them, may be a function of organizational policy. Generally speaking, providing refreshments and break times helps to create a welcoming atmosphere that supports learning. Without refreshments or breaks, learners may go in quest of them and become self-distracted, when they should be focused on learning.

Break times also create the opportunity for learners to interact informally with each other and even discuss issues that arose during the planned learning event. Facilitators can encourage that interaction by providing some structure to support it (like tables with name tents with topics assigned) or allow it to occur informally. For instance, in some organizations, people are arranged in groups and asked to talk about what they are learning over lunch or break.

> *I had a cadre of 25 branch managers that I would visit on a monthly basis asking how their participants were performing after they returned back to the branches. Then, I would ask if there were any adjustments or things that were resonating to continuously improve our process.*
>
> **–Scott A. Critchfield, CFP**
> *Coach, Learning Professional*

4.3.6 Event Evaluation

Nearly, all organizations conduct some form of participant evaluation. That sometimes takes the form of a reaction sheet completed by learners at the end of a training session. Evaluation is done to determine how much learners liked what they learned, how comfortable they felt in the environment (physical place or electronic space), how much they learned from the experience, what they will take back and apply to their jobs, what productivity improvements or cost savings resulted from the learning experience, and what impact the training had on achieving business results.

> *I'd have a lunch with several participants, and ask for their feedback and insight on the program they just attended – what were two or three things that stuck out for them that were key takeaways, and what were two things they would tweak to the program… what would that be?*
>
> *–**Scott A. Critchfield, CFP***
> *Coach, Learning Professional*

Event evaluation can also be used to create an impetus for change back on the job by encouraging learners to create action plans or "to do lists" about what they plan to do differently when they return to their work settings. It can also be used to surface likely barriers to training transfer and encourage learners to consider ways to knock down barriers that may keep them from applying what they learned.

4.4 Creating a Supportive Learning Environment

Creating a supportive learning environment requires more work than it might appear (Weller 2007), and the learning environment design may be a function of the learning and development department structure (discussed in Chapter 3, "Structure for Accountability"). For instance, some learning organizations with a corporate university or federated structure create learning centers where employees may drop in at any time to get real-time help on work challenges. Many organizations have information centers or online Web sites, which serve as libraries of the education offerings made available to employees. One key is to make learning experiences both visible to potential learners for selection and accessible to employees for enrollment.

But if other managers will not permit workers to leave their work areas to seek the help in learning centers, or permit workers to have access to learning offered online, then the notion of providing real-time help to workers as learners is defeated. It can demonstrate a lack of a supportive learning environment or else a compliance-driven philosophy of employee education.

Creating a supportive learning environment means that learning and development managers must clarify what is required to design and plan the full physical or electronic space dedicated to employee development. Managers must then determine what resources need to be provided and take actions to ensure that the learning environment is sustained and accessible to employees.

4.5 Conclusion

Training is an internal function, in which both managers and resources need to support employees from across varied business units as learners. Learning managers are challenged with aspects of establishing a proper environment for learning, be it an online webspace or a residential setting, and this environment may be vastly different from the learners' workspace. For accreditation, the training environment must be managed proactively as a comfortable physical and psychological environment, which is carefully designed, and which contains adequate support to learners.

Manager Tips

A. Involve learners and instructors in identifying what is needed to create a supportive learning environment. Ask your employees to examine carefully both your physical learning environment (training center) and your online or electronic learning environment (Web site). Seek learner input on how the environment can better support learners. Be willing to provide the necessary money, time, staff, and other resources to create and sustain both your physical and your psychological environment.

B. Identify what barriers to learning the organization creates—intentionally or unintentionally—to learning. Then take steps to knock down the barriers. *Example*: The organization requires each worker to have an Individual Development Plan (IDP). But if no action is taken during the year to implement the IDP, nothing happens. That is a barrier to an effective learning environment. *Example*: The organization offers several learning modules online but fails to publish the access procedures for logging-in or completing the training online. This, too, can be a barrier to an effective learning environment.

C. Broaden the notion of the learning environment to include issues affecting online learning, peer learning, and experience-based learning.

Examples: Does the organization take steps to minimize interruptions to learners as they engage in online learning while at their desks? Does the organization encourage the use of Internet-connected devices that can be taken off-site for individualized e-based learning or make learning experiences available on mobile devices such as smartphones? Does the organization offer interactive webspaces where peers can share lesson learned?

D. Communicate the importance of a supportive learning climate to other managers across the organization. While some operating managers accept the notion of "creating a learning organization," they may not realize that creating such an environment also means encouraging employees in climates conducive to education, as well as task execution.

Supplement

Directions: Use this instrument to determine how well the organization's climate supports real-time learning to solve work-related problems. For each condition listed in the left column, indicate in the right column how much you perceive that condition to exist at present in your organization. Use the following scale:

1 = This condition is *not applicable* to this organization.
2 = This condition is *never true* in this organization.
3 = This condition is *sometimes true* of conditions in this organization.
4 = This condition is *usually true* of conditions in this organization.
5 = This condition is *always true* of conditions in this organization.

There are no absolutely "right" or "wrong" answers to these questions. Answer as you perceive the conditions to exist in your organization. When you finish the assessment, add up your scores and then consult the table at the end to determine next steps.

Supplement Tool 4A: Tool to Assess the Organization's Learning Climate

Part I: Assessment

CONDITIONS		In this organization at this time, this condition is …				
		NOT APPLICABLE	NEVER TRUE	SOMETIMES TRUE	USUALLY TRUE	ALWAYS TRUE
		1	2	3	4	5
1	There is enough money to support learning to solve job performance-related problems in real time.	1	2	3	4	5
2	There is enough time to support learning to solve job performance-related problems in real time.	1	2	3	4	5
3	Workers are sufficiently engaged to solve job performance-related problems in real time.	1	2	3	4	5
4	Managers support workers to solve job performance-related problems in real time.	1	2	3	4	5
5	Workers feel they will be rewarded if they learn in real time to solve work-related job performance problems	1	2	3	4	5
Total all the scores from items 1-5 above and place the sum in the box at right →						

Part II: Scoring

If your score was between:	Then:
25-21	Grade the organization's learning climate an "A." The conditions in your organization are most supportive of workplace learning. While some improvements can still be made in the spirit of continuous improvement, your workplace-learning climate is exemplary.
20-16	Grade the organization's learning climate between a "B" and "C." The conditions in your organization *usually* support workplace learning. Examine carefully those items on which you scored your organization below a 5. Pinpoint specific areas for improvement and take action to improve them.
15-10	Grade the organization's learning climate an "D." The conditions in your organization *sometimes* support workplace learning. Examine carefully those items on which you scored your organization below a 5. Pinpoint specific areas for improvement and take action to improve them.
9 and 0	Grade the organization's learning climate an "F." The conditions in your organization never support workplace learning. Examine carefully those items on which you scored your organization below a 5. Pinpoint specific areas for improvement and take action to improve them.

References

Rothwell, W. (2002). *The workplace learner: How to align training initiatives with individual learning competencies.* New York: Amacom.

Rothwell, W., Benscoter, B., King, M., & King, S. (2016). *Mastering the instructional design process: A systematic approach* (5th ed.). New York: Wiley.

Weller, M. (2007). *Virtual learning environments: Using, choosing and developing your virtual learning environment.* London: Routledge.

Part II

Planning the Environment and Educational Events

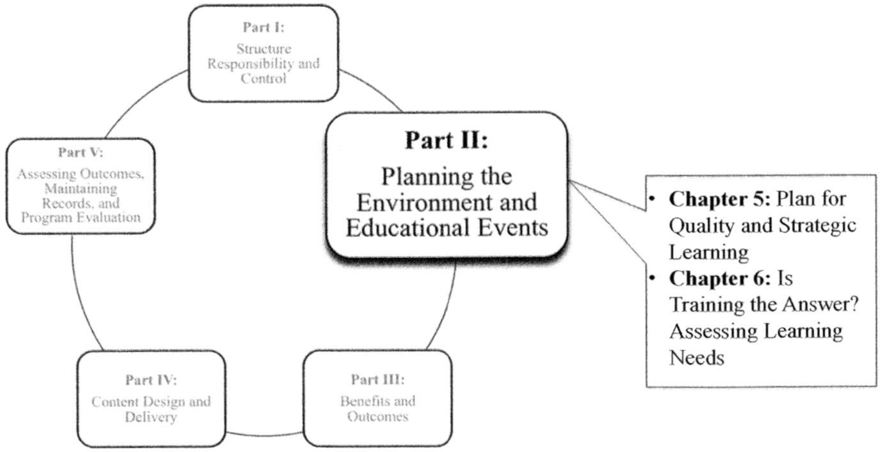

Fig. 1 Chapter organizer

An individual's motivation to grow in the workplace is strongly influenced by the organization's learning environment. Companies that have been successful in developing a learning culture have improved productivity, promoted innovative solutions, and enhanced employee engagement. Organizations must be prepared to upskill and reskill their employees, as well as develop new skills that have not yet been identified. Companies must be prepared to develop future talent for jobs that do not yet exist, where the knowledge, skills, and abilities to be successful are still unknown. Re-skilling will be a lifelong process for tomorrow's workforce. Quality training programs must provide learning solutions that are agile, adaptable, and are continuously updated to meet the moving target of a competent workforce. Therefore, it benefits every organization to invest time and resources in creating an optimal learning atmosphere with specific plans for setting the direction of learning as a strategy for employee development.

The previous part described structuring an organization for the learning and development (L&D) department. Part II, "Planning the Environment and Educational Events", describes structuring the product of the learning and development department—its educational output. Providing a program that is accredited will require a structured plan to ensure quality (defined by continuous improvement), and a pre-defined curriculum of training products—not just a haphazard collection of courses. Structuring a curriculum requires forethought of the department's educational philosophy and the development of a Learning Blueprint, which codifies the learning plan. The goal is to tie the educational effort of the learning and development department to the strategic plan of the organization and help the organization meets its challenges and succeed in its marketplace.

The Learning Blueprint is the learning and development department's strategic plan that maps out the long-term training process earmarked for employees. Much like an architectural blueprint which codifies plans for floors, rooms, and systems (i.e., plumbing and electricity), the Learning Blueprint codifies plans for training programs and courses, as well as plans for support systems, which link learning directly to the organization's strategic plan. In architecture, the end result of a well-codified building blueprint is a complete physical structure. In learning and development, the end result of a Learning Blueprint is a complete learning program structure. Accredited learning and development departments also establish a process for creating the individual workshops and courses—the hallways, floors, and rooms within the blueprint. Designing each course or learning event requires a single process which is systematic, consistently used, and includes an evaluation component. Both the Learning Blueprint and course design process are discussed in Chapter 5, "Plan for Quality and Strategic Learning".

Before creating individual sessions or courses, the overall employee education program must meet the particular and unique needs of the organization. Those needs must be fully scoped out and investigated in order for the learning and development department to be able to defend against internal pressures regarding resource allocation and ensure that learning events are not subjected to the whims of managers. Unique organizational needs are either existing deficiencies, gaps in productivity and effectiveness, or opportunities for employees to grow and excel. However, training may not always be the best solution. Identifying the opportunities or deficiencies in learning is a diagnostic process, referred to as a *needs assessment*, discussed in Chapter 6, "Is Training the Answer? Assessing Learning Needs". In needs assessment, the root causes of performance gaps are investigated, analytically deciphered, and communicated proactively to leaders. Learning strategies are then designed and developed to close the gaps.

In spite of a well-thought-out plan, not all learning strategies are created equal. An accredited training provider ensures that the learning strategies meet the standards of a reputable accrediting institution. Thus, through accreditation, learners are assured that the learning and development program provides high-quality training outcomes.

5

Plan for Quality and Strategic Learning

Dwight D. Eisenhower is credited with saying that plans are useless, but planning is essential. His point was that a plan, as a work product, is often not used. But the planning process is essential to encourage people to think about what they need and why they need it. The same point applies to learning and development. In managing a learning and development department, leaders must anticipate, prepare, and be proactive. The planning process for learning, and aligning training to organizational strategic plans, is critically important. This chapter focuses on strategic planning for learning and recommends creating a Learning Blueprint. Accreditation is driven by a quality approach to learning—both in the overall curriculum design and in the planning process to create and build courses. Overall, the notion of quality learning and development has shifted from an episodic intermittent activity in response to an internal request to a more continuous ongoing learning strategy, which is pursued and implemented by the learning and development leadership. The Learning Blueprint is the documented plan which aligns the learning structure with the organization's business plan. Learning organizations will not achieve accreditation unless both planned learning and a secure instructional design process have been established, documented, and consistently implemented. Thus, the learning and development department needs a structured plan for how it approaches learning to assure quality, and a process to establish its learning products. The Learning Blueprint builds a learning strategy so the department can train proactively to meet organizational business needs, as opposed to training as a reaction to mistakes or gaps.

W. J. Rothwell et al., *Increasing Learning & Development's Impact through Accreditation*,
https://doi.org/10.1007/978-3-030-14004-5_5

5.1 Quality Management Background

Attaining quality is an ongoing practice. The theory of quality management explains it as a systematic "procedure to determine product conformance or nonconformance" (see p. xxi in Mauch 2009). Organizations recognize that quality management can enhance competitive advantages in the marketplace. Total Quality Management (TQM) philosophies have been applied to the academic setting through an Academic Quality Consortium formed by the American Association for Higher Education. In health care, the TQM model is applied to continuous medical education activities (Shortell et al. 1998).

Popularized by the Japanese auto industry, TQM is a strategy for continuous improvement that builds on the work of W. E. Deming, an American engineer and management consultant (Ferris and King 1996). TQM is the term generally used to describe quality practices within organizations and can be characterized by three core principles: continuous improvement; customer focus; and employee involvement.

5.1.1 Continuous Improvement

Accreditation from an organizational perspective, ensures that people, processes, and systems are all aligned that they're focused on continuous improvement as an organization.

—Laureen Kaczmarek
ISACA
Senior Director,
Product Development and Content

Continuous improvement, also known as Kaizen, is the philosophy of continually seeking ways to improve products, services, or processes through incremental changes. It is an ongoing effort initially aimed at reducing waste to streamline factory work, but which now is applied to work procedures and processes in a variety of industries. There are several structured approaches to continuous improvement, such as Six Sigma, Lean Six Sigma, Agile, or Scrum. A foundational concept of quality is the cycle for learning and continuous improvement, as illustrated in (Fig. 5.1) Deming's Wheel (PDSA cycle).

Implementing the Plan-Do-Study-Act (PDSA) cycle in the learning and development effort can significantly improve organizational learning and facilitate problem-solving activities by employees in the workplace (Choo et al. 2007). The work problem is identified and analyzed in the (P) planning

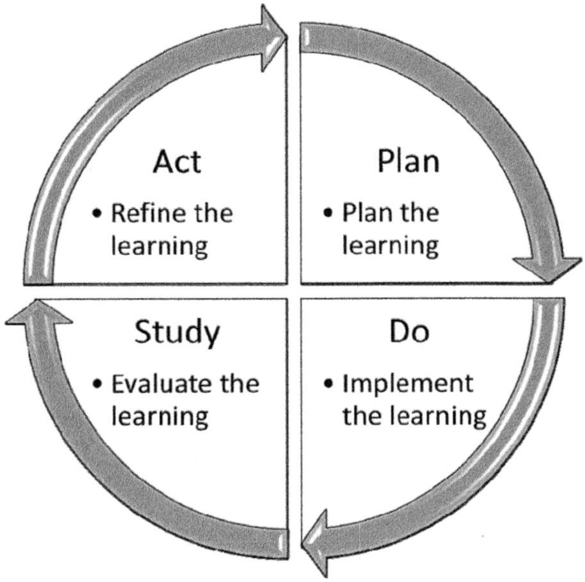

Fig. 5.1 Deming's Wheel (PDSA cycle) (Adapted from W. Edwards Deming, [1993])

phase, solutions are implemented in the (D) doing phase, and the results are evaluated in the (S) study phase, resulting in refined learning solutions in the (A) acting phase. This continuous learning design cycle supports the development and revisions of training interventions.

5.1.2 Quality and Continuous Improvement in the Context of Learning

Grounded in the world of business, TQM was originally discounted within the training field because it was, unfortunately, viewed as commoditization of education. Using key terms such as value-added, output, input, process, and benchmarking, educators resisted the model. However, as the concept of organizational learning emerged (Argyris and Schön 1997), the TQM approach was incorporated as a primary characteristic of human resource management and as a critical business function to optimize the human element.

Quality and continuous improvement in the context of training and learning, emphasizes a step-by-step practice for carrying out the course design with an evaluation strategy aimed to improve the learning outcomes. The evaluation of training moves beyond the verification of "did the employee learn?" into a self-correcting system where the learning and development department examines itself and identifies where both programmatic and operational changes are needed to improve the learning outcomes (see Chapter 13, "Program Evaluation and Records").

5.2 Quality Approach to Training—Strategic Planned Learning

Training in today's organizations involves both the learning and development department's overall programs (curriculums), and the individual steps for creating separate courses. A quality approach to training means there are two underlying structures: a plan for creating the overall curriculum and a process for creating each learning event produced. An accredited provider is required to have both:

1. A structured learning plan (or referred in this book as a Learning Blueprint)
2. A systematic process to create and build individual courses.

5.2.1 Clean Up the Talk

Terms and nomenclature can get confusing in the learning and development field. Learning and development departments will often offer a series of workshops or sessions to cover multiple aspects of one topic, and the series itself might be termed a training "*program.*" For example, if the series topic was Sales Skills, and if it was used for employees to build quality interactions with customers, the series might include several courses such as "Serving Customer Needs," "Determining Customer Wants," "Negotiating Price," and "Relationship Building." All the courses in the series would make up a "*program*" on Sales Skills. If the topic was a series on Leadership, the series might include several courses such as "Goal Setting," "Providing Subordinate Feedback," "Writing Appraisals," "Managing Group Projects," and "Ongoing Team Guidance." All the courses in this series might constitute a "*program*" on Leadership Skills. A series of courses offered by the learning and development department might also be called an extended Training Workshop or a Training Series. The individual sessions can be termed courses, classes, or units. Importantly, all the series of topics offered, all the *programs* taken collectively, along with all the individual courses, constitute the department's entire learning curriculum.

5.2.2 Don't Say Curriculum!

The word *curriculum* is derived from the Latin, meaning "to run a race." It is commonly understood to mean a learning plan. While Latin terms can be confusing, the point is that planned learning is like a race. There should be a definable beginning, middle, and end to planned learning. *Curriculum planning* is thus the process of determining the beginning, middle, and end of the program your learning and development department offers.

Most people encounter the term *curriculum* in school. *Curriculum* is a common term in education and refers to the teacher's instructional plan. However, in business, the word *curriculum* is not used at all because operating managers do not understand the term *curriculum* in a business setting. Therefore, as a learning and development manager, don't use the word *curriculum*. Instead, create a term useful to your organization, which describes the comprehensive learning plan for your organization. That comprehensive term might be the "Learning & Development Plan," the "Plan for Learning," or the "Learning Blueprint." Whatever term you use, make sure they carry meaning as the entire collection of programs, series, and sessions produced by your learning and development department.

5.2.3 Structured Learning Plans—The Learning Blueprint

To achieve accreditation, your firm's overall training scheme must be based on structured learning plans, what we are calling *Learning Blueprints*. Just as a blueprint is an architectural plan for building a physical structure, a Learning Blueprint is an educational plan for building a training structure. Having a learning plan, or Learning Blueprint, is the same thing as a training strategy for planned employee growth through at-work education, and it is one of the most critical elements of accreditation.

The Learning Blueprint, sometimes called the Learning Map, is the learning and development department's codification of the long-term training effort for employees specific to your organization. Much like an architectural blueprint which codifies plans for floors, rooms, and systems (such as electrical and plumbing), the Learning Blueprint codifies plans for training programs and courses, as well as supporting systems which link learning to the organization's strategic plan. As depicted in Fig. 5.2: *The Learning Blueprint* is grounded within your organization's mission, vision, and employee values discussed in Chapter 2, "Align Learning and Development

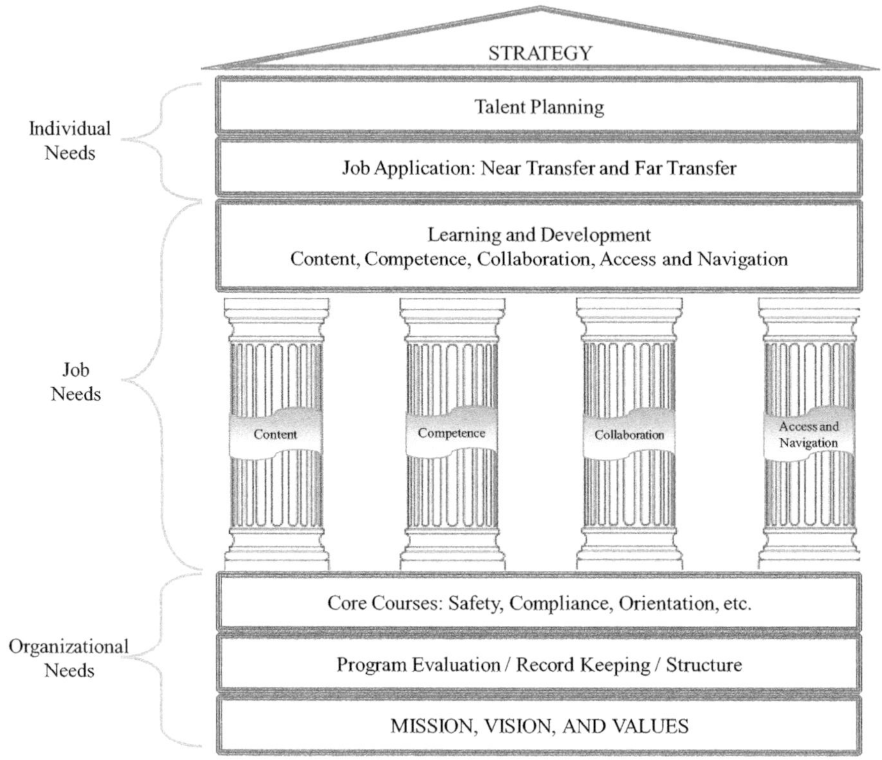

Fig. 5.2 The Learning Blueprint

with Organization Mission and Values". Upon this is built your learning and development business structure and your educational philosophy. Within the core of the Learning Blueprint lie your training programs, workshops, and courses, built to address job needs. Here, training is designed to address job content, the collaboration needed by workers conducting interdependent jobs, special competencies needed for unique jobs (such as technical engineering jobs, medical jobs, and certified skill jobs), and allowance for access and navigation to the training offerings (discussed in Chapter 10, "Deciding What to Include"). Enhancing the learning products beyond job needs are the plans for training to meet individual needs. These are depicted at the top of the Learning Blueprint diagram. Here, your learning and development department is involved in the job application of content taught—to assure near transfer and far transfer application (see Chapter 12, "Learner Feedback and Job Application"). Your learning and development plan also addresses leadership needs and plans for developing leadership skills and talent to guide the organization. Finally, the Learning Blueprint must align and coordinate with the organization's strategy, depicted at the peak of the Learning Blueprint diagram. As shown, the final result of a Learning Blueprint is a complete learning structure.

5.2.3.1 Organizational, Job, and Individual Needs

Each Learning Blueprint, or learning structure, should be tied to organizational needs, job needs, and individual needs. *Organizational needs* can be focused on what all people must know, do, or feel to achieve strategic organizational goals. As a simple example, a business that is implementing statistical process control in every operating unit might mandate training on the topic for all of its employees to address critical organizational needs. In this example, statistical process control training would constitute one of the foundation training courses for the organization, just like the foundation drawing for a building blueprint—it is needed for the structure to stand. Training addressing organizational needs are shown in the Learning Blueprint diagram as one of the foundational elements, particularly noted in core courses.

Job needs are focused on what groups of people must know, do, or feel to carry out a job category in ways that meet expected competencies. Every job description lists expected work duties and requirements. Training designed to help individuals carry out the duties or responsibilities listed within their job descriptions would meet job needs. As an example, all jobs which deal directly with customers might become more effective following training on handling interpersonal conflict. This training would help job performance where people interface with customers. The Learning Blueprint in this example would include a plan for training all persons in jobs which deal with customers and would be depicted as a competence pillar on the blueprint for learning across a variety of roles.

Individual needs are what individual people must personally know, do, or feel to be effective in their work. Not all individuals enter jobs equally prepared to carry out the required responsibilities. Training can close individual gaps so that all employees meet minimum job requirements. Training can also be offered to maintain job skills amid changing business conditions. Training can also be a means for preparing individuals to guide the organization in the future by providing management and leadership skills to certain individuals. In our example, individual leadership training might be designed as specific topics in the Learning Blueprint, much like designing specific rooms in an architectural building plan.

5.2.3.2 Planning the Learning Blueprint (*Shhh!—Curriculum* Planning)

Many philosophies guide the structuring of learning plans or Learning Blueprints. One philosophical approach asks: Should instruction be focused around subjects, objectives, or questions? A *subject-centered curriculum (blueprint)* is organized around course titles. Adult students in a community college may, for example, study history, english, mathematics, and so forth. Those are subjects. A subject-centered curriculum is organized around the courses (or other experiences) that experts believe people should understand.

An *objective-centered curriculum (blueprint)* is organized around learning objectives. What targets (objectives or goals) should learners achieve to be capable of doing their jobs well? *Instructional objectives* are targets for employee accomplishment by the end of a training program. It is also possible to establish objectives for lessons, units, or bigger blocks of learning—such as an entire degree program or an entire organizational need (such as a High Potential or a New Manager program).

An *inquiry-based curriculum (blueprint)* is organized around questions. What questions should learners be encouraged to explore? An inquiry is directed according to what is necessary to encourage learners to think through what issues are worthy of exploration.

5.2.3.3 Writing a Learning Blueprint (Shhh!—*Curriculum* Design)

The first step of Deming's Cycle, PDSA, is "Plan." In this step, a business-driver approach is used to inform and create the Learning Blueprint, or the plan for learning at your organization. Your Learning Blueprint will be unique to your organization based upon the drivers of your business. Drivers of the business may be the technicalities of the industry, the changing demands of customers, the speed of technology improvements, or any other forces that seriously impact your organization's business strategy. Overall, the Learning Blueprint will be based on the needs of your unique workforce to flex with the changing business drivers and be adaptable in the future.

Unlike education, which can be carried out in many different organizational settings, Learning Blueprints are drawn to help workers perform their jobs in one unique organizational setting within one corporate culture. The learning and development manager's job is to determine the unique qualities of the organization and to design a unique Learning Blueprint aligned with both the strategy of the organization and the performance needs of the employees.

To design a subject-centered Learning Blueprint, learning and development managers would simply ask line managers what courses workers should take, and then design pages of the blueprint for each topic. Some courses would be necessary to perform a job, but other courses might be intended to meet legal obligations for compliance, or requirements for safety. Still, other courses might be intended to help build general workforce awareness on subjects tied to organizational goals—such as workplace ethics, core company values, harassment avoidance, or other topics relevant to the organization's culture.

To design an objective-centered Learning Blueprint, learning and development managers would focus on performance levels that employees (as learners) can transfer to their work. The line manager would examine what targets would need to be met to help workers reach minimum job requirements, maintain their job performance as technology changes, or prepare for advancement to higher levels of responsibility. In the example above, both the "Selling Skills" program and the "Leadership" program would fall under an objective-centered Learning Blueprint.

High-quality Learning Blueprints are a combination of subject-centered and objective-centered training designs aimed to help workers meet all performance requirements by linking educational efforts to the strategic plan of the organization. An example of a subject-centered and objective-centered Learning Blueprint would be one that codifies both organization-wide training events on topics such as safety or regulation as courses available for all employees, and a series of training events on topics which are objective-centered and designed for specific jobs. Objective-centered training events might be focused on technology topics, customer service topics, or product feature topics because these topics are needed by workers across different jobs. Whichever form your Learning Blueprint takes, you need to hold to a philosophy of learning and use that philosophy as the foundation for planning the Learning Blueprint. Top learning and development managers know the foundations of their learning, they know how their learning is designed, and they use the written Learning Blueprint to maintain solid, and dependable, learning programs.

We direct all the learning programs, especially our online programs. I get involved early to plan the programs to be sure everything is done properly and meets our protocols - whether it's a business-line need or whether it's for organization-wide training.

–Reg Bonfoco

Canadian Financial Securities Company Continuing Education Specialist

5.2.3.4 Formalize the Learning Blueprint

Similar to a project map, an organization's Learning Blueprint is a document that displays the comprehensive structure to the learning and development department offerings. Some parts of your Learning Blueprint may focus upon subjects, such as software tools or delivery timing. Other parts may focus on objectives or inquiries, such as supervisory competence building, or collaboration. This is like designing a building with different floors and hallways, off of which the rooms will differ. The Learning Blueprint should be written, perhaps authorized formally into policy, and made available for access by both organization leaders and learning and development professionals. A sample Learning Blueprint is offered at the end of this chapter.

5.3 Creating Courses—A Design Process

Workers are hired or promoted at one level of ability and must then be trained—that is, put through a series of instructional experiences—to achieve the next level of job abilities or next level of needed performance. For accreditation, the learning and development department must have a defined process for the building of individual training courses that help workers to learn. Each course is like an individual room on the blueprint; what is required is a process for course development. This is the "Do" part of the PDSA cycle. Creating courses of quality requires a design process that is systematic, representing a consistent method of doing things, and which includes a component of continuous improvement. Your learning and development department must always use just one method for designing its courses, and should be used continually. The course design process should also be one that is known to learning and development professionals as a method for constructing quality lessons, and the process should include an evaluation component.

One of the big things I do is look at a course before it goes live to make sure that every part is included that needs to be there. I get rid of all the fluffy stuff, and make sure that each component is completed to satisfy our various requirements.

–Reg Bonfoco

Canadian Financial Securities Company Continuing Education Specialist

5.3.1 Instructional Systems Design (ISD)

Instructional Systems Design (ISD) is a good process focused on a step-by-step design. ISD evolved from research conducted during World War II to create effective technical training for new recruits to the military. Later, the ISD process was used in business and industry as a method to achieve behavior change in workers under a variety of industrial settings. The process consisted of four phases, which were completed with an evaluation loop used for course revision and improvement. Instructional System Design process is deeply rooted in adult learning principles, and several process models have emerged from it. Today, ISD is an approach for both the assessment of needs and the development of courses—specifically for the purpose of creating and delivering workplace training. Several models that use the ISD approach as a foundation are the ADDIE model, the Dick and Carey model, and the Successive Approximation Model (SAM) the successive approximation model.

A lot of it (accreditation process) was really just examining what we were doing. Having a process and being able to show information and begin to look at the programs we need to develop. It was very much kind of like educating people on the ADDIE model.

–Peter Finn

Society of Women Engineers

Deputy Executive Director and Chief Learning Officer

5.3.1.1 ADDIE Model

The ADDIE model is essentially the standard instructional design framework used most often in creating training courses. The ADDIE model is an adaptation of the ISD process based upon the notion that using a step-by-step approach to design training systematically will create the most effective results for the business. The training will be specific to the organization's workers, and their job function needs to effectively change the employee's work behavior.

ADDIE is an acronym for the five phases—Analyze, Design, Development, Implementation, and Evaluation—to build one course or class. It provides a step-by-step process for analyzing specific needs, designing content, developing course materials, implementing the instruction, and evaluating the results of the course. The phases of the ADDIE model are summarized as follows:

- **Analyze**: This first phase of the creation process is arguably the most important. It enables the instructor to identify the key elements needed for the content of an effective course, such as performance expectations, the job requirements, and the worker profile. The instructor analyzes job tasks and compares them to the knowledge, skills, and attitudes of the current workers. This phase explores and assesses the root cause(s) of an identified business need and determines if the acquisition of new knowledge, skills, and/or abilities by the workforce via learning event(s) is the most appropriate solution to the need.
- **Design**: During the design phase, instructors start planning and structuring the content. Objectives linked specifically to the necessary acquisition of knowledge, skills, and/or abilities identified in the "analyze" phase are established, and instructional methods for learners to achieve each objective are determined. This includes the conceptual design of visuals, activities, exercises, assessments, and interface (electronic or in person). An evaluation plan is also designed. The document produced during this phase detailing all these decisions is called a storyboard and serves as a guide for creating the course.
- **Develop**: The development phase is where instructors use the storyboard created in the design phase and actually produce the activities, exercises, graphics, etc., to be used by both the learners and the facilitator. If a learning management system (LMS) was developed for the instruction, it is installed during this phase. This phase also involves beta testing and debugging any issues that turn up, both forms of continuous improvement.
- **Implement**: In this phase, the instruction is actually delivered to the learners, whether recorded electronically, offered through an in-person facilitator, or both. Activities of the course in operation may be observed for making improvements. This is the phase where an e-learning course is uploaded to a learning management system (LMS) or put online so learners can access it.

- **Evaluate:** After the implementation phase, the course is evaluated to measure how well it achieved the objectives detailed in the design phase. Evaluation is actually a continuous process, which may have formative, summative, or confirmative purposes. This phase will result in revisions and updates of the course (see Chapter 12, "Learner Feedback and Job Application", and Chapter 13, "Program Evaluation and Records").

5.3.1.2 Dick and Carey Systems Approach Model

The Dick and Carey Systems Approach is a design instruction model from a "systems" standpoint (Dick and Carey 2001). The development phase is emphasized, and instruction is broken down into smaller components. This model is centered on the learner; therefore, characteristics of the target audience are critical factors in the design process. According to Dick and Carey, "Components such as the instructor, learners, materials, instructional activities, delivery system, and learning and performance environments interact with each other and work together to bring about the desired learning outcomes." Impact upon the worker-learners in a training course is a key element to designing individual courses. The components of the model include the following (Dick 1996):

- Assess needs to identify goal(s),
- Conduct instructional analysis,
- Analyze learners and contexts,
- Write performance objectives,
- Develop assessment instruments,
- Develop instructional strategy,
- Develop and select instructional materials,
- Design and conduct formative evaluation of instruction,
- Revise instruction,
- Design and conduct summative evaluation.

5.3.1.3 Successive Approximation Model (SAM)

The Successive Approximation Model (SAM) is an instructional design model that emphasizes agility and approaches learning from repeated small steps to address practical design issues, such as budget constraints and time restrictions. The model includes constant evaluation, which is depicted as iterative steps. The iterative steps allow for continual adjustments based on practical project limitations. The SAM process is divided into three phases, each containing deliverable milestones:

- Preparation phase,
- Iterative design phase, and
- Iterative development phase.

Each phase's purpose is to move the learning project toward completion. It works through small steps, frequently taking quick diagnostics as evaluation measures. Thus, the intention of continuous improvement is included in the SAM model. SAM focuses more on the participant experience, engagement, and motivation, rather than on the content or the presentation of information. The SAM model was created by Michael Allen as an alternative to the ADDIE model.

5.4 Plan to Evaluate

Evaluation is a critical part of quality as it forms the basis for continuous improvement. Quality checking is an essential part of establishing a Learning Blueprint, and the process of quality checking can be included at many stages of course creation. Continuous quality checking is an inherent feature of the evaluation phase of both the ADDIE model and the Dick and Carey model. Regardless of the design method utilized, a continuous improvement process, or continuous evaluation, should be used to maintain quality. This is the "Study" part of the PDSA cycle. Plan to calculate a baseline of training costs and results. Incorporate built-in checks and measures of progress in each phase of course design to ensure the quality. The emphasis in evaluation is on the ending result of improved performance for the individual worker when they are back on the job. Conducting evaluation work is a profession of its own and an independent field of expertise within the learning and development field. Frequently, good evaluation work needs to be assisted by an accountant who can interpret findings into explainable costs and benefits, and who can calculate the return on investment (ROI) of your training efforts. Specific information about the different types and purposes of evaluation is described in Chapter 12, “Learner Feedback and Job Application”, and in Chapter 13, “Program Evaluation and Records”.

5.5 Conclusion

Accreditation requires organizations to have a learning plan, or a Learning Blueprint in writing for their learning and development department. The Learning Blueprint links business’ operational strategies to the overall educational structure and the design of individual courses. The design of individual courses should follow a selected design process, and that process needs to be consistent for all courses and programs created by the learning and development department. High-quality learning and development departments also document both Learning Blueprints and course design procedures and infuse those plans with evaluations for continuous improvement. Through the planning and design effort, the learning and development department can be proactive and anticipatory in serving the organization.

Manager Tips

A. Don’t use the word *curriculum*.
B. Differentiate your organization’s use of training terms such as a program, series, learning event, and course. Your training staff should use your organization’s terminology exclusively.
C. Make training quality intentional.
D. Create a structured Learning Blueprint to which all the department’s training programs are aligned.
E. Use one, standard process for creating individual training courses. For accreditation, make sure that process is systematic and is used consistently by instructional designers.
F. Include an evaluation feature in the creation of both training events and training programs.
G. Evaluate using hard data numbers whenever possible. Hire an accountant to assist in calculating costs, expenses, and revenues.

Supplement

Supplement Tool 5A: *Job Needs—Job Learning Blueprint (JLB) Worksheet*

JOB NEEDS: Job Learning Development Blueprint (JLB)

Directions: The purpose of this worksheet is to align the job's learning requirements with the organization's strategic objectives. It outlines the basic courses needed to do a standard job, bringing individuals to adequate levels of performance. When you have completed this tool for key jobs across departments within your organization, complete Supplement Tool 5B to organize your organization's overall learning needs.

Issue	Job Title: ______________________
Title(s) of Learning Events pertinent to this job.	
Purpose of the Learning Events (knowledge, skill, affective improvement)	
Objectives of the Training for this Job	*Upon completing all the learning events, employees in this job will be able to:* • • •
Prerequisites (*list if any training must be completed before job starts*)	
Relationship of Job to the Organization's Strategic Goals	
Targeted Learners *(characteristics of those qualified to start this job)*	
Performance Assessment expected by unit post-training	

Supplement Tool 5B: *Organizational Needs—Organizational Learning Blueprint (OLB) Worksheet*

Organizational Needs: Organizational Learning Blueprint (OLB)Worksheet

Directions: This is just one example of a possible format for an Organizational Learning Blueprint (OLB). An Organizational Learning Blueprint like this should be completed for *each department*. For each job category listed in the left column below, list the *title of a learning experience* that would be appropriate at each stage of an individual's experience in the job. Training topics might reflect experiences like "a tour of the facilities," planned learning events like courses, or efforts in mentoring or coaching. "Entry" means "upon entry to the job category." "Intermediate" means "after 1-2 years." "Advanced" means "after the individual has been in the job category for 3-5 years." There are no "right" or "wrong" answers. The aim of the activity is to begin to scope the organization's learning requirements by examining learning needs per unit or department.

Job Category	Entry Job Needs	Intermediate Job Needs	Advanced Job Needs

***Supplement Tool 5C**: Individual Needs—Individual Learning Blueprint Worksheet*

Individual Needs – Learning Blueprint (Individual Development Plan-IDP)	
Directions: Complete the form below for each employee and then schedule a meeting between worker and his or her immediate supervisor. The Individual Development Plan (IDP) is intended to customize the Organizational Learning Blueprint, tailoring it to the needs of each employee.	
Name of Employee:	**Name of Employee's Immediate Supervisor**
Today's Date:	**Period Covered by This Plan:**
Job Category of Employee:	**Department:**
Employee Needs	
Employee Learning Experiences	
List learning experiences that the employee should participate in over the period covered by the plan. Indicate planned experiences (such as training online or onsite), coaching, mentoring or other social learning-oriented experiences, and on-the-job work experiences designed to build learner competence.	

Time, Resources and Evaluation Methods

For each learning experience, indicate how much time, resources and evaluation methods should be allocated for it.

Experience	Time Period	Resource	Evaluation

Signature of Employee/date	Signature of Supervisor/date

Supplement Tool 5D: *Sample Learning Blueprint*

Introductory Courses	**Workplace Tool Programs**
• Orientation to ______ • Start Work/Core Values • ______ • Safety Regulations for ______	• Microsoft Office Products • Employee Interfaces (using Skype) • Personal Work Management • ______ • Subconscious Bias in Workplace
Objective-based Programs	**Inquiry-based Programs**
• ____Officer Training Program • Associate Engineer Basics • Beginning Logistics • Basic Selling Skills • Advanced Presentation Skills • Managing Customer Relationships • ______ • Supervisory Skills 101 • Basic Leadership Techniques • Advanced Leadership • Managing Projects • Delegation and Feedback	• Envisioning Our Future • Goal Setting • Visioning with Clients • ______ • Promoting Respect/Social Media • ______ • Industry Advances in 20XX • ______ • Community Footprint
Department Specific Programs	**Programs Open to Others**
• Etc.	• Etc.

References

Argyris, C., & Schön, D. A. (1997). *Organizational learning: A theory of action perspective. Reis*, (77/78), 345. https://doi.org/10.2307/40183951.

Choo, A. S., Linderman, K. W., & Schroeder, R. G. (2007). Method and psychological effects on learning behaviors and knowledge creation in quality improvement projects. *Management Science, 53*(3), 437–450.

Deming, W. E. (1993). *The new economics: For industry, government, education.* MIT: Cambridge.

Dick, W. (1996). The Dick and Carey model: Will it survive the decade? *Educational Technology Research and Development, 44*(3), 55–63.

Dick, W., & Carey, L. (2001). The systematic design of instruction: Origins of systematically designed instruction. *Classic Writings on Instructional Technology, 2*, 71–80.

Ferris, G. R., & King, T. R. (1996). Politics in human resources decisions: A walk on the dark side. In G. R. Ferris & M. R. Buckley (Eds.), *Human resources management; perspectives, context, functions, and outcomes* (3rd ed., pp. 44–53). Englewood Cliffs, NJ: Prentice-Hall.

Mauch, P. D. (2009). *Quality management: Theory and application.* CRC press. www.pqm-online.com/assets/files/lib/books/mouch.pdf.

Rothwell, W., Benscoter, B., King, M., & King, S. (2016). *Mastering the instructional design process: A systematic approach* (5th ed.). New York: Wiley.

Shortell, S. M., Bennett, C. L., & Byck, G. R. (1998). Assessing the impact of continuous quality improvement on clinical practice: What it will take to accelerate progress. *The Milbank Quarterly, 76*(4), 593–625.

6

Is Training the Answer? Assessing Learning Needs

Assessing needs is more difficult than ever, particularly as a plethora of haphazard information becomes readily available. Old information becomes obsolete; new knowledge, skills, and abilities emerge, and time continues to be scarce. Organizations must pursue quality information and abilities, often mistaken for compliance, by focusing on real efforts to improve the knowledge and skills of employees. But how can you identify training as the appropriate solution to a need? Training is one of many ways to improve employee performance so that the work can be done more effectively or efficiently. Working more effectively means greater collaboration, higher product quality, or increased customer satisfaction. Working more efficiently means a faster pace, fewer steps, or reduced errors. To make such improvements, how do you know when training is needed versus other ways to improve performance, such as skill refinement, memory jogging, or coaching? Before determining the training solution, what is most needed must first be specified. This is the effort of assessing the real performance need, the process of needs assessment. This chapter focuses on assessing the learning needs to identify root causes of the performance problem and to determine if training is the best solution for addressing a business challenge.

W. J. Rothwell et al., *Increasing Learning & Development's Impact through Accreditation*,
https://doi.org/10.1007/978-3-030-14004-5_6

6.1 Assessing the Real Need—Determining the Business Problem/GAP

In a lot of cases, we weren't doing any kind of needs assessment. Some of our programs were based on a lot of assumptions and the sample of one. So, we wanted to make sure that we're moving away from that and started doing some surveying and doing some focus groups.

–***Peter Finn***
Society of Women Engineers
Deputy Executive Director and Chief Learning Officer

Assessing the real performance need means scoping out the complete situation at the enterprise so that the actual work problem and its source can be named. Scoping out the enterprise means determining the business problem and framing it if one exists. Framing the problem means to inquire if the source of the issue stems from a change in the business—a change in the way the organization operates; or a change in how it serves its customers.

There are many different kinds of needs. A business need implies an issue affecting the enterprise. A performance need implies an issue affecting work results. A learning need implies a lack of knowledge, skill, or attitude essential to achieve necessary work results. The needs of a learner focuses on individuals and implies knowledge, skill, or attitudes (KSA) that individuals lack to do their jobs. Identifying business needs require information about organizational targets and desired milestones, such as strategic goals. Identifying performance needs require the distinciton between the desired work outcome targeted versus the actual work result. Identifying learning needs require an assessment of the existing knowledge, skills, or attitudes. Identifying learner needs require making comparisons between what individuals currently know, do, or feel to exactly what they must know, do, or feel to achieve necessary results.

Note that each of these needs implies a gap or deficiency that is best addressed through training. Thus, identifying training needs requires examinations of business, performance, learning, and learner needs. A gap exists when actual performance differs from the desired performance. Naming the problem and describing its depth and breadth are called determining the gap. The work is not being done as effectively or as efficiently as it might be, and someone needs to diagnose why. Therefore, needs assessment is a process of scoping out business needs, performance needs, learning needs, and learner needs. Undertaking the needs assessment process is much like a doctor taking a health history before diagnosing a medical condition or like an accountant conducting a financial audit to uncover the source of mistakes in calculation.

Importantly, training needs are different from training wants. Let's be sure to know the difference. A training need is a gap between what employees currently know, do, or feel and what they must know, do, or feel to meet the job requirements. In contrast, a training want is the desired situation, perhaps something that managers or employees wish workers could do or possess. Ask managers and workers what knowledge, skills, or attitudes are *necessary* to do the work, and you will surface training needs; ask managers what they *wish they were getting* from workers and you will surface training wants. Wants and needs are not the same things. Wants are "nice to have"; needs are "essential to have."

Real performance problems, or actual training needs, might surface in situations such as late deliveries, high production rejects, inconsistent service levels, or increased customer complaints. While these types of situations are broad indicators of areas with performance problems, they may not be situations that training can solve. We don't really know if training can solve a performance problem until we thoroughly explore the business problem/need. A thorough exploration involves framing the problem/need, identifying the type of need being presented, and investigating for root causes.

6.1.1 Framing the Problem

Framing the problem is inquiring about the source of the organization's issue or the change being experienced. How did the work change for employees? Was there a new aspect added to the production process that altered how work was to be done—such as a new software system, a new feature to a product, a new device on a machine, or a new application to incorporate? Framing the performance problem might involve responding to recent business events—such as a decline in sales, an increase in returns, or an uptick in customer complaints. Framing the business problem might arise from a strategy move at the organization requiring people to think collectively, manage large projects, or make collaborative decisions. While instructors and training designers may tend to call all of these "performance problems," the framing is really an investigation of the enterprise—scoping out the enterprise job changes that may arise because the organization is engaging in new opportunities, new methods, or new production/service processes.

6.1.2 Type of Need

Type of need falls into six identifiable categories which are used when conducting a needs assessment or gap assessment, because they represent characteristics that surface from a broad viewpoint of the organization and its environment. In other words, something might be happening outside the organization that people inside are reacting to. The six types of needs are: normative needs, comparative needs, felt needs, expressed needs, anticipated needs, and critical incident needs.

A normative need arises when the organization's output or quality is compared to a target or national standard, such as ISO 9000, Transportation Safety Standards, or Occupational Safety and Health Administration (OSHA) standards. Normative needs frequently exist in regulated industries such as transportation, financial services, or medicine. In these industries, the standard is usually available from professional associations or trade groups.

A comparative need arises when the organization or enterprise unit compares its results to peer groups or target groups—competitors or businesses within the same profession. However, the target group results must be measured using comparable data in order to determine a true difference. A comparative need will exist when there is a gap between the measurement of the target group average and your organization's result. Responding to a comparative need should be taken with care, however. You want to be focused on correcting a real difference rather than merely trying to "keep up with the neighbors."

A felt need is a desire on the part of individuals to do their jobs better—to improve their own performance. Felt needs surface in interviews with employees or through personnel surveys using open questions about opportunities in the job(s). Felt needs among employees are real performance needs because the individuals self-identify the knowledge or skills they need to perform more effectively or efficiently.

Expressed needs are felt needs, which have been acted upon by employees. Here, employees don't wait for the organization's learning and development department. Rather, individuals take action to improve their own production. Expressed needs are evidenced by employees attending outside classes, enrolling in structured courses, or placing their names on waiting lists for training programs. Expressed needs are a good training manager's dream, and these types of employee demands should be addressed as soon as possible.

Anticipated needs are foreseen future performance shortfalls because of an upcoming process change, production or delivery re-tooling, or organizational restructuring. Here, good training managers anticipate training needs by identifying organization changes that will take place in the future and estimating the impact those changes will have upon employee production. Foreseeing changes in software, mechanics, processes, regulation, quality, or customer demand are identifying future needs that will drive work changes for employees. Any aspect of the organization that is expected to be altered should be examined carefully because anticipated needs are very likely to drive training demand.

Finally, critical incident needs are those which stem from a major failure or emergency. Employees need to react to emergency situations safely and accurately and will need skill training to respond appropriately. While critical incidents are rare, the resultant losses to personnel and facilities can be devastating to an organization. Critical incident needs are identified by asking "What if…?" questions in order to analyze potential catastrophes, and design pre-emptory or preventative training.

6.1.3 Investigating Root Causes

Investigating root causes means pinpointing the problem. For training to be effective, it must be focused on the particular problem as it exists among specific workers within the organization. Finding root causes is a process which identifies the source of the issue—what caused the problem—in efficiency or effectiveness; it identifies why employees are not working to their full potential. Investigating root causes is a key step in the needs assessment completed by training managers, particularly because it helps to address the real issue. A learning and development manager can avoid addressing issues which are not important to achieve in employee productivity or which are only problems perceived or suggested by others. Root causes of job difficulty (workers' performance problems) can lie at both the individual worker level and a broader organizational level.

6.1.3.1 Individual-Level Root Causes

Individual-level root causes can be found in missing knowledge, employee skill, or employee attitude. Knowledge is the individual's comprehension, understanding, and use of information to mentally conduct a particular job. Skill is the individual's capability to take action to perform the physical aspects of a job. Attitude is the individual's approach to the work itself, which impacts the individual's engagement in the job. Each of these individual-level root causes can be the source of performance problems. Alternatively, the combined knowledge, skills, and attitude of workers can be viewed together as a combination of root causes.

> *Root Cause Example*
>
> When a new radiation expeller is purchased for a cancer treatment lab in a hospital, oncology nurses must learn the new terminology associated with the expeller, they must learn to physically operate the machine, and they must address their own attitude towards using the equipment on cancer patients. This is a combined need for new knowledge, new skills, and an attitude examination on behalf of the nurses.

During the needs assessment process, a root cause in knowledge describes missing comprehension, understanding, or recall about specific topics. The assessment identifies such items as: "employees do not retain all necessary facts," or "employees do not understand the steps for …," or "employees do not know the difference between X and Y."

A root cause in skills describes specific actions which are needed to execute the job, but which are not being exhibited by workers. An assessment of skills needed might describe "button not pushed completely," or "drops the sterile instrument," or "document converted incorrectly."

A root cause in attitude describes specific behavior, which exemplifies a negative or nonchalant emotional perspective about performing the job. The assessment of attitude might describe: "non-contaminant gear improperly worn after break time," or "waiting customers are ignored," or "impartial about understood deadlines."

6.1.3.2 Organization-Level Root Causes

Organization-level root causes can be found in environmental factors, management conditions, and interpersonal relations. Discovering these root causes uncover real business needs.

Environmental factors in the workplace setting and its physical conditions include access, equipment availability, noise, odor, and lighting. Environmental factors are evidenced directly within the production area, office space, place of entry/exit, or shared common spaces. A root cause based on environmental factors might surface as "late arrivals because parking lot has insufficient spaces for drivers," or "air quality not consistent between floors," or "reflective overhead lighting impacts laptop visibility." Environmental factors, while they can significantly deter performance, cannot be resolved by training. Rather, improving the physical condition of the workplace should be addressed.

Management conditions involve giving direction, observing employee performance, offering feedback, and time of supervision—basically the guidance provided to workers by their bosses. Lack of supervision and guidance to workers can easily deter employee performance. Root causes based on insufficient management might surface as "direct supervision is not possible due to the remote location of the immediate boss," or "limited direction is provided by the supervisor to second shift workers," or "manager fails to provide direction for marketing calls expected toward potential clients." In these instances, training the employees further will not resolve the issue. Rather, a change in management or training in supervisory practice is needed.

Interpersonal relations involve the availability and relationship of all persons on a team or project. Each individual may well be able to conduct his/her job duties adequately, while the overall performance is problematic due to interpersonal issues. People may just not be getting along with each other. Without team direction and support for team efforts, lack of cooperation between workers can negatively impact performance. Root causes based on interpersonal relations surface in observations such as: "work group dispersion causes progress to falter," or "poor communication among team members hamper team success," or "competitiveness among staff members disrupt attention to tasks." Again, when root causes are identified as organization-level causes, formal learning or training is not likely to be a successful solution.

Learning and development managers must carefully discern causes and address only the root causes for which training can be a solution. Learning and development managers must also be direct in expressing to executives the reasons why changes in management practices or other adjustments need to be made to help employee performance. Table 6.1 provides a summary of root causes to employee performance problems and offers suggested solutions, many of which are not training suggestions.

To help name the problem and identify its root causes, a *Needs Assessment Diagnostic Checklist* is provided at the end of this chapter.

Table 6.1 Root cause examples and sample solutions

Root Cause	Symptom/Example	Solution
Lack of Knowledge	Production workers do not know speed setting on beltline. New personal bankers do not know requirements for loan application.	Train – beltline settings. Train – loan application documents and use.
Lack of Skill	City maintenance workers cannot operate refuse crusher at municipal waste site. Administrative assistants cannot save legal documents for lawyers in pdf format.	Train – Refuse crusher controls and operation. Train – use of Adobe and Word software functions.
Lack of Attitude	Safety goggles not worn by all workers in food processing plant. Team members not prepared for group project meetings.	Train – food handling safety and organization safety values. Re-order Team Structure and/or offer incentives for team project participation.
Environmental Factors	Professional staff experiencing back pain at new workstations. Lighting in shop causing errors in watch repair work.	Modify environment or adjust workstation configuration. Modify environment lighting.
Management Conditions	Supervisor fails to observe full production run 5x per shift. Senior executives speak English to office personal; do not speak Spanish to plant personnel.	Change management practice or coach supervisor. Train – executives in Spanish, or hire bi-lingual executive.
Interpersonal Relations	Rivalry between credit managers limits loan approvals. Managers from original firm distance themselves from managers of second firm absorbed during merger.	Provide coaching/conflict resolution for managers. Change management practices or change titles and incentives.

6.2 Conducting a Needs Assessment

As a result of the accreditation process, we improved our process of needs assessment… We used to rely very heavily on the subject matter experts, particularly the concepts that somebody needed. But it wasn't rigorous; it wasn't backed-up by surveys, it wasn't backed-up by site observation. It was overly reliant on the opinion of a single subject matter expert. But you've got to really understand the needs analysis, for the courses to be relevant to the users.

–***Clyde Seepersad***
Linux Foundation
General Manager,
Training & Certification

Conducting a formal needs assessment within the organization requires a planned process for seeking information, assuring that all the information has been requested, and obtaining the information thoroughly. A needs assessment is usually carried out as a seperate project. The project consists of conducting an "audit" of the work situation for the job or jobs in question, which requires a project plan. One simple needs assessment plan falls into six areas: setting the limits; determining the data needed; identifying sources of information; selecting methods for data collection; collecting and analyzing the data; and communicating needs assessment results.

6.2.1 Setting the Limits

Setting the limits means determining in advance how much time, money, and staff will be devoted to the assessment project. Resource allocations for assessments need to be balanced against resource constraints. The project of conducting a needs assessment does not involve making changes or improvements, however, the other managers may grow impatient with the assessment process and may want to move directly to new training. Thus, time and demands of other managers may cause limits to the scope and extent of any assessment effort you want to pursue.

6.2.2 Determining the Data Needed

Determining the data required to conduct the needs assessment involves thinking about the job and identifying information that is unclear and should be clarified. Is the needed information about the worker's knowledge? Worker's skills? Worker's attitudes? The data should help to determine exactly what the needs are at the worker level. Don't depend upon the managers for this information. Going straight to the workers for input into their job needs is the best way to determine the exact breadth and depth of information needed. It simultaneously gives the workers a hand in helping to determine the learning program that is ultimately designed for them. Most important is the information concerning the nature of the employees' work situation as it presently exists. The work situation includes the job responsibilities, the job performance expectations, the reporting structure of the work situation, and the aspects of the job that are knowledge or skill related. At this point, it is important to plan how to get answers—plan out the types of questions that will be useful, how will the questions be distributed, what sources will be used to collect the data, and who will collect the data information.

6.2.3 Identifying Sources of Information

Identifying sources of information means naming the places where job-related information can be obtained. Some information may be written down in job descriptions or in work procedure documents. Information related to job expectations may be obtained through policy reviews or regulation requirements. Information related to job conditions may be obtained through employee records, grievance reports, documented accidents, or service records. Some information may not be documented at all and will need to be obtained firsthand from persons in the job(s) or from samples of the work produced from the completed job(s).

6.2.4 Selecting Methods for Data Collection

Selecting methods for data collection means determining how the information needed about the job can be reasonably collected. A variety of techniques are used to gather assessment information. These include observation of persons conducting the job(s), questioning the workers themselves (through surveys, interviews, or small group discussions), testing the individuals currently conducting the jobs for knowledge or procedural facts, reviewing documents and records, and taking work samples. Each technique carries various advantages and disadvantages, including the time needed and the thoroughness demanded by the organization's leaders. With ample time and resources, information can be collected that thoroughly describes expectations for job performance and completely documents job production as currently conducted. However, most organizations do not have unlimited time and resources, making a selection of methods for collecting data a function of your organization's culture.

In a culture of openness and sharing, enough information may be obtained through a few interviews, informally directed at key persons who are trusted to be forthcoming. Conversely, in a culture of closed communication and reluctant collaboration, information may best be obtained in formal, but anonymous ways, such as written employee surveys, documentation reviews, or examinations of work samples.

6.2.5 Collecting and Analyzing the Data

Collecting and analyzing the data means obtaining both hard and soft data and interpreting it for logical comprehension. Not all situations are ideal, and practical obstacles to obtaining key job data are likely to be encountered. If possible, use a combination of techniques (quantitative and qualitative) but don't spend excessive time waiting for exact data. Pursue data that is obtainable within your specific organization. Analyzing the data involves applying quantitative methods (such as statistics), qualitative methods (such as thematic word comparisons), or a mixed–method (both statistical analysis and word analysis). Data analysis may include a step where business, performance, learning, and individual learner needs about what is (current situation) are compared to what should be (desired situation).

6.2.6 Communicating Needs Assessment Results

Once the information has been obtained and analyzed, a clear distinction can be made between the optimal performances needed for the job(s) and the actual performance exhibited by the worker(s). The difference between optimal performance and actual performance is the job gap. Using the needs assessment results, you can communicate that gap to impacted persons internally through town hall meetings, executive presentations, web site announcements, written reports, or a combination of these. For high-quality learning and development that is accreditation worthy, the organization must have an established process for both identifying needs and communicating those needs inside the organization. Do not sit on your findings. How you communicate actual training needs will influence the motivation of line managers and workers toward the training programs.

> *We are totally dependent upon the needs assessment based upon the organization's quality management system. If there are any identified risks or issues that come up during the assessment process, depending upon the level of the risk or the issue identified, there will be a remediation plan created.*
>
> –***Jessica Burnett***
> *Senior Product Manager*
> *ISACA*

6.3 Issues in Needs Assessments

As a manager, you should actively oversee the needs assessment process. Inexperienced instructors sometimes get so carried away with collecting data about training needs that they forget the goal is to isolate gaps between the knowledge, skills, and attitudes that employees already possess and those they must possess to perform their jobs successfully. It is easy to see how that can happen. It is not a simple thing to prepare, implement, and analyze numerous surveys, interviews, observations, or other data. As instructors do that, they become easily distracted by the minutiae of the data collected, or they become biased by sympathizing with co-workers' stories. Instructors may end up forgetting the goal is to determine what many people must know, do, or feel to perform successfully and to build readiness among managers to plan and carry out learning efforts to meet training needs.

It is important to remember that training needs stem from business, performance, learning, and learner needs. Those four areas should be examined to identify gaps. And then training should be chosen as a way to close the gaps only when it is the most cost-effective way to do so, since there are many other ways to close gaps that are simply faster, cheaper, or even more effective. Consider, for instance, changing how people are selected for jobs, how the jobs are defined, how employees are given feedback on their performance, and how employees are rewarded for results. Changing selection methods, job design, feedback systems, or reward systems can sometimes be faster, cheaper, and easier than designing training.

6.4 Planning for Strategic Organizational Learning Beyond Needs Assessment

Planning for strategic organizational learning is more work than it appears. Inexperienced learning and development professionals may think that their jobs end with naming training needs, pinpointing root causes, and outlining the instruction needed on new knowledge, skills, or attitudes. But it is not that simple.

For one thing, organizational leaders want results and not just learning. Learning will not solve all of the organization's problems. In fact, training will solve only about 10 percent of all organizational problems with employees. Effective learning and development managers will thus be thinking beyond planned training to include any procedure that helps to improve employee job performance. For example, how are workers recruited, selected, rewarded, appraised, and promoted? Answers to these questions may affect job performance more than training. It is thus important—in fact, it is best practice—to precede training needs assessment with an effective performance analysis in which problems are sorted into those that training will solve and those that training will not solve. Generally, learning and development professionals refer to the difference as "training needs" versus "management needs."

How can learning and development professionals, or managers, determine what is a training need and what is a management need? The answer is relatively simple. If workers have previously demonstrated successful job performance, then they do not need training. But if workers are new to the job and have never demonstrated successful performance, then training is required. As a simple example, a new hire will need training because he or she has not demonstrated successful job performance. But a twenty-year veteran worker does not need training if he or she ever did the job right one time. Problems with the veteran's performance may call into question issues about the feedback being received, the reward system, worker motivation, management engagement, and so forth. One key for you, as the manager of the learning and development effort, is to both discern these differences and hold firm in not designing training for worker problems that truly rest with management.

6.5 Conclusion

Needs assessment is a key step in the effective design of learning and development programs. Without it, the organization may end up wasting time, money, and effort. A need is a gap or deficiency between what is (actual) and what should be (desired). Needs may exist at the organizational/business, performance, learning, or learner levels. Needs assessment is the process of identifying what training is needed to address root causes that cannot be more quickly or easily addressed through alternative solutions such as changing selection methods, reward systems, feedback systems, or other methods. A simple needs assessment plan falls into six areas: setting the limits; determining the data needed; identifying sources of information; selecting methods for data collection; collecting and analyzing the data; and communicating needs assessment results.

Manager Tips

A. Involve other managers, employees, and learning and development professionals in identifying training needs and separating problems that training can solve from problems that training cannot solve.
B. Conduct a problem diagnosis before spending the resources on a full training needs assessment. Find the root causes of any perceived problem.
C. Resist efforts by managers to tell the learning and development department what learning is necessary without any analysis. Managers are often tempted to do that because they think they already know training needs and wish to save time and money. But skipping the needs assessment process will often result in a training need reaction rather than a training needs analysis.
D. Conduct the full needs assessment work as a project. Identify a project team and actively direct the team's work with a project plan.
E. Facilitate the process of developing a full assessment of the behavior changes needed, and clearly describe the new behavior in terms of business results. Without these, senior managers will question "why are we undertaking this training experience, and how does it relate to achieving business needs?" Always be prepared to answer these questions.
F. Communicate proposed training from a basis in organizational goal achievement, and the employee behaviors needed to fit that goal in order to achieve strategy.
G. Know when training will not solve an employee performance issue. Stand firm in your refusal to design training for problems that training cannot fix.

Supplement

Supplement Tool 6A: Needs Assessment Diagnosis—Where Is the Real Problem?

Directions: Fill in the right hand column to determine the real need at your organization.

Framing the Problem (what is its source?)		
	New equipment. machinery, computers, software, etc.?	
	New people in (jobs)	
	Re-assignments of employees into (jobs)	
	Strategy change toward	
Type of Need (name what needs fixing)		
	Normative: need to meet a target (explain)	
	Comparative: need to meet the competition (explain)	
	Felt need: managers worried about	
	Anticipated Need: future will bring	
	Critical Incident: we might mess up at	
Root Causes at Our Organization – lack of		
	Individual Knowledge:	
	Individual Skill:	
	Individual Attitudes toward:	
	Combined K, S, & A:	
Root Causes at Our Organization want		
	Strategy will Help Us:	
	All Employees expected to:	

Supplement Tool 6B: *Checklist to Guide Training Needs Assessment*

Directions: Use this checklist to guide preparation of a training needs assessment project plan. For each item in the left column below, indicate in the center column whether the step has been planned. In the right column, indicate notes about how you or your team plans to carry out the step.

Steps in Training Needs Assessment		Has the Team Completed the Step?		Notes About How You or Your Team Plans to Carry Out the Step
		Yes	No	
1	Clarify training needs assessment objectives			
2	Set the limits (time, money, people)			
3	Determine the data requirements			
4	Select data collection approaches from a range of approaches			
5	Collect data			
6	Analyze data			
7	Communicate results			
8	Establish learning objectives based on learning needs			

References and Additional Resources

Barbazette, J. (2006). *Training needs assessment: Methods, tools and techniques*. San Francisco: Pfeiffer.

McGoldrick, B., & Tobey, D. (2016). *Needs assessment basics*. Alexandria, VA: Association for Talent Development.

Rothwell, W. (2015). *Beyond training and development: Enhancing human performance through a measurable focus on business impact* (3rd ed.). Amherst, MA: HRD Press.

Rothwell, W., Benscoter, B., King, M., & King, S. (2016). *Mastering the instructional design process: A systematic approach* (5th ed.). New York: Wiley.

Rothwell, W., Benscoter, B., Park, T., Woocheol, B., & Zabellero, A. (2014). *Performance consulting: Applying performance improvement in human resource development*. New York: Wiley.

Rothwell, W., King, S., & Hohne, C. (2018). *Human performance improvement: Building practitioner competence* (3rd ed.). London: Routledge.

Rothwell, W., Stopper, A., & Myers, J. (Eds.). (2017). *Assessment and diagnosis for organization development: Powerful tools and perspectives for the OD practitioner*. London: CRC Press.

Sleezer, C., & Russ-Eft, D. (2014). *A practical guide to needs assessment* (3rd ed.). Alexandria, VA: American Society for Training and Development.

Part III

Benefits and Outcomes

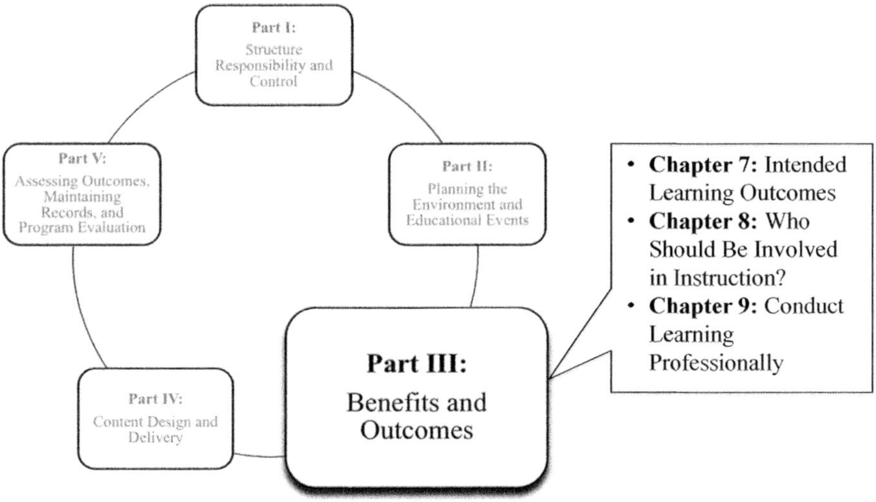

Fig. 1 Chapter organizer

Based upon your organization's needs assessment, training goals, which broadly describe the upcoming challenge for employees, and objectives that set parameters for employee performance, are established. Training goals carefully describe the new normal for the organization—what the organization will become and how the organization will benefit. Performance objectives set the parameters for what the employees will be able to accomplish after the training—what new actions will be consistently taken by employees. Training objectives, or instructional objectives, describe the new learning by employees expected to take place during training and accomplished by the training itself. Instructional objectives are set within the domains of knowledge, action, or emotion. Together, both training goals and instructional objectives set the plan of outcomes to result from the training and set the boundaries for the development of the respective training classes. Learning and development departments can become accredited if they set goals for each training program and plan the outcomes for each course, using instructional objectives. Accreditation focuses on sustained learning through carefully determined objectives that ensures the quality of the training program.

Setting goals for training programs and writing performance objectives for the purpose of modifying employee behavior require competent learning and development professionals. Competent instructors may qualify as subject matter experts, or as experts in the educational skills needed to effectively build meaningful classes. Skills to create effective training rest in planning and needs assessment (see Chapter 6, "Is Training the Answer? Assessing Learning Needs"), or in the tasks of producing the training itself—such as course design, courseware development, course delivery, or evaluation. The organization must legitimately own and protect its training products—its educational curriculum and courses. Accredited training providers produce learning products which are legally owned, and their delivery is assured as non-discriminatory. Finally, the learning and development department's products must be carefully held as intellectual property in order to protect the organization's educational assets and help it to remain competitive.

Setting training goals and establishing performance objectives for changed employee behavior involves analyzing various jobs and setting training goals (Chapter 7, "Intended Learning Outcomes"). Staffing the learning and development department with qualified professionals who can accurately carry out the work of planning and delivering training is the responsibility of training managers (Chapter 8, "Who Should Be Involved in Instruction?"). Protecting the organization's intellectual property and assuring the rights of all employees to continued education is the job of all learning professionals (Chapter 9, "Conduct Learning Professionally").

7

Intended Learning Outcomes

Assessing needs and planning resources for learning and development efforts are no match for positive and sustained change in employee behavior. Today, workers must do their jobs differently—working smarter and with a broader array of talents and tools. Anticipatory and accreditation-worthy training providers work to capitalize on employee talent, introduce new tools, and produce employees ready for change. This chapter focuses on the need for learning and development programs need to achieve learning outcomes based upon goals for workplace change and objectives for improved employee performance.

As in all endeavors, establishing a goal and setting objectives to meet that goal are two different procedures. A training goal is a general statement about the intended overall organizational change which new learning by employees will accomplish. Establishing training goals will focus the learning and development department on workplace performance outcomes and to tackle only what training can fix. Setting performance objectives will focus the instruction on achieving sustained behaviorial changes in employees.

> *Accreditation allowed us to speak to the fact that we really understand the needs analysis, we really think about learning styles, we really think about what the appropriate way is to evaluate the skills. We think about what's the breadth of quiz and checks relative to delivering content.*
>
> **–*Clyde Seepersad***
> *Linux Foundation*
> *General Manager,*
> *Training & Certification*

W. J. Rothwell et al., *Increasing Learning & Development's Impact through Accreditation*,
https://doi.org/10.1007/978-3-030-14004-5_7

7.1 Name the Program Goal

The organization's desired needs assessment documents the performance based on the current circumstances (Chapter 6, "Is Training the Answer? Assessing Learning Needs"). That needs assessment becomes the basis for establishing a training goal. After a thorough analysis of the future workforce needs, a clear purpose should arise for establishing new employee behaviors, hence, the goals for training. Remember not all job problems are solvable with training (see Solutions in Table 6.1), so be sure you are addressing an issue that training can fix. Nevertheless, the purpose for training will address the gap(s) identified in the Needs Assessment Final Report.

7.1.1 Training Program Goal Looks to the Future

The training goal is written evidence that shows the relationship between the performance need (or performance gap in the Needs Assessment Report, see Chapter 6, "Is Training the Answer? Assessing Learning Needs") and the expected outcomes of the to-be-developed training. The gap identified the deficiency; the training goal rewrites that deficiency into a reason for new training. The goal is basically written as a simplified statement that either points toward a resolution of the performance problem or promotes a new endeavor that the organization is undertaking to execute a new strategy. The goal is written in the future tense—a Vision Statement of sorts for the course or program—as a condition that "will be" for the trained workers. Examples of training goals, written in the future tense, are:

- "All employees will recognize the value of ethical treatment of…"
- "Customer service personnel will create…."
- "Payments will be processed through the finance and accounting units such that…"
- "Workers in the Z region will adjust tariffs according to…."
- "Sales personnel will consistently offer…"
- "Employees will discern differences between…."

7.1.2 Training Program Goal Covers Broad Changes

Each learning event offered by your organization does not require a separate training goal. A good training goal may suggest several separate learning events, sessions, or workshops. If the training need is the result of a strategic business move (such as improving organization-wide quality, workplace ethics, or corporate citizenship), one broad training goal can overarch a series of learning events to address that business strategy across different departments and workers. In this case, the goal would be singular, while the objectives for the workers in different departments would be customized. However, the rationale and reasons for planning training events would still be based upon the overarching business goal which surfaced from the needs assessment, in this case, one that arose from a new corporate strategy. Remember, the needs assessment always documents changes needed in the worker's skill, knowledge, or attitude. The new training goal must clearly state the anticipated the worker's new behavior based on skill, knowledge, or attitude.

7.2 Differentiate Goals and Objectives

Goals for learning programs and objectives for training events with employees are related, but different, directives. Goals are descriptions of the broad change (or the new environment), as described above. Objectives set forth the needed result at the worker level and are written as active, specific, and measurable worker outcomes. Documented objectives, which articulate the individual behavior to be mastered and executed upon completion of the training, need to detail the worker's action and the worker's situation. Post-training employee behavior needs to be clearly described in as few words as possible.

As a learning and development manager, you will most likely be directly involved in goal setting or in framing a learning goal based upon the final needs assessment and the identified performance gap (see Chapter 6, "Is Training the Answer? Assessing Learning Needs"). However, you may not be as directly involved in setting specific objectives. Objectives are well-articulated descriptions of the behavior to be expressed by workers—after the training session or workshop. Good objectives are detailed in action and specific to learning topics.

Objectives serve different purposes for learners, designers, and line managers. Employees refer to the objectives to understand what they will learn, do, or assimilate differently into their jobs after training. Each learning event, or session, will contain several objectives that set out new behaviors for employees to do on the job after training. Employee-focused objectives for back on the job are referred to as *performance objectives.*

Designers on the training team need objectives in order to guide what to include within the training instruction. Designers use the term *instructional objectives*, which are the same as performance objectives for workers, but are used to guide the designer's writing of the course. Instructional objectives help to clearly distinguish between topics that need to be covered within the training and topics that can be excluded from the training. Designers can then create a highly focused unit of learning for the target employees.

For line managers, performance objectives serve as a guide for evaluating the training to measure the impact of the training on the worker, in the workplace. This chapter focuses on establishing a training goal for a program and analyzing jobs to determine effective performance objectives. Writing effective instructional objectives for designing training content is explained in Chapter 11, "Methods to Achieve Consistency". Using objectives to evaluate training's impact is addressed in Chapter 13, "Program Evaluation and Records".

7.3 Analyze Jobs to Determine Performance Objectives

Determining the entire knowledge base, level of skills and attitude required of a worker performing a job is called *job analysis*, *task analysis*, or sometimes *performance analysis*. These terms are used interchangeably in the learning and development field. The *job analysis* is conducted when a production problem stems from a lack of employee knowledge, skill, or attitude. In these cases, a full and complete examination of the job is made by the learning and development staff in order to gather a comprehensive understanding of all aspects of the job function.

7.3.1 Job Analysis

Job analysis is the process of digging into the gaps between what the employees in the job currently know, do, or feel—and what they must know, do, or feel in the future to perform the job effectively and efficiently. There will often be differences in the current performance levels for jobs and the needed performance levels. The complete training need comprises all the gaps between what people presently know, do, or feel (what is happening today) and what they must know, do, or feel in the future (what should be happening), in order to perform at levels needed by the organization. Consider a simple example of job analysis related to a typist job.

Example

A manager initially has trouble with her workers, who are all typists, writing effective letters. So, she visits the training department to ask for help. Trainers do not automatically assume that the workers need training, nor do they immediately schedule training. Instead, the trainers will meet with the manager, as well as current workers, to understand all the knowledge, skills, and attitude characteristics needed to perform the letter-writing job well. During those meetings, the trainer will ask some important questions. Those questions illustrate a job analysis in action. For instance, the trainer might ask:

- What are the standards for well-written letters?
- How are the standards for well-written letters communicated to workers?
- What actions have been taken to address the problems with workers' letter-writing, and what were the results of those actions?
- Have workers ever produced documents (letters or other communications) that were written to the manager's satisfaction?
- Who seems to have trouble writing letters? What particular problems do those persons have?
- When did these problems first surface?
- Where (by unit or geography) do the letter-writing problems seem most noticeable?

Through the job analysis, specific gaps will be uncovered in the performance of the job, and this is where the learning and development effort will focus. Some parts of the job may be done quite well, while other parts may have errors or production difficulties. Performance objectives which describe the parts of the job being done well may already be in place and used by the workers and line managers. Using the specific gaps which have been identified, performance objectives are written to describe the areas of the job that need to be improved. The entire series of performance objectives constitute the job analysis. This job analysis becomes the basis for describing the skills needed by the workers performing that job.

Example

(In our job analysis for letter-writing): Only when the answers to the questions posed to the manager, and the typists, and observations of letters currently written seem to indicate that the letter-writing problem stems from lack of worker knowledge, or skills or attitudes will the training department begin a project to create and conduct training on letter-writing. The workers may already exhibit adequate skills in basic typing and keyboard knowledge.

Analysis establishes the framework that describes a job completely and that identifies areas of deficiency. Learning and development professionals who perform analysis poorly—or who skip it entirely—will usually discover previously unknown job steps are not performed properly. This can be a problem because line managers often discourage learning and development professionals from spending time on analysis since: (1) the line managers believe they already know what is needed, and (2) the line managers worry that both job analysis and learning and development determinations will add unnecessary time, money, and effort to a project. Line managers sometimes prefer that learning and development professionals "take the manager's word" that training is needed and should be scheduled and delivered, even if the class or workshop only covers one skill area.

I always have a sample of the typical practice done in one of our divisions. I match that practice up against the training request to see if it meets what everybody in the job deals with. If it doesn't, we go back to the content people and revise sections.

–Reg Bonfoco
Canadian Financial Securities Company
Continuing Education Specialist

7.3.2 Performance Objectives in Domains

Performance outcomes for job behavior are called performance objectives, and when designing training, they are called instructional objectives. Performance objectives can be grouped into three categories or domains: cognitive, psychomotor, and affective. Each domain contains levels of specificity or levels of difficulty in expression. Good performance objectives describe a detailed outcome that workers will perform according to a level of difficulty depicted within a domain.

7.3.2.1 The Cognitive Domain

The cognitive domain addresses a person's knowledge and ability to articulate the intellectual aspects of work. Bloom's taxonomy is a widely used depiction of increasingly harder levels of mental functioning—depicted in a sequence (Bloom et al. 1956). Bloom labeled the lowest level simply "knowledge," meaning the ability to recall information. Higher levels of mental functioning are categorized as harder thinking processes and sequence to comprehension, application, analysis, synthesis, and evaluation. Figure 7.1 provides descriptions of the related mental activity performed at each level of Bloom's taxonomy and the corresponding actions to be performed by the learner at each level (adapted from Brown and Green 2016; Morrison et al. 2012).

One of the challenges to job analysis is to discern performance objectives that specifically describe mental activity by workers at one of the five higher levels of mental functioning—higher than "knowledge." Many times, jobs are only designed for recognition or repetition, where employees are only expected to function at the knowledge level. This simple approach to basic mental functioning, however, does not help a worker or manager to really distinguish the more complex job functions. As an example, a performance objective which states: "Remembers the processing forms and their uses" is a much more basic cognitive performance objective than "Distinguishes among processing forms to select the one appropriate for the situation." Clearly, a higher level of mental acuity is described in the second performance objective. Talent, which requires mastery at a higher level of mental functioning, such as analysis, synthesis or evaluation, needs to be set down in performance objectives which specify the exact mental acumen needed for the job. Determining and writing correct performance objectives is a key skill of good learning and development professionals.

7.3.2.2 The Psychomotor Domain

The psychomotor domain addresses a person's ability to use physical motion (motor skills) to accomplish tasks. Physical skills are the use and coordination of muscles and skeleton to perform the action. In the workplace, physical skills include operating equipment, manipulating processes, and constructing objects. Builing on Bloom's taxonomy, a grouping of psychomotor skills was constructed by Dave (1975), which depicts a taxonomy of physical skills based on increasing degrees of precision and coordination. Figure 7.2 depicts the five levels of psychomotor actions and a description of each accompanied with the corresponding action-verbs at each level.

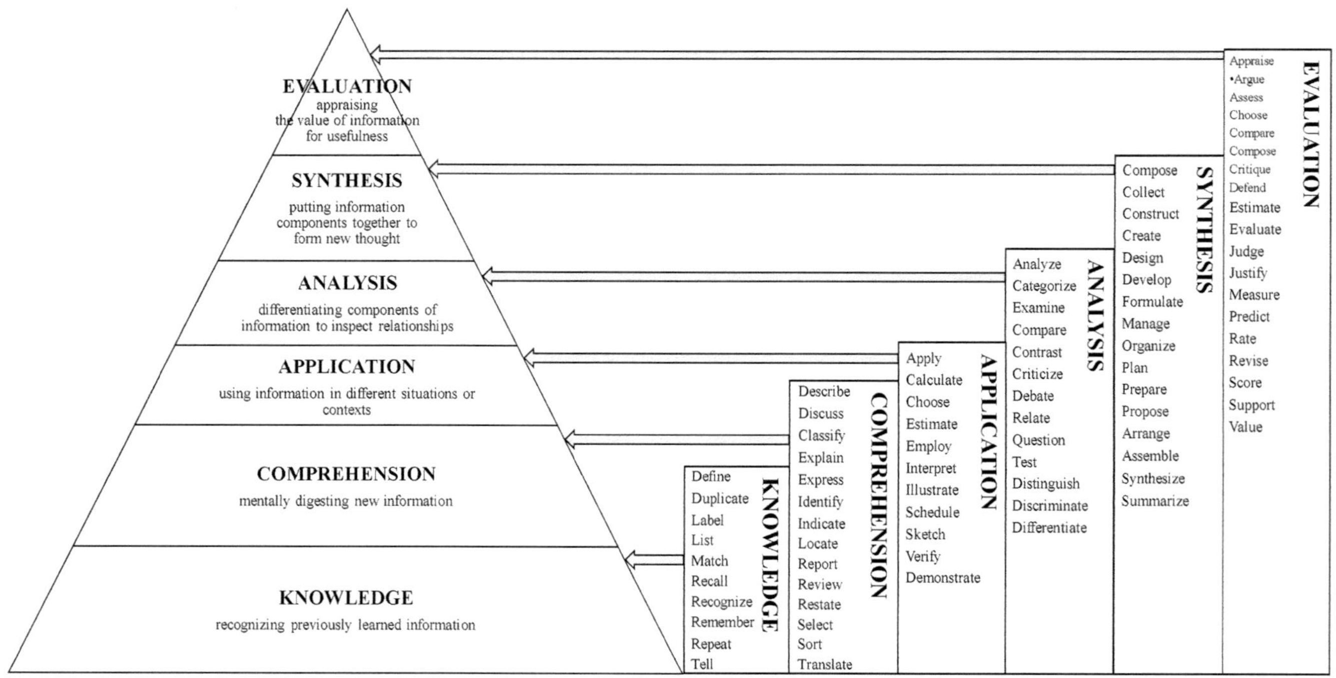

Fig. 7.1 Bloom's taxonomy of the cognitive domain (Adapted from Brown and Green [2016]; Morrison et al. [2012])

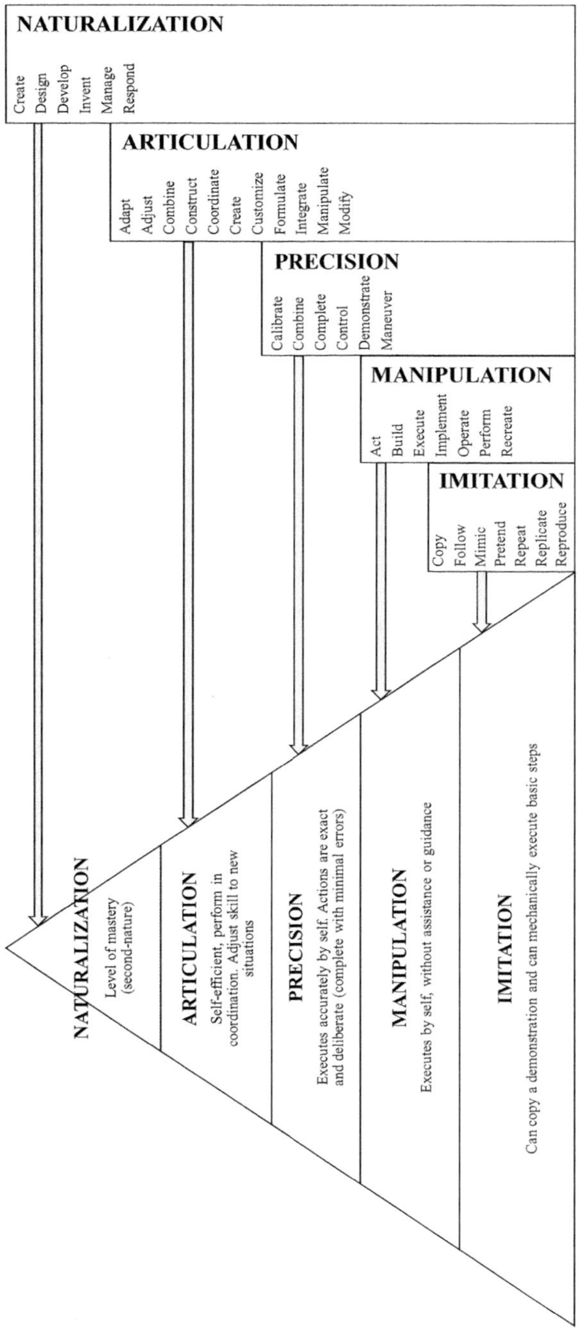

Fig. 7.2 Psychomotor domain levels (Adapted from Dave [1975])

Each higher-level of psychomotor activity represents a harder degree of physical difficulty. Jobs designed to build skills for physical action, or the doing of work, need to be expressed in performance objectives which clearly express the level of difficulty required. Objectives for psychomotor skills must specify the level of precision needed. For example, an objective of "Manipulates a jackhammer to break up concrete walkways" is different from an objective stating "Integrates proper safety procedures when operating the jackhammer to break up concrete walkways while avoiding damage to curbs, signs and light posts." Again, performance objectives for the purpose of a job analysis must carefully articulate the exact psychomotor action required by specifying the level of physical agility need for the job.

7.3.2.3 The Affective Domain

The affective domain addresses a person's feelings or approach to the work undertaken. Affections by employees are dispositions toward or against the experience of the work required and represent basic attitudes such as enjoying, conserving, and respecting. The affective domain has also been organized into levels of specificity according to response, and these human responses form a continuum of attitudinal behavior. The five affective levels are: receiving; responding; valuing; organizing; and characterizing value (Krathwohl et al. 1964). These responses range in emotion from simple awareness to inclusion into a person's value system. Each higher affective level is a different form of reaction and response, leading ultimately to personal integration. Figure 7.3 depicts the five levels of attitudinal behaviors, affective domain and offers a brief description of each accompanied with corresponding actions for each level.

Performance objectives within the affective domain focuses on attitudes, appreciation, values, and beliefs. At the higher levels, positive affections translate into core values held by persons, which in turn guide that person's behavior toward others. Affections and values intrinsically direct an employee's actions at work and forms the basis for an individual's belief about "ought to" behaviors in the workplace. Affective domain behaviors are very important to cultivate in learning and development efforts, but too often they are left unaddressed. An example of an affective performance objective is: "Appreciates the value of good customer relations by seeking to answer all customer phone inquiries." Difficulty in creating accurate affective descriptions has caused them to be less used in performance objectives for job analyses. However, in today's diversified organizations which are encouraging

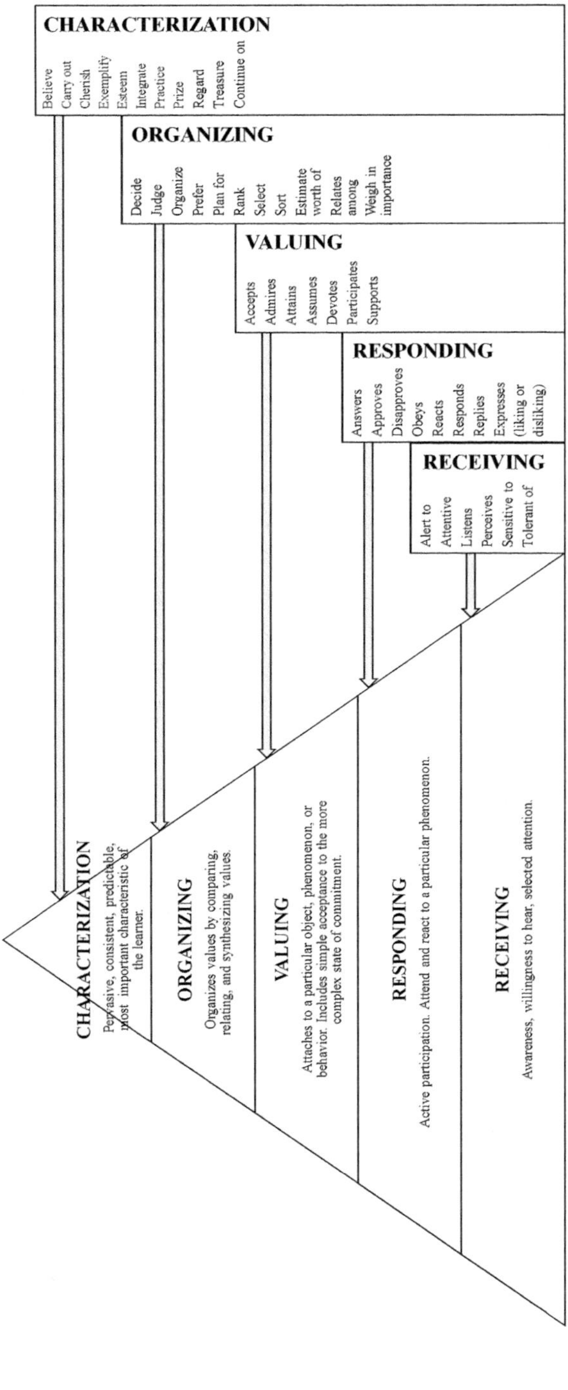

Fig. 7.3 Affective domain levels (Adopted from Krathwohl et al. [1964])

exchanges across employee cultures and experiences, affective development is becoming critical to full job performance.

As an accreditation reviewer, we're looking to see if there's higher levels of Bloom's taxonomy versus lower levels of Bloom; if there are getting the affective and the cognitive pieces. We look at how they are structuring their course. How they created their objectives. Are they using Bloom's taxonomy? I go into their learning management system and look for this stuff.

–Dr. Maureen C. Jones
The Pennsylvania State University
Accreditation Coordinator for the MHA Programs

7.3.3 Using Domains in Performance Objectives

Depending on the need to be met and the performance gap to be described, the taxonomy provides a useful model to describe specific and focused performance objectives. Performance expectations can be focused on the cognitive, psychomotor, and affective domains. Further, each level within the domain is accompanied with a list of verbs depicting a behavior by a person, and this represents a performance action. Thus, learning and development professionals use the taxonomies of each cognitive, psychomotor, and affective domain to name the specific levels of knowledge, skill, or attitude needed in job performance.

Bloom's taxonomy helped me communicate better with my e-learners in my e-curriculum because I could explain how we take the language in the knowledge we are pushing out at them, and help them build stories, and then help them apply it to what they do in their jobs.

–Scott A. Critchfield, CFP
Coach, Learning Professional

7.4 Write High-Quality Performance Objectives

Performance objectives address the workplace setting where employees must apply the training. The value of performance objectives is to emphasize results in the setting of the job, where environmental conditions can complicate the employees' ability to apply what was learned in training (see Chapter 4, "Establish the Learning Environment").

7.4.1 Marrying Performance Objectives and Instructional Objectives

Learning and development professionals know that instructional objectives might be met during training courses, but when people return to their jobs, they are not always able to apply what was learned. This is the *transfer of learning problem*, and a commonly cited statistic states that only 8% of off-the-job training is transferred back to the job in changed behavior. Transfer of learning is hampered because people forget what they learned, their immediate supervisor does not insist they apply what was learned, or the environment does not support the application to the work. To increase transfer, learning and development professionals will marry *instructional objectives* to *performance objectives* and partner with line managers to encourage on-the-job application by worker trainees. Performance objectives make clear exactly what should be applied on the job (note: performance objectives for individual workers are sometimes referred to as individual outcomes or expected performance outcomes).

7.4.2 Descriptors in Every Performance Objective

Writing high-quality performance objectives is essential for training accreditation. Accreditation-worthy performance objectives are specific in component features and follow a consistent method for writing the descriptors. Some performance objectives can contain three features: condition, behavior, and criterion, as developed by Robert Mager (1984). Condition refers to resources the employee uses to demonstrate the new behavior at work; behavior is the action the employee should demonstrate after training; and criterion has to do with the measure of behavior effectiveness or efficiency. Alternatively, some performance objectives follow the ABCD formula and contain four features: audience, behavior, criteria, and depiction. Still, others follow the SMART formula. The nuances of these descriptions are detailed more fully in Chapter 10, "Deciding What to Include", which describes writing good instructional objectives. Whichever method your learning and development effort uses, the descriptors should be consistent and the method for writing performance objectives continuously followed.

Sample Objective

(from our letter-writing situation): Suppose the trainer is about to create instruction on letter-writing. One instructional objective might indicate:

By the end of the training, learners will be able to "use a software program and a computer to type at 30 words per minute with 3 errors or less." In this example, the behavior is type; the condition is using a software program and a computer; and the criteria are both speed (quantity: 30 words per minute) and quality (3 errors or less).

In general, by incorporating conditions, behaviors, and criteria, performance objectives can be of high quality and accreditation worthy. Writing quality performance objectives supports both the job analysis being undertaken and add to the professionalism of the learning and development organization.

7.5 Uses for Performance Objectives

When written succinctly, and including the features discussed above, performance objectives provide clear descriptions about the expected behaviors which the training course will produce. The value of performance objectives is to emphasize training results in the context of job situations—in other words, to move the learner's new behavior from a training environment to the workplace itself—which is of keen interest to executives and line managers. In this way, good performance objectives for the new job become instructional objectives for training.

As a learning and development manager, you should use the written performance objectives as evidence to line managers and executives of the direct influence of training in both accurately describing job expectations and creating new employee behaviors. Performance objectives are estimates of what the training will accomplish, but good objectives also help communicate training's purpose to others within the organization. This sets expectations for what the learning and development effort can accomplish, and adds value to the entire organization. Further, employees obtain clarity about job performance expectations and understand the rationale for participating in training courses. Learning and development professionals can work together to produce instruction that is specific, concise, and unique to your jobs and your workplace. Thus, the subsequently produced training courses will meet your organization's goals and positively change your employees' performance.

We rely heavily on Bloom's taxonomy for our learning objectives, and our course descriptions have been altered to include these objectives, so this communicates to the manager and the end users.

–Dr. J. Kevin Perry
Society of Automotive Engineers (SAE) International
Director, Professional Development

7.6 Creating Evaluation Methods to Test Objectives

If the learning assessment is a true/false quiz, but you tell me that the competency is analytical thinking... then that's a mismatch, because there is no really analytical thinking involved in T/F types of questions and there's no way to demonstrate it.

–Dr. Maureen C. Jones
The Pennsylvania State University
Accreditation Coordinator for the MHA Programs

How do line managers, instructors, and learners know that instructional objectives have been achieved and thereby ensure that training needs were met? The answer is to create evaluation methods to test for objectives. Perhaps a simple example will serve to illustrate. Recall the instructional objective in the typing course was to type 30 words per minute with 3 errors or less. One way to evaluate whether that instructional objective was met is to administer a typing test at the end of the training session. If learners can demonstrate they have achieved 30 words per minute with only 3 errors or less, then the instructional objective has been met. If learners can demonstrate the ability to consistently perform to that level back on the job (when a re-test is administered to them as an employee), then a performance objective has also been met. Testing learners for the accomplishment of performance objectives occurs during the evaluation phase of the ADDIE model and is fully described in Chapter 12, "Learner Feedback and Job Application".

7.7 Preparing Learning Outlines or Storyboards

Once objectives have been identified, then instructors can prepare a learning outline to show how the performance objectives will be achieved. Again, training designers will refer to *performance objectives* as *instructional objectives.* A logical relationship should exist between the instructional (or performance) objectives and the outline items. Using our example, if an objective indicates ability to type letters for the organization, then some content elements in the training outline would include topics of appropriate logos or font sizes, uses of organizational email and memos, typing speed and typing accuracy.

7.7.1 Instructional Plan or Storyboard

Frequently, an outline for training is called an Instructional Plan or a Storyboard. This document is a listing of <u>all</u> the objectives to be addressed within one training session, or one learning event, along with other training information such as session length and module names. Outlining the objectives into an Instructional Plan or Storyboard becomes the tool for designing the complete training course. It is used to provide organized content information for planned learning events and to distinguish the content addressed per session. A good storyboard starts with a complete set of objectives.

Key to your success as a manager is to assure that each training event structured in your learning and development department follows an Instructional Plan or Storyboard that is clearly based upon a finite set of instructional objectives. The finite set of instructional objectives will guide the topics covered and keep the training session specific to the skills needed.

Example

In our letter writing example, several objectives would be set for the training on letter writing, and this set of objectives would outline the course, indicating at the end of training employees will be able to:

- "Use a software program and a computer to type at 30 words per minute with 3 errors or less."
- "Select corporate logos from the company website and insert each at the correct location for formatting a letter, memo, or email with 100% accuracy."

- "Identify font sizes and colors restricted for typefaces deemed appropriate for XYZ company correspondences."
- "Differentiate the format, salutation, and paragraphing appropriate for XYZ company correspondences when creating letters, emails and memos."

7.8 Writing, Buying, or Buying and Modifying Instructional Materials

In business, line managers always have a choice to either make what they need, buy what they need, or buy what they need and modify it to meet specific requirements. The same principle applies to learning. When learning and development professionals identify a training need, they have the option of creating the training by writing the content from scratch (write a training program), buying the training from another source (such as a publisher or training vendor), or purchasing a license from a vendor but then modifying the training materials to meet the unique needs of the organization.

Learning and development managers today have many options to find materials to meet instructional objectives. A plethora of free material is available on the web, including a host of videos and print material. At the same time, learning and development managers may also examine online or onsite workshops that may be regularly offered by third parties, such as TED Talks or Prager Videos. This online material may be useful in meeting all or part of workers' learning needs. Of course, great care should be taken to honor copyrights, patents, and trademarks in this adaptation process when meeting unique organizational needs.

7.9 Communicating Training Events as Opportunities

Employees—and other stakeholders such as line managers and executives—need to be convinced that it is important to attend training events and meet new performance levels. After all, training is expensive and can take productive time away from serving customers or making products. For that reason, learning and development managers should take steps to communicate training needs as learning opportunities—for employees and for others. That message needs to be delivered on a continuing basis and not just announced one time and thereafter forgotten.

How can that be done? One way is to include a description of the target audience. For example: "This course is a beginner-level session intended for employees with little-to-no familiarity with Personal Financial Management" or "This course is intended for seasoned managers with multiple telecommuting direct reports." Another way is to build an explanation of talents to be gained into descriptions of the training courses, using the written objectives.

7.9.1 Communicate to Employees

As previously mentioned, objectives can be used to inform employees of the knowledge and skills to be gained by them during training events. Use the performance objectives in your communications about the training opportunity. Tie the description of the training event directly to jobs and to people, using the objectives. Explain what will be gained—specific knowledge, skills, and attitudes—and how that learning will help employees better execute their jobs. In this manner, the learning to be accomplished is explained in the course description directed to the employees.

Example

A description of the letter-writing course might say:

"Learn to type company letters, memos, and email quickly and with few mistakes in order to build your communication skills both internally and with customers."

7.9.2 Communicate to Other Managers

Learning can also be explained in efforts to build individual development plans to increase employee professionalism and learning transfer. In this way, the skills learned are not only taken back to jobs, but are of real benefit to the individual learners by improving their personal skill sets and talents.

Example

(In our typing case): The description might also say:

"Use your improved typing skills to improve the effectiveness and professionalism of all your written communications."

For the best learning transfer, application rarely involves just the learner. Full use of learned skills on the job involves the line managers, colleagues, course instructors, and many others for both pre-course work and follow-up verification of abilities. Here, the Individual Development Plan, negotiated between an employee and his/her manager, would strive toward both improved communication skills for the typist on the job, and the training course would be tied into that person's individual communication skills.

The important point is to make a concerted effort to communicate the benefits of the training course to all affected persons—both employees and line managers—in a manner that explains the skills to be achieved. Learning and development managers must actively express not only what the training content covers, but the improved skill sets that will result across the organization. Failure to do so may end up jeopardizing the learning and development function or causing a course to be eliminated or unfunded.

7.10 Conclusion

High-quality learning and development programs successfully achieve new outcomes-based upon both descriptive goals for training and detailed objectives for employee performance. Accreditation-worthy goals for new training address performance gaps identified in previously conducted needs assessments. Quality performance objectives detail the new skills needed on the job and are written by the learning and development department in specific terms and precise language. The value of quality objectives is to train only on what is needed and to move changed employee behavior from a training environment to the workplace itself—thus, assisting in the transfer of learning to the job. Quality performance objectives are also useful as descriptors to executives of the precise talents needed in the workplace, as key components for designers when creating courses or classes, and as communicators to employees to clearly express the talents they will gain from learning events.

Manager Tips

A. Write only a few goals, but focus them on the change needed—the gap identified in the needs assessment.
B. Don't address as a goal, nor accept as a directive, a problem that training cannot fix.
C. Goals are broad statements of proposed problem resolution across bands of workers.
D. Objectives are specific employee behaviors that will result from learning events.
E. Know the distinction between performance objectives and instructional objectives.
F. Make sure every performance objective fully depicts a behavior and a level of precision for work deemed adequate on the job.
G. Combine related objectives into one learning event or course, outlined in an Instructional Plan (Storyboard), to meet the training goal.
H. Use both the training goal and the performance objectives as promotional tools to explain the influence and value of training to line managers and the benefits of training to learners within the organization.

Supplement

Supplement Tool 7A: Instructional Objectives Worksheet

	Cognitive	Psychomotor	Affective
Conditions of performance *(given/using)*			
Behavior Performance expected *(action verb)*			
Criteria • *Level of accuracy,* • *Degree of completeness,* • *Measure of quality, etc.*			
Important Learner Information...			

At the end of training, learners will be able to:

1.

2.

3.

4.

References and Additional Resources

Bloom, B. S. (Ed.), Engelhart, M. D., Furst, E. J., Hill, W. H., & Krathwohl, D. R. (1956). *Taxonomy of educational objectives, Handbook I: The cognitive domain.* New York: David McKay Company. www.cft.vanderbilt.edu/guides-sub-pages/blooms-taxonomy/.

Brown, A., & Green, T. D. (2016). The essentials of instructional design: Connecting fundamental principles with process and practice (3rd ed.). New York: Routledge.

Dave, R. H. (1975). Psychomotor levels. In R. J. Armstrong (Ed.), *Developing and writing behavioural objectives* (pp. 33–34). Tucson, AZ: Educational Innovators Press.

Krathwohl, D. R., Bloom, B. S., & Masia, B. B. (1964). *Taxonomy of educational objectives, Handbook II: Affective domain.* New York: David McKay Company. ISBN 0-679-30210-7, 0-582-32385, 1.

Krathwohl, D. R., Bloom, B. S., & Masia, B. B. (1973). *Taxonomy of educational objectives, the classification of educational goals, Handbook II: Affective domain.* New York: David McKay Company. www.nwlink.com/~donclark/hrd/Bloom/affective_domain.html.

Mager, R. F. (1984). *Developing attitude toward learning* (2nd ed.). Belmont, CA: Lake Publishing.

Morrison, G. R., Ross, S. M., Kalman, H. K., & Kemp, J. E. (2012). *Designing effective instruction.* Hoboken: Wiley.

Simpson, E. J. (1972). *The classification of educational objectives in the psychomotor domain.* Washington, DC: Gryphon House. www.nwlink.com/~donclark/hrd/Bloom/psychomotor_domain.html.

8

Who Should Be Involved in Instruction?

Alexander the Great credited his father for his life but credited his teachers for learning how to live well. His point was: teachers influence how people think, feel, and perform. The quality of the teacher, therefore, influences how well people learn to live. The same point applies to instructors and facilitators. Those who design, lead, or facilitate training must be competent—or even exemplary—because they influence the employees who are trained. Instructors are role models for those they train. Instructors must be competent in the subject matter and/or competent in the theories and principles of learning itself. The learning and development department should not be the resting place for those looking to glide into a peaceful retirement or the last refuge of the incompetent employee. This chapter addresses the question: Who should be involved in instruction? What competencies are essential for learning and development professionals to bear in order to analyze, design, develop, implement, and evaluate learning experiences? How do organizations document learning staff qualifications? An accredited learning and development organization actively provides opportunities for their learning staff to continuously develop, improve and demonstrate their skills through appraisals and documented skill updates.

> *The trainers go through both a knowledge base assessment, as well as, a teaching base assessment which again is very important because those who may be the best subject matter experts in the field, might not have the skills as an effective*

W. J. Rothwell et al., *Increasing Learning & Development's Impact through Accreditation*,
https://doi.org/10.1007/978-3-030-14004-5_8

facilitator or communicator. So, the trainer assessment really shows proof that they can communicate the key principles, and they're aligning what they're talking about to what the actual learning objectives and learning outcomes are.

–*Jessica Burnett*
Senior Product Manager
ISACA

8.1 Qualifying as a Learning and Development Professional

Should learning and development professionals be subject matter experts, instructional design experts (IDE), or both? Subject matter experts (SMEs) possess the education, experience, and other qualifications in the content of what they teach. For instance, an engineering SME possesses engineering qualifications. Similarly, an IDE possesses the education, experience, and other qualifications in the training process. For instance, an IDE has expertise in analyzing training needs, designing instruction, developing training methods and materials, utilizing instructional technologies, delivering or facilitating learning experiences, and evaluating training results. Possessing a degree of skill in all these areas—perhaps with additional experience in one or two specific tasks—qualifies a person to be an instructional designer or part of the training staff.

It is also possible to prepare training using teams. Teams may be necessary when the subject matter is highly technical and/or the media to be used are blended. Team members may collectively possess expertise in the subject matter, in elements of instructional design, or in technical delivery. Training team members may also possess other relevant qualifications. For instance, in preparing e-learning, it may be necessary to have team members who are proficient in graphic design skills, multimedia skills through which the training is presented, and language skills (if training is to be translated for wording and concepts into multiple languages).

8.2 Knowledge, Skills, Attitudes, and Other Competencies Essential for Learning and Development Professionals

For many years, the American Society for Training and Development (ASTD)—more recently called the Association for Talent Development (ATD)—has undertaken research on the knowledge, skills, and attitudes (and such other competencies as motivation levels) that are necessary for learning and development professionals to be well qualified. An important assumption in ATD's research is that more skills are necessary to conduct effective training than mere expertise in the subject matter. It is also understood that the requirements to be a well-qualified instructor change over time and do not remain static because business conditions are dynamic, and technology is ever-evolving.

Over the years, it has been concluded that the burden on learning and development professional to increase their skill sets continues to grow. In other words, what it takes to be a well-qualified learning and development professional is growing more daunting. The reason is simple. Employers want more than training from instructors. Employers want improved worker productivity and positive worker attitudes.

> *Because one component of the standard talks about making sure that the subject matter experts who teach courses are qualified, we created a more serious and complete set of criteria that have to be met before you become one of our instructors.... It led us to be a little more rigorous about who teaches our courses. We require 10 years of industry experience, ideally in the content area that they're proposing to teach a course on and..., we require them to show some evidence of teaching evaluations or some kind of documentation that they've already been successful presenting technical information.*
>
> **–Dr. J. Kevin Perry**
> *Society of Automotive Engineers (SAE)*
> *International*
> *Director, Professional Development*

8.3 Learning and Development Professionals Skills

In reality, what it takes to train people has not changed much over the years, even though it is also true that employers expect "trainers" to do more than just training and that is why requirements in the learning and development field keep changing. One reason that the requirements for good trainers have remained relatively stable is that human beings do not change much despite staggering changes in the nature of work and workplaces. Professional learning and development skill requirements center around needs assessment and the skills to create and execute an instructional design system (IDE skills). Needs assessment skills involve identifying what the organization needs broadly to achieve its strategic goals (see Chapter 6, "Is Training the Answer? Assessing Learning Needs"). Creating and executing instruction involves skills in job analysis, instructional design, course development, and implementation (see Chapter 10, "Deciding What to Include", and Chapter 11, "Methods to Achieve Consistency").

8.3.1 Needs Assessment Skills

Well-qualified learning and development professionals can assess worker situations and analyze training requirements, a process called needs assessment or performance analysis. Needs assessment work separates the problems training can solve from those requiring management actions, such as a change in supervision, management guidance, or physical conditions (see Chapter 6, "Is Training the Answer? Assessing Learning Needs"). Training, after all, is carried out within a broader context of human resources that include employee recruitment, candidate selection, job design, organizational design, reward systems, feedback systems, employee support systems, and much more. Changes in all of these elements within HR systems can affect training requirements. As a simple example, the decision of who to recruit for a job vacancy (candidates bearing certain levels of experience or competencies) will affect how much and what type of training is necessary for the new recruit. If new recruits bear adequate skills and expertise in a job function, perhaps the training can focus upon internal processes or organizational nuances.

Learning and development professionals conducting needs assessment must be able to survey employees, interview persons setting the organization's direction, conduct external research on competitors, and understand practices in the organization's business functions. Needs assessors must be capable of perceiving business risks, analyzing internal and external pressures, and identifying trends. Importantly, learning and development personnel who conduct needs assessments must possess a keen appreciation for the functional components of the organization, such as marketing, finance, IT, and executive management and must understand the inter-dependencies of these functions. Needs assessors must be capable of gaining the confidence of organizational leaders to conduct intimate conversations about future business risks, strategic plans, and management concerns. Professional staff jobs in needs assessment include consultant, needs assessor, risk analyst, big data specialist, organization development specialist, change manager, and assessment manager.

8.3.2 Job Analysis Skills

Well-qualified instructional designers should be able to conduct a professional job analysis. Job analysis involves deciphering training requirements arising from employee situations within specific functions (see Chapter 7, "Intended Learning Outcomes"). Instructional designers must be able to identify what individuals need to meet work requirements and what job skills are required to achieve essential work results. Instructional designers conducting job analysis must be able to create surveys, administer surveys, conduct interviews with both managers and employees, facilitate focus groups, examine job-related documents, observe workers performing their jobs, and importantly write performance objectives. Key skills for job analysts are attentive listening and keen observation. Job analysts must also be able to document the requirements of jobs and categorize requirements into the domains of knowledge (cognitive domain), behavior (psychomotor domain), and attitude (affective domain). Failure to conduct a good job analysis will mean that the training which is offered is probably not properly targeted, resulting in wasteful uses of time and other resources. Training staff titles in job analysis include job analyst, task analyst, focus group guide, workflow observer, data collection agent, data analyst, analytics manager, content diagnostician, survey administrator, and subject matter expert.

8.3.3 Design Skills

Design means that plans are written, and courses are outlined for the instruction. Targets for success are established in the form of instructional objectives, which (when achieved) indicate that training has met its goals, and gaps or deficiencies have been addressed (see Chapter 11, "Methods to Achieve Consistency"). Typical actions during design include setting objectives, preparing testing methods to measure how well objectives were achieved, formulating modules or syllabi, and selecting media by which to deliver training. Training staff titles in the design of learning include curriculum writer, storyboarder, instructional strategist, graphic designer, instructional designer, curriculum associate, and methods expert.

8.3.4 Development Skills

Development is about moving from design to preparation for delivery. Learning and development professionals can create, purchase, or buy and modify instruction. If designers create the course, skills are needed to write content for delivery, be it online, onsite, or some blended delivery format. Designers may pilot test a course to see if all the components and sub-components are working. Pilot testing can help a designer to make modifications to improve the quality of the training before it is rolled out to groups of learners. Professionals in material development have titles that include media expert, materials developer, materials coordinator, videographer, editor, courseware coordinator, and session reviewer.

8.3.5 Implementation Skills

Implementation means delivery, though it can also include training administration such as admission, record keeping, issuing certificates, and even setting up classrooms and equipment. The implementation may take place onsite (in classrooms), online (electronically), or in blended formats that combine many media. Delivery skills include procedures for professionals functioning as facilitators or as instructors. Instructors tell learners what they must know; facilitators ask learners, encouraging them to deliberate and think out their own solutions.

Delivery requires special skills. Performing effectively as a training facilitator requires public speaking skills, which are sometimes called platform skills. Those skills can be honed by practice and by coaching from others. Further, performing effectively as an online instructor is different from public speaking as a classroom instructor, and requires innovative ways to get learners to interact and engage electronically. Blended delivery, which relies on both onsite and online modes, further requires facilitators who are flexible and creative enough to use varied instructional approaches. Training staff titles in delivery include facilitator, senior facilitator, e-learning instructor, technical instructor, site coordinator, conference manager, facilities planner, and logistics coordinator.

> *One of my favorite victories when I worked at a (Construction Engineering and Procurement Company), I was up against a lone subject matter expert and I was trying to get him to move from a four-day contracts workshop with hundreds and hundreds of slides to a blended learning solution using online delivery. And when he saw how things were working, he came up to me and said 'Wow, pretty good!'*
>
> ***–Anonymous***
> *Corporate Learning & Development/*
> *CEU Program Lead*

8.3.6 Evaluation Skills

While there are a plethora of evaluation models, the traditional view of training evaluation stresses skills in the four "levels" of training evaluation associated with the well-known Donald Kirkpatrick model of training evaluation. These levels include reaction, learning, behavior, and results. To pursue evaluative answers to these four "levels", training evaluators gather both qualitative and quantitative data, analyze that data, relate the descriptive statistical findings with deeper resonant findings, and summarize the data to form an evaluation answer.

In recent years, however, instructors have also had to go beyond these four levels. Employers would like to know more information about return on investment (ROI), otherwise known as cost-benefit analysis. ROI means determining training benefits (usually in productivity improvement or cost savings) minus the costs of training itself (see Chapter 13, "Program Evaluation and Records"). Thus, learning professionals have had to find hard measures of productivity improvements or efficiency increases within the functional operations of the organization, along with numerical evidence of costs for designing and delivering the training programs. None of these benefits or costs is easy to quantify, thus making the skills needed by a training evaluator analytically varied.

Training staff titles in evaluation include evaluator, evaluation designer, tester, test administrator, collection agent, input coordinator, data analyst, accountant, evaluation reporter, and evaluation communicator.

8.4 Documenting Learning and Development Professional Qualifications

Professional qualifications for learning and development personnel should be documented, of course. Job descriptions should be written for all training staff positions, and those descriptions should name the job title to which the position reports and list the duties, tasks, and responsibilities of the position. Learning and development departments should also list the educational qualifications or experience (years) needed by individuals to be considered qualified for a training staff position. Duties, tasks, and responsibilities will differ for the variety of positions needed in a quality training organization. Learning and development department positions that require a writing emphasis, such as curriculum or program associate, will have an emphasis on verbal skills. Positions requiring technical or artistic expertise, such as graphic designer, will require a technical design skill or media education emphasis. Documenting learning and development staff qualifications, per position, should not be much different from documenting qualifications for any employee position within your organization. Sample job descriptions for learning and development professionals can easily be found on the web, and they indicate required and desirable qualifications.

8.5 Developing Learning and Development Professional Skills

The individuals on the learning and development team who are involved in creating, developing, or delivering courses should, themselves, participate in ongoing professional development activities. It is important for learning and development staff to stay current about effective instructional methods, to fine-tune personal skills, and to upgrade user skills as technology demands. The skill needs of your learning and development staff can be determined through either formal or informal appraisals, which should take place at least annually. Formal appraisals might involve training work logs, skill tests, reviews of needs assessment reports, or sample course designs. Informal appraisals might occur through conversation or observation. Accredited organizations not only appraise the skill needs of the learning and development staff, but also provide opportunities for staff members to improve their skills by attending conferences, participating in professional association meetings, or obtaining particular certifications. Accredited organizations ensure that learning and development staff members, particularly those involved in the design and delivery of courses, keep current in instructional methods and enhance their related delivery skills. Learning organizations also need to document this commitment to staff development through professional development planning, funding, and assurance that time for staff attendance will be made available.

8.6 Ensuring a Well-Qualified Learning and Development Team

How do learning and development managers ensure a well-qualified team of assessors, analysts, IDE, facilitators, and evaluators? One approach is to recruit from within the organization. That means promoting someone from an operating department and then developing the training skills in that worker. ATD, for instance, offers many courses to train the instructor. These courses can be especially helpful to workers who have significant business expertise but have no prior exposure to training practice, adult learning fundamentals, or training specialities.

Another approach is to recruit professional staff from outside the organization. This means recruiting and selecting someone from a graduate or undergraduate learning and development program or someone with training expertise from an outside organization. Many universities offer degree programs in learning and development or related fields. Professional instructors hired from outside the organization can bring specific expertise in design skills, data interpretation, facilitation, or evaluation. Any workers recruited from outside the organization will, of course, require appropriate onboarding to be effectively socialized in your corporate culture and will need to learn more about the organization's business mission and purpose.

Neither approach—that is, recruiting from outside or promoting from within—is foolproof. Mistakes can be made. Quite often learning and development managers find it more useful to combine both staffing tactics—promote some people from within and recruit others externally. In this way, the learning and development department is staffed by those who understand the organization's culture and perspective on employee development (see Chapter 2, "Align Learning and Development with Organization Mission and Values") and those who bring with them greater expertise and professional training talents from outside the organization.

8.7 Conclusion

Who should be involved in instruction? This chapter addressed that question. It also addressed such other questions as: (1) What competencies are essential for learning and development professionals to analyze, design, develop, implement, and evaluate learning experiences? (2) How do organizations document professional learning staff qualifications? Expectations for learning and development professionals have been growing for many years, in part, because times change, and also because employers expect more from people and have placed a greater value on the human talent of their organizations.

Manager Tips

A. Involve line managers, learners, and instructional design experts in preparing job descriptions for professional staff positions within your learning and development department.

B. Keep job descriptions accurate and documented for all positions within your learning and development department.

C. Resist efforts to move problem performers from operating divisions into the learning and development department. Instructors should be the best performers—and not those nearing retirement who wish to ride out a few years with low-stress jobs, nor problem performers who cannot work effectively within operating departments.

D. Commit to developing your learning and development staff as professionals. Do not assume that assessors, designers, or facilitators need minimal skills or do not require updating. Skills date quickly, and learning skills need to be kept current.

E. Assess learning and development professional staff skills both formally and informally, and document professional staff development actions.

Supplement

Supplement Tool 8A: Checklist to Review Instructor Qualifications

Directions: Use this checklist to review instructor qualifications—and how well the organization ensures that instructors are well qualified. For each item in the left column below, indicate in the center column whether that action is taken. In the right column, indicate any relevant notes for additional discussion or review.

Reviewing instructor Qualifications	Is This Action Taken?		Notes
	Yes	No	
Was a job description for the instructor position prepared by discussing requirements with managers, instructors and other relevant stakeholders?			
Was an instructor selected from inside the organization with knowledge of the organization or from outside the organization with knowledge of the training field and training process?			
Were instructors who were promoted given effective train-the-instructor experiences and were instructors who were hired from outside given an effective on boarding experience?			
Are instructors encouraged to participate in professional development experiences to keep their skills updated?			

References

Arneson, J., Rothwell, W., & Naughton, J. (2013). *ASTD competency study: The training and development profession redefined*. Alexandria, VA: Association for Talent Development.

Hirudayaraj, M., & Baker, R. (2018). HRD competencies: Analysis of employer expectations from online job postings. *European Journal of Training and Development*. https://doi.org/10.1108/EJTD-04-2018-0036.

Rothwell, W., Stopper, A., & Zaballero, A. (2015). *Building a talent development structure without borders*. Alexandria, VA: ATD Press.

9

Conduct Learning Events Professionally

Learning and development as a field has evolved and grown in its importance, particularly because of its impact on job performance and organizational outcomes. Learning and development practitioners have the responsibility of developing strategies for the organization to prosper through learning, and are essential to overall employee development. They are critical to the organization's talent pipeline and indispensable to the skill standards of the national workforce. Therefore, it is vital to professionalize training. Professionalizing the function of learning and development requires the recognition of a unique body of occupational knowledge, adherence to a set of established standards, expectations to hold learning professionals accountable, and a commitment to a professional code of conduct. This chapter will build upon the previous chapter's discussion about trainer qualifications. The evolution of the training profession will be briefly reviewed. Educational accomplishments, work experiences, and competencies needed to become an effective learning and development professional will be further explored. Finally, this chapter will address the importance of maintaining high professional standards, including disclosure of conflicts of interest and non-discriminatory behavior in conducting trainings. Accredited learning and development programs disclose any perceived or actual conflict of interest in performing training duties, and ensure that learning and development practitioners are professionally qualified to execute instructional tasks.

W. J. Rothwell et al., *Increasing Learning & Development's Impact through Accreditation*,
https://doi.org/10.1007/978-3-030-14004-5_9

9.1 Historical Evolution of the Learning and Development Profession

To understand the profession of learning and development, specifically training in the workforce, it is important to review the history and the evolution of training. Dating back to antiquity, workforce training took the form of apprenticeships and on-the-job instruction. The "instructor" was actually the work itself. The master-apprentice relationship did not involve a curriculum or learning objectives, but followed cultural traditions where seniors taught a family member the craft of their forefathers or experienced artisans taught their proteges. The main objective was to transfer skills from one generation to the next.

During the nineteenth century, the need for a larger skilled workforce arose due to the industrial revolution. This led to the development of organizational training classes. Replicating a formal education classroom structure, where a group of learners were led by a single instructor, structured on-site training emerged. This format facilitated the development of large groups of people simultaneously and efficiently, where only a few trainers were required and learning and training departments became a norm.

In 1962, Leonard Nadler completed the first occupational study of instructors. Nadler interviewed training directors, subordinates, and administrators and concluded that training directors performed the following tasks (pp. 1–2):

- obtain and control a budget;
- choose, purchase, and evaluate training equipment;
- provide leadership and supervision to training staff;
- determine needs;
- plan a curriculum based on work requirements;
- conduct training and evaluations;
- share information about the outcomes of training.

The US Civil Service Commission (USCSC) conducted another foundational study of instructors in 1973, which provided a foundation for roles, competencies, and tasks in the federal government (Rothwell 2002). The American Society for Training and Development (ASTD) conducted a US nation-wide study pertaining to what a human resource development (HRD) professional actually does. Models for Excellence (McLagan 1983) defined training and development's focus as "identifying, assessing–and through planned learning– helping develop the key competencies which enable individuals to perform current or future jobs" (pp. 2–3).

As organizations have become more aware of the value of the people executing the work, training has shifted from an episodic learning event to take on a more strategic focus, giving learning professionals a seat in the C-suite. New executive positions have emerged, including Chief Learning Officer (CLO) and Chief Talent Officer. According to Elkeles et al. (2017), CLOs "often take responsibility for all employee development and effectiveness functions including recruitment, training, succession planning, retention, and enterprise-wide process improvement" with a continuous aim of "adding value" to the organization (2017).

The training function has generally been part of the human resource department; however, organizations have evolved into a dedicated learning and development department employing professionals with backgrounds in workforce education, human resource development, industrial psychology, and adult training and development (see Chapter 3, "Structure for Accountability").

9.2 Learning and Development Professionals

According to the US Department of Labor, the job prospects for training and development professionals—instructional designer and related positions—are better than average and are projected to grow at a steady rate of 11% from 2016 to 2026 (U.S. Department of Labor, Bureau of Labor Statistics 2018a, b, c). These occupations are projected to have 100,000 or more job openings within the next decade.

In addition, the Occupational Information Network (O*NET), a free online database sponsored by the US Department of Labor/Employment and Training Administration (USDOL/ETA), designated training to likely change as a result of the green economy (National Center for O*Net Development 2018). Technologies and activities in the green economy are increasing the demand and reshaping the work and worker requirements, generating new and emerging occupations. Therefore, new tasks, skills, knowledge, and credentials will be needed, and training professionals will play an important role to help workers be relevant and employable. Training programs related to efficiency, recycling, or other issues with environmental impacts will continue to be in high demand now and in the future.

Learning and development professionals are designated with different titles, including: Assistant L&D Manager, Learning Manager, Training Manager, Program Manager, Corporate Instructor, Senior Training Manager, Internal Learning Consultant, Head-Capability Development Manager, Performance Development Coordinator, Talent Development Consultant,

Talent Transformation Consultant, Talent Manager, Chief Learning Officer, and Chief Talent Officer.

9.2.1 Occupational Profiles

The skills needed by learning and development practitioners are varied but focus upon designing and developing educational curricula appropriate for the employee base. Instructional design experts (now sometimes called learning experience design experts) are skilled in adult learning, educational program design, method use, learning strategies, and evaluation. Instructors deliver training sessions using lectures, group discussions, team exercises, videos, self-guided instructional manuals, or online applications, just to name a few. Training may also be collaborative, designed for employees to connect informally with experts, mentors, and colleagues. This requires skills in managerial relations, recruitment, and program management. According to O*NET, learning and development occupational roles include, but are not limited to (National Center for O*Net Development 2018):

- **Training and Development Specialist**: Design and conduct training and development programs to improve individual and organizational performance. May analyze training needs. Sample of reported job titles: *Computer Training Specialist; Corporate instructor; E-Learning Developer; Job Training Specialist; Management Development Specialist; Senior Instructor; Supervisory Training Specialist; Technical instructor; Instructor; and Training Specialist.*
- **Instructional Designers and Technologists**: Develop instructional materials and products and assist in the technology-based redesign of courses. Assist faculty in learning about, becoming proficient in, and applying instructional technology. Sample of reported job titles: *Chief Technology Officer; Director, Educational Research, and Product Strategy; Instructional Designer; Instructional Technologist; IT Senior Analyst (Instructional Technology Senior Analyst); Lead Performance Analyst; Learning and Development Specialist; Senior Instructional Designer; Team Lead, Teacher Support; and Student Intervention Specialist.*
- **Distance Learning Coordinators**: Coordinate day-to-day operations of distance learning programs and schedule courses for distance learning. Sample of reported job titles: *Coordinator*

of Online Programs; Director of Distance Learning; Distance Education Faculty Liaison; Distance Learning Coordinator; Distance Learning Technician; Distance Learning Unit Leader; Head of Academic Technology; Online Facilitator; and Program Director for Distance Learning.

- **Training and Development Managers**: Plan, direct, or coordinate the training and development activities and staff of an organization. Sample of reported job titles: *Learning and Development Manager; Education and Development Manager; Education Director; Learning and Development Director; Learning Manager; Staff Training and Development Manager; Training and Development Coordinator; Training and Development Director; Training Director; and Training Manager.*

9.2.2 Required Qualifications

> *We assess our instructors. Beyond a CV, we will oftentimes sit in on something that they've done and also have them show us what they have done in the past, such as, samples of positive outcome of a program that they've been involved in. We're trying to generate more evidence that supports why we're bringing in this instructor.*
>
> **–Peter Finn**
> *Society of Women Engineers*
> *Deputy Executive Director and Chief Learning Officer*

As stated in Chapter 8, qualifications for learning and development professionals should be documented, and training staff members must stay abreast of current instructional/learning methods to develop their skills continuously. Learning and development professionals usually need several years of work-related experience, on-the-job training, and/or a bachelor's degree. Specialists may have a variety of educational backgrounds, but most have a bachelor's degree in training and development, human resources, education, instructional design, or workforce development. Others may have a degree in business administration or a social science degree, such as education or organizational psychology. In general, work-related experiences are important for learning and development practitioners. Many positions require work experience in areas such as training and development or instructional design or in related occupations, such as human resources or teaching. Employers may prefer to hire candidates with previous work experience within the industry in which the company operates, or with experience in e-learning, mobile training, or technology-based education. However, more employers are requiring candidates with a master's degree or higher and/or professional certifications such as a Certified Professional in Learning and Performance (CPLP) or a Certified Performance Technologist (CPT).

9.2.2.1 Credentials, Certifications, and Certificate Programs

Many industries have developed an industry-recognized credential to connect individuals to the skills they need to enter into and advance in their careers. For a learning and development practitioner, obtaining a professional credential is akin to a training program obtaining accreditation, and both are based on predetermined standards. As a designation for a trade or profession, a credential is awarded by a third party that will attest to an individual's level of knowledge, proficiency, and professionalism in a given field. Possessing a credential validates an individual's baseline level of competency, and it ensures the employer that the individual is equipped to carry out his or her duties. Obtaining a credential requires: passing a proctored exam, meeting minimal levels of education, and providing proof of experience. Most credentials, like accreditation, will expire after a period of time. The credential holder must also submit evidence of continuing education in order to renew the credential.

Certification is another form of validation. Obtaining a certification requires a formal process that recognizes and validates an individual's qualifications in a certain subject. The certification is designed by an accreditation body to meet needs and requirements which are more specific than those of a credentialed program. Certifications must be renewed periodically, generally through completed continuing education units.

A certificate (often of completion) builds individual capacity and recognizes the acquisition of specific topical learning. Certificates do not carry the weight of a credential or a certification, but provide the learning and development practitioner with evidence of knowledge to complement his/her existing experience. Certificates are usually issued at the end of a course, and no additional renewals are required.

9.2.2.2 Learning and Development Credentials

Obtaining a training credential will distinguish learning and development practitioners and validate your professionalism in the training industry.

There are many certifications available; however, not all credentials are created equal. Selecting the appropriate credential will depend on the individual practitioner's eligibility and career goals. Usually tied to a specific industry, certifications are usually offered by a professional organization or a company that specializes in a particular field (i.e., Certified Life Underwriter; Certified Public Accountant; Certified Nurse Practitioner). Some employers require a certification in order to be eligible for a job; this is particularly true in health care, in engineering, and in the financial industry. Many professionals obtain specialty certifications to help advance their careers. According to CareerOne Stop's Certification Finder, sponsored by the US Department of Labor, there are 1434 certifications available from 468 organizations for training and development.

Certified Professional in Learning and Performance (CPLP)

For learning and development professionals who are interested in advancing their careers to the next level, the CPLP is a logical step. The CPLP is a broad-based credential and the highest level of certification for a talent development professional. More employers are listing it as a preferred or required qualification for incoming learning and development staff. The CPLP credential legitimizes a talent development professional's competency in 10 specific areas of expertise, with a focus on global application as defined by the latest Association for Talent Development (ATD) Competency Model. (For more information visit the following website www.td.org/certification/cplp/introduction)

Associate Professional in Talent Development (APTD)

For learning and development professionals who may have stumbled into a training position or who are in the early part of their careers, the APTD is a good option. Unlike the CPLP, the APTD primarily focuses on a few areas of expertise from the ATD Competency Model, specifically: Instructional Design; Training Delivery; Learning Technologies; Evaluating Learning Impact; and the foundational competency of Global Mindset. These five competencies were identified to be the core building blocks for early-career talent development professionals. The competencies included in the APTD are the basics of talent development that professionals can use every day, no matter the level with an organization or company. It may be a destination for some or a step to the CPLP for others. (For more information visit the following website www.td.org/aptdlearnmore)

Certified Performance Technologist (CPT)

Unlike the CPLP that requires both the passing of a knowledge-based exam and a peer-reviewed work product, the CPT relies solely on a portfolio-based submission package as an attestment to prove proficiency. The CPT is based on the International Society for Performance Improvement (ISPI) standards with a technology focus and is based on the human performance technology model of outcomes, systems thinking, analysis, design, development, implementation, and evaluation (ISPI 2018). Thus, the CPT represents a specialized view and skill set, whereas the CPLP represents a broader and more generalist view of workplace learning. (For more information visit the following website www.ispi.org/ISPI/Credentials/CPT_Certification/Apply_for_CPT.aspx)

Alternate Credentials

Many organizations categorize learning and development (or training) as an essential part of the human resource department. Therefore, it is not uncommon for learning and development practitioners to have a certification in human resources. The Professional in Human Resources (PHR) certification or the Senior Professional in Human Resources (SPHR) certification. Both the PHR and the SPHR are general human resources certifications for those who have also demonstrated mastery of the strategic HR body of knowledge. The Global Professional in Human Resources (GPHR) demonstrates a professional's expertise of multinational HR responsibilities. These human resource (HR) certifications are awarded by the Human Resource Certification Institute (HRCI) to individuals who meet the eligibility requirements and pass the certification exam. More recently, the Society for Human Resource Management has launched its own certifications—including the SHRM Certified Professional (SHRM-CP) and SHRM Senior Certified Professional (SHRM_SCP) for HR generalists.

9.2.2.3 Eligibility for Credentials

Eligibility for the learning and development credentials is based on both work experience and education. Table 9.1 summarizes the requirements to earn the above-mentioned credentials.

Table 9.1 Learning and Development (L&D) Credentials

Training Credential	Organization	Required Years of Experience	Exam	Work Product	Recertification
CPLP (Certified Professional in Learning and Performance)	Association for Talent Development (ATD) www.td.org/certification/cplp/introduction	• Have at least five (5) years of full-time professional work experience in the talent development or related fields; OR • Have at least four (4) years of full-time professional work experience in the talent development or related fields AND one year of college or university study in talent development; OR • Have at least four (4) years of full-time professional work experience in talent development or related fields AND successful completion of an ATD Master Series program.	Knowledge Exam **Exam time:** 3 hours **Exam length:** 150 questions covering all 10 areas of expertise **Exam type:** Multiple choice questions Skill Application Exam **Exam time:** 3 hours **Exam length:** 100 questions focusing on one of area of expertise **Exam type:** Multiple choice, multiple select and short answer	No work product	Every 3 years 60 recertification points
APDT (Associate Professional in Talent Development)	Association for Talent Development (ATD) www.td.org/aptdlearnmore	• Three years of work experience in the talent development field or related discipline. Related disciplines include human resources, higher education or similar OR • Two years of work experience in the talent development or related field PLUS one year of college/university study in talent development or related discipline OR • Two years of work in the talent development field PLUS successful completion of the ATD Master Instructional Designer or the ATD Master instructor program.	Knowledge Exam **Exam time:** 2 hours **Exam length:** 115 questions covering 3 main areas of expertise **Exam type:** Multiple choice questions	No work product	Every 3 years 40 recertification points

(continued)

Table 9.1 (continued)

Training Credential	Organization	Required Years of Experience	Exam	Work Product	Recertification
SHRM Senior Certified Professional n (SHRM-SCP)	Society for Human Resource Management www.shrm.org/certification/about/AboutSHRMCertification/Pages/SHRM-SCP.aspx	• Less than a Bachelor's Degree ⇒ HR-Related Program - 6 years in HR role ⇒ Non-HR Program - 7 years in HR role • Bachelor's Degree ⇒ HR-Related Degree - 4 years in HR role ⇒ Non-HR Degree - 5 years in HR role • Graduate Degree ⇒ HR-Related Degree - 3 years in HR role ⇒ Non-HR Degree - 4 years in HR role	Knowledge Exam **Exam time:** 4 hours **Exam length:** 160 questions **Exam type:** (95 knowledge items/65 situational judgment items)	No work product	Every 3 years 60 recertification points
SHRM Certified Professional n (SHRM-CP)	Society for Human Resource Management www.shrm.org/certification/about/AboutSHRMCertification/Pages/SHRM-CP.aspx	• Less than a Bachelor's Degree ⇒ HR-Related Program - 3 years in HR role ⇒ Non-HR Program - 4 years in HR role • Bachelor's Degree ⇒ HR-Related Degree - 1 year in HR role ⇒ Non-HR Degree - 2 years in HR role • Graduate Degree ⇒ HR-Related Degree - currently in HR role ⇒ Non-HR Degree - 1 year in HR role	Knowledge Exam **Exam time:** 4 hours **Exam length:** 160 questions **Exam type:** (95 knowledge items/65 situational judgment items)	No work product	Every 3 years 60 recertification points
Senior Professional in Human Resources (SPHR)	HR Certification Institute www.hrci.org/our-programs/our-certifications/sphr	• Have at least four years of experience in a professional-level HR position + a Master's degree or higher, • Have at least five years of experience in a professional-level HR position + a Bachelor's degree, OR • Have at least seven years of experience in a professional-level HR position + a high school diploma	Knowledge Exam **Exam time:** 3 hours **Exam length:** 150 questions **Exam type:** mostly multiple choice questions	No work product	Every 3 years 60 recertification points

(continued)

Table 9.1 (continued)

Training Credential	Organization	Required Years of Experience	Exam	Work Product	Recertification
Global Professional in Human Resources (GPHR)	HR Certification Institute www.hrci.org/our-programs/our-certifications/gphr	• Have at least two years of experience* in a global professional-level HR position +a Master's degree or higher, • Have at least three years of experience* in a professional-level HR position (at least two in global HR) +a Bachelor's degree, OR • Have at least four years of experience* in a professional-level HR position (at least two in global HR)+a high school diploma.	Knowledge Exam **Exam time:** 3 hours **Exam length:** 140 questions **Exam type:** mostly multiple choice questions	No work product	Every 3 years 60 recertification points
Professional in Human Resources (PHR)	HR Certification Institute www.hrci.org/our-programs/our-certifcations/phr	• Have at least one year of experience in a professional-level HR position + a Master's degree or higher, • Have at least two years of experience in a professional-level HR position + a Bachelor's degree, OR • Have at least four years of experience in a professional-level HR position + a high school diploma.	Knowledge Exam **Exam time:** 3 hours **Exam length:** 150 questions **Exam type:** mostly multiple choice questions	No work product	Every 3 years 60 recertification points
Certified Performance Technologist (CPT)	The International Society for Performance Improvement (ISPI) www.ispi.org/ISPI/Get_Certified/CPT_Certification	• Minimum of 3 years of experience		Description of 3-7 projects to demonstrate ability to satisfy CPT standards Attestations by employers or clients for projects	Every 3 years 40 recertification points

9.2.3 Competencies of Learning and Development Practitioners

Our subject matter experts (SMEs) are scientists with PhDs or master's degrees in their specific technical area. We have a competency list and associated development activities for growing and evaluating the SMEs' instructor and facilitation skills.

–Anonymous
Multi-National Energy Corporation
Technical Learning & Development Manager

The identification of competencies of learning and development practitioners has been undertaken several times. Galbraith (1998) identified questioning as the single most influential training behavior, because of its potential to facilitate learning. Stolovitch and Keeps (1999) selected listening to be the most important instructor skill as a tool to redirect the participant's attention to more reflective thinking. Wlodkowski (1993) considered relevant feedback to be the most important skill of an instructor. Knowles (see p. 224 in 1980) is stated that, "What happens in the first hour or so of any learning activity, largely determines how productive the remaining hours will be." Individuals do not learn from experience per se, they learn from reflecting on their experience (Knowles 1990; Thiagarajan and Thiagarajan 1999). Rothwell et al. stated that the analyst role functions to provide proof of the necessity of both training and shifts in employee behavior. Performance analysis combines traditional skill assessment and an intuitive ability to recognize training needs within an organization. Recognizing strong and weak worker competencies and identifying where key skill training is needed are important facets of the analyst role.

Average learning and development practitioners have a repository of experiences for use at particular times, but effective instructors regularly examine them, looking at the lessons they learned, and search for effective ways to express them. Reflection allows us to "know what it is that we know," as well as "knowing what it is that we don't know," and is the basis for effective performance as an instructor. The ATD Competency Model helps guide an organization in the hiring and selection process for learning and development practitioners. Managers can select competencies from several studies that focused on identifying the competencies which provides employees a pathway to enhance their performances as they move into better career positions within your organization (Table 9.2).

Table 9.2 Learning and Development (L&D) Competencies

Research	Trainer Competencies		
2013 ATD Competency Study (Arneson. Rothwell, & Naughton)	• Performance Improvement • Learning Technologies • Integrated Talent Management • Change Management Foundational competencies • Business skills • Interpersonal Skills	• Instructional Design • Evaluating Learning Impact • Coaching • Global Mindset • Personal Skills	• Training Delivery • Managing Learning Programs • Knowledge Management • Industry Knowledge • Technology Literacy
According to Gauld (2015), the following list of trainer competencies is a compiled list fromselected authors and researchers(Lindeman 1926, 1938; Grabowdki,1976; Pinto & Walker 1978; Knowles 1980; Knox, 1979, 1986; Jacobs, 1987; Olson, 1994; Leach, 1996; Thompson,2001, instructors Network, 2009;CSTD, 2012; ASTD, 2013)	• Set goals and objectives • Develop lesson plans • Keep current and up-to-date • Conduct needs assessments • Counsel students about other matters • Blend different training techniques • Use questioning to involve learners • Facilitate group learning activities • Build Relationship	• Attend to individual differences/ diversity • Evaluate effects and impact of training • Analyze course materials/ learner information • Assure preparation of training site • Establish/maintain trainer credibility • Possess content knowledge/skill taught • Understand training and development • Apply research skills	• Demonstrate effective communication skills • Demonstrate effective presentation skills • Support learner needs/feedback/ transfer of learning • Use media effectively • Evaluate learner performance • Evaluate delivery of training • Report evaluative information • Understand program development
Marquardt (2014) identified ten competencies of a successful global instructor	• Knowledge of One's Own Culture (Cultural Self-Awareness) • Knowledge and Appreciation of Other Cultures • Global Perspective and Mindset	• Respect for the Values and Practices of Other Cultures • Cultural Flexibility, Adjustment, and Resiliency • Ability to Acculturate Learning Programs and Events	• Communication Skills • Cultural Empathy • Patience and a Sense of Humor • Commitment to Continuous Learning

Despite these identified trainer competencies, skilled people who have a history of good behavior, but lack experience in dealing with certain conditions, often commit ethical violations. A competent tactical professional does not equate to trustworthy conduct of behavior and they are not immune to unethical actions. Doing wrong or causing harm must be avoided. The following section will focus on maintaining high professional standards when administering training and conducting training work under a code of ethics.

9.3 Professional Conduct and Code of Ethics

Codes of ethics and professional conduct reinforce public trust in the training profession and guide the professional conduct of learning and development practitioners. Training ethically involves making reasoned decisions about what to do in order to achieve the most good for all learners. These choices involve a complex interchange between business context, professional experience, and personal beliefs/values. Moral and ethical choices are deliberate, intentional, and grounded in our beliefs: beliefs about ourselves, beliefs about others, beliefs about the past, beliefs about the current reality, and beliefs about the future (Caldwell et al. 2002). However, ethical conduct is not as simple as choosing right from wrong. Choices are often paired with values such as: truth versus loyalty; individual rights versus the collective needs; short term versus long term; or justice versus mercy. A learning and development professional must be able to mitigate real or perceived conflicts of interest, abide by confidentiality requirements, interact with all stakeholders in an unbiased and professional manner, and ensure the highest level of integrity, while aligning to organizational mission, vision, and values. This can be a difficult balance to maintain. It is important for both learning and development managers and learning and development practitioners to differentiate between situations bearing legal or ethical implications or both. Just because something is not illegal does not mean it is ethical.

9.3.1 Professional Obligations

Learning and development professionals are responsible for adding value to the organizations they serve holistically and to contribute to the success of each individual learner. Using the organization's values as guidepost, learning practitioners must abide by the highest standards of professional behavior, while complying with the law. Learning and development professionals must bear accountability for their individual decisions and actions and commit to a high standard of responsible adult education. See Chapter 2, "Align Learning and Development with Organization Mission and Values", and Chapter 8, "Who Should Be Involved in Instruction?"

9.3.2 Confidentiality

Learning and development professionals aim to create a safe and supportive environment, where learners may share personal or professional information; however, a common challenge that practitioners face is confidentiality. Learning and development practitioners often collect a significant amount of personal data and information from a broad cross-section of learners (associates, co-workers, executives, clients, suppliers, etc.), and this data must be handled in accordance with privacy laws and corporate policy. Data should only be collected if expressly authorized by the learner. Maximum care must be implemented when collecting and storing personal data, and data maintenance must be in accordance with an established policy. No personal data or professional information can be disclosed to an unauthorized third party. Priority should be given to the security of personal data and the confidential management of information.

Learning and development practitioners must also be careful to protect organizational assets and intellectual property through responsible and ethical behaviors that are in line with the organization's operating procedures. It is important to avoid improper use of company information and to properly secure passwords and identification codes to prevent unauthorized access. Organizational data and information should not be reproduced for external use unless authorized to do so. Training professionals may directly or indirectly obtain confidential information regarding the organization, including but not limited to: strategies, activities relating to research and development, industrial practices and processes, technical and production data, commercial and marketing plans, promotional or sales data, financial and operational results, or information about internal associates. It is the responsibility of the learning and development manager to protect and manage all such organizational information with utmost care and caution.

9.3.3 Professional Boundaries and Limitations

Professionalism at the managerial level is also paramount. It is imperative for learning and development managers to resist political influences on training demands and training delivery. Accredited learning programs serve the employees first, focusing upon employee learning needs, and not the demands of line managers. Accredited training programs are fair to all employees as learners or potential learners. Therefore, do not use the learning and development manager position for undue influence or preference for educating distinct operating areas to the detriment or neglect of other areas (i.e., do not play favorites).

9.3.4 Professional Integrity

Learning and development practitioners must always act in an honest, professional, and ethical manner, both personally as a talent development professional and professionally as an agent of the organization. Learning and development practitioners should actively promote a climate of trust and fairness in all training activities and among learners of training programs. Professional integrity is a critical aspect of ethical and professional conduct for all jobs and professions. A lack of professional integrity is simply professional dishonesty, and it is often reflected in attempts to deceive. Common acts of professional dishonesty in training involve the fabrication of data and the falsification of assessment results to portray inaccurate training outcomes. However, the most common violation of professional integrity in training is plagiarism.

Plagiarism is the appropriating and subsequent passing off of another person's work as one's own. If the work of another is used, acknowledgment of the original source must be made. Although ideas cannot be copyrighted, instructors often misrepresent content and materials as their own. Often unintentional, professional reports, training manuals, and presentation materials may include copied content without appropriate citation. Copied content that has not been appropriately cited from an outside source, regardless of intentional or unintentional copying, is plagiarism. Use of plagiarized materials can lead to legal disputes. Training professionals must assure all training products are legitimate. Obtaining copyrights on proprietary instructional creations, titles, documents, published exercises, forms, etc. are important, and learning and development practitioners must seek guidance on copyright infringement when necessary.

9.3.5 Maintain Intellectual Property

The issue of intellectual property rights is one of growing importance, particularly as large amounts of content are available online. Legal questions and concerns become more crucial as learning professionals maneuver through various content management systems, implement the delivery of content on multiple platforms, and disseminate information using social media. Most instructors search the web for resources that can help demonstrate a concept or an idea using YouTube videos, music montages, photo memes, infographics, and other illustrative materials that can stimulate a visual and auditory response from the learners. It is important to always consider copyright and intellectual property laws for all materials sourced electronically. Unwittingly, instructors put their organizations in compromising positions that can lead to liability issues if the courseware used contains music, images, or videos which have been acquired without all proper legal permissions.

9.3.6 Inclusionary Practices

Inclusionary practices also have legal implications, which can impact talent development practices. The legal aspect pertains to ensuring that equal opportunity exists in all aspects of employment, including learning opportunities at work. For most US employers with 15 or more employees, this means following guidelines set by the Equal Employment Opportunity Commission (EEOC). One such law is Title VII of the Civil Rights Act, which protects applicants and employees against discrimination or retaliation for filing a complaint, based on race, ethnicity, gender, religion, national origin, or pregnancy. This includes the categories protected by federal, state, and local laws. Title VII also explains prohibited employment practices, including unlawful harassment and discrimination, and details the investigation process and protection from retaliation. Other laws enforced by the EEOC include the Equal Pay Act, the Age Discrimination in Employment Act, the Americans with Disabilities Act, and the Genetic Information Nondiscrimination Act.

9.3.7 Conflicts of Interest

Learning and development professionals must maintain a high level of trust and protect the interest of all stakeholders with professional integrity. Potential conflicts of interest may include personal, material or financial gain, or preferential treatment of others in the design, development, or delivery of education. A conflict of interest may arise when a learning professional has personal or private interests that interfere with or benefit from an organization sponsored activity at his/her employer. It is important to note that interest does not have to be monetary to create a conflict (i.e., outside business interest, such as consulting may pose a conflict of interest). A conflict of interest can arise when not acting in the best interest of the organization, or there is inappropriate personal gain. In cases of potential conflicts, disclosure to relevant stakeholders (Chief Talent Officers, key executives or legal counsel) should be addressed.

9.4 Conclusions

The learning and development profession has evolved from training large numbers of workers to the careful and planned development of education to meet both specific employee (learner) and organizational (strategic) needs. This evolution has altered the job of traditional trainers and significantly expanded the skills needed for a learning and development professional. Further, with today's access to data, information, and educational materials, the professional and ethical conduct of learning and development practitioners becomes of greater concern. Both training personnel and learning and development managers must promote professional integrity, ethical behavior, and the confidential treatment of learner data. Accredited programs adhere to high standards of information security, ethical conduct, and the avoidance of conflicts of interest.

Manager Tips

A. Take responsibility for your work and actions, do what needs to be done, and don't leave it for others.
B. Work to develop the skills and competencies of your professional learning and development personnel.
C. Encourage professional credentialing, certification, and competency evidencing in the talent development arena.
D. Never share confidential, privileged, employee or client information unnecessarily.
E. Do not tolerate or justify dishonest conduct by others. Report any conflicts of interest immediately.
F. Seek help from legal counsel and advice on the handling of potential conflicts of interest, if needed.
G. Ethical conduct is doing the "right" thing at all times, regardless of where you are and who you are with. Always report suspicious conduct or violations of company policies or illegal actions.

Supplement

Supplement Tool 9A: Professional Development Activities for L&D Personnel

Directions: Use this worksheet to track professional development activities of the learning and development staff. List all training and continuing education-related events.

	Continuing Education Events			
	Educational Institution or Host Organization	Date	Course Event	CEU
	Speaking and Instruction			
	Educational Institution or Host Organization	Date	Presentation Title	
	On-the Job Professional Development			

References and Additional Resources

Bassi, L., & McMurrer, D. (2007). Maximizing your return on people. *Harvard Business Review, 85*(3), 115–123.

Caldwell, C., Bischoff, S. J., & Karri, R. (2002). The four umpires: A paradigm for ethical leadership. *Journal of Business Ethics, 36*(1/2), 153–163. https://doi.org/10.1023/A:1014230002724.

CSTD (Canadian Society for Training and Development). (2012). *Competencies for Training and Development Professionals.* Canada: CSTD Press.

Elkeles, T., Phillips, J. J., & Phillips, P. P. (2017). *The chief talent officer: The evolving role of the chief learning officer.* New York, NY: Routledge.

Farrant, P., Cohen, S. N., & Burge, S. M. (2008). Attributes of an effective instructor: Implications of the views of U.K. dermatology trainees: Attributes of an effective instructor. *British Journal of Dermatology, 158*(3), 544–549. https://doi.org/10.1111/j.1365-2133.2007.08394.x.

Galbraith, P. L. (1998). System dynamics and university management. *System Dynamics Review, 14*(1), 69–84. https://doi.org/10.1002/(SICI)1099-1727(199821)14:1<69::AID-SDR139>3.0.CO;2-T.

Gauld, D. (2014). The competencies of effective trainers and teachers. In K. Kraiger, J. Passmore, N. R. Dos Santos, & S. Malvezzi (Eds.), *The Wiley Blackwell handbook of the psychology of training, development, and performance improvement* (pp. 117–135). Chichester, UK: John Wiley & Sons, Ltd. https://doi.org/10.1002/9781118736982.ch7.

Gordon, W., & Sork, T. J. (2001). Ethical issues and codes of ethics: Views of adult education practitioners in Canada and the United States. *Adult Education Quarterly, 51*(3), 202–219. https://doi.org/10.1177/07417130122087241.

Gould, D. (2014). The competences of effective instructors and teachers. In K. Kraiger, J. Passmore, N. R. Dos Santos, & S. Malvezzi (Eds.), *The Wiley Blackwell handbook of the psychology of training, development, and performance improvement.* Chichester: Wiley.

Grabowski, S. (1976). *Training teachers of adults: Models and innovative programs.* Syracuse, NY: National Association for Public Continuing and Adult Education.

International Society of Performance Improvement (ISPI). (2018). CPT Certification. Silver Spring, MD: ISPI. Retrieved August 23, 2018 from www.ispi.org/ISPI/Get_Certified/CPT_Certification/ISPI/Credentials/CPT_Certification/CPT_Certification.aspx?hkey=6e82efde-8956-4b8d-aad2-64c5aa02c367.

Jacobs, R. L. (1987). *Human performance technology: A systems-based field for the training and development profession.* Information Series No. 326. Columbus, OH: ERIC Clearinghouse on Adult, Career, and Vocational Education; National Center for Research in Vocational Education, Ohio State University.

Knowles, M. S. (1980). *The modern practice of adult education from pedagogy to andragogy.* Englewood Cliffs, NJ: Cambridge Books.

Knowles, M. (1990). *The adult learner.* A neglected species. Houston, TX: Gulf.

Knox, A. B. (Ed.) (1979). *Enhancing proficiencies of continuing educators.* New Directions for Continuing Education, No 1. San Francisco: Jossey-Bass.

Knox, A. B. (1986). *Helping adults learn.* San Francisco: Jossey-Bass.

Leach, J. A. (1996). Distinguishing characteristics among exemplary trainers in business and industry. *Journal of Vocational and Technical Education, 12*(2), 5–18.

Lindeman, E. C. (1926). *The meaning of adult education.* New York: New Republic.

Marquardt, M. J. (2014, November). Successful global training. *td at Work: Tips, Tools & Intelligence for Developing Talent, 31*(1426). Association for Talent Development (ATD).

McLagan, P. A. (1983). *Models for excellence: The conclusions and recommendations of the ASTD training and development competency study*. American Society for Training and Development.

Nadler, L. (1962). *A study of the needs of selected training directors in Pennsylvania which might be met by professional education institutions* (Doctoral dissertation, Teachers College, Columbia University).

National Center for O*Net Development. (2018). *O*NET OnLine Help: Find Occupations*. O*NET OnLine. Retrieved August 07, 2018, from www.onetonline.org/find/quick?s=training.

Olson, S. J. (1994). Competencies of two-year college technical instructors and technical trainers: Similarities and differences. *Journal of Industrial Teacher Education, 32*(1), 65–85.

Pinto, P. R., & Walker, J. W. (1978). *A study of professional training and development roles and competencies*. Madison, WI: ASTD.

Rothwell, W. J. (2002). *The workplace learner: How to align training initiatives with individual learning competencies*. Amacom Books.

Rothwell, W. J., Arneson, J., & Naughton, J. (2013). *ASTD competency study: The training & development profession redefined*. American Society for Training and Development.

Stolovitch, H. D., & Keeps, E. J. (1999). *Handbook of human performance technology. Improving individual and organizational performance worldwide*. San Francisco: Jossey-Bass.

Sundstrom, E. D., Lounsbury, J. W., Gibson, L. W., & Huang, J. L. (2016). Personality traits and career satisfaction in training and development occupations: Toward a distinctive T&D personality profile. *Human Resource Development Quarterly, 27*(1), 13–40. https://doi.org/10.1002/hrdq.21223.

Thiagarajan, R., & Thiagarajan, S. (1999). *Experiential learning/jolting learners*. Training 1999 Conference, Chicago, February.

Thompson, K. D. (2001). *Adult educator effectiveness with the training context: A study of trainee perception of effective trainer characteristics*. Ph.D. Thesis. University of Wyoming.

U.S. Department of Labor, Bureau of Labor Statistics. (2018a). *Occupational outlook handbook-Instructional coordinators*. Washington, DC: Government Printing Office. Retrieved August 07, 2018 from www.bls.gov/ooh/education-training-and-library/instructional-coordinators.htm.

U.S. Department of Labor, Bureau of Labor Statistics. (2018b). *Occupational outlook handbook-Training and development managers*. Washington, DC: Government Printing Office. Retrieved August 07, 2018 from www.bls.gov/ooh/management/training-and-development-managers.htm.

U.S. Department of Labor, Bureau of Labor Statistics. (2018c). *Occupational outlook handbook-Training and development specialists.* Washington, DC: Government Printing Office. Retrieved August 07, 2018 from www.bls.gov/ooh/business-and-financial/training-and-development-specialists.htm.

Wlodkowski, R. (1993). *Enhancing adult motivation to learn: A guide to improving instruction and increasing learner achievement.* San Francisco: Jossey-Bass.

Part IV

Content Design and Delivery

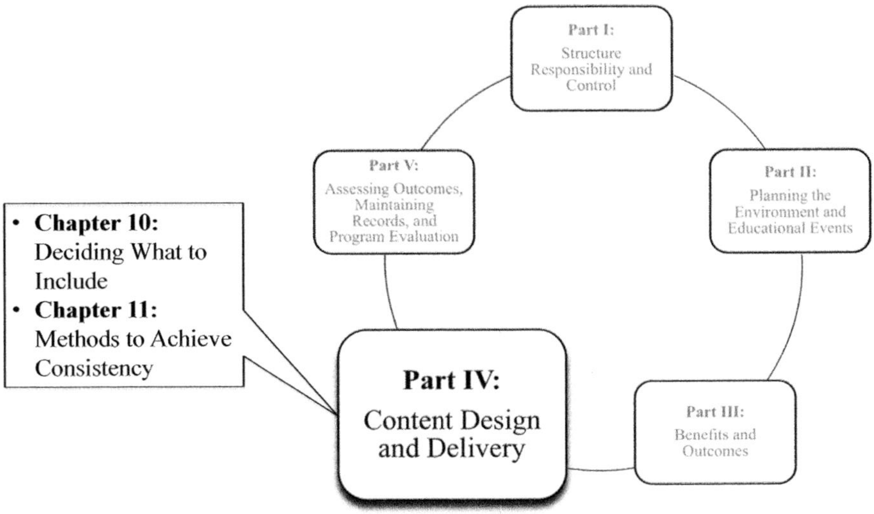

Fig. 1 Chapter organizer

Accredited learning and development programs organize educational information and plan adult learning in a logical manner. Workshops, sessions, and courses are structured based upon the domains of cognitive, behavioral, and affective learning, which together form the cornerstones of quality adult education. Based upon these fundamentals, training curricula are built around goals, objectives, and expected changes in employee behavior. For accredited learning and development programs, the goal is not simply employee learning, but employee application of knowledge and skill on the job. Based upon a defined need for workplace improvement, objectives for learning are set and carefully linked to improve performance on the job.

High-quality learning and development programs also design content and use instructional methods in an efficient manner, seeking to provide talent which is useful for the organization and which can be further sustained. When determining content and choosing methods for instruction, accredited training programs focus upon the employees as learners. Content is ordered in a logical manner, which adults can relate to, and training methods are carefully selected to sustain employee interest. Content is also fine-tuned around employees particular to the organization, in order to ease the shift needed for specific work talents. Course design, methods, and media always strive for excellent participant experiences during training in an effort to achieve sustainable talent improvement and long-term performance change.

The chapters in this part will focus on: setting goals and organizing learning events which are specific and relevant for the employees unique to your organization (Chapter 10, "Deciding What to Include"), and designing courses in which content is logical and methods are consistent to assure that employee change is achievable (Chapter 11, "Methods to Achieve Consistency").

10

Deciding What to Include

Selecting content and organizing information to logically change employee behavior is an important process for an accredited learning and development provider. Deciding what to include in training involves event planning specific to learners within the organization (your employees) and setting instructional objectives for accurate training outcomes. Accreditation requires a logical alignment of adult teaching strategies with expected learning outcomes—thus leading to lasting change in employee behavior. Importantly, the outcome from any training must be appropriate for the specific employees within your organization.

> *You have to ask yourself if your course descriptions and objectives align with the skills and abilities that are needed in the workplace and what is needed in the industry. Especially now, when relevance seems to have a two-year life cycle.*
>
> ***–Dr. Maureen C. Jones***
> *The Pennsylvania State University*
> *Accreditation Coordinator for the*
> *MHA Programs*

10.1 Planning Training for Your Employees and Your Workplace

> *After a request comes in, then we determine if it's a training need … and even more importantly, will training solve the problem.*
>
> ***–Anonymous***
> *Corporate Learning & Development/*
> *CEU Program Lead*

W. J. Rothwell et al., *Increasing Learning & Development's Impact through Accreditation*,
https://doi.org/10.1007/978-3-030-14004-5_10

Thinking and behavior are complex processes, which are inherently different between adults. To create effective training for all the adult workers in your organization, an understanding of your employees as learners is essential. When creating learning events, you want to teach your employees skills relevant to the work they will be doing inside your organization. Therefore, it is important to critically understand the persons employed by your organization as adults with unique learning characteristics and capabilities. Fully characterizing the traits of the employees within your organization means understanding your workers in two areas: general/demographic characteristics and current abilities or competencies.

10.1.1 General/Demographic Characteristics

General/demographic characteristics describe the people internal to your organization as they are. The persons to be trained are your target audience. It is important to know this target audience because you want to design training that is appropriate for building skills with the particular people inside your organization. Demographic and general characteristics include age ranges; gender; educational background; primary language; and ethnicity. It is important to have as much broadly definable information about the target audience as possible, so your training can be focused to meet the characteristics of these learners. Training designs and instruction to employees will differ for young workers in their 20s with no experience, versus workers who are in their 40s or 50s with much experience. A real challenge for training designers is the mixture of persons representing diverse backgrounds and experiences who are now found across many of today's employee groups.

The most often used demographic characteristic is education because education level indicates a proclivity for reading and comprehension. Grade of schooling completed will be important in designing materials that are understandable to your target audience and instructions that are clear to the majority. Indeed, the entire design of created training may alter depending upon the speed of reading or other cognitive skills of your target audience. Much of the education information on target audience employees is attainable from personnel records and job requirement data.

Due to the diversity of today's workplaces, attention also needs to be paid to the needs of culturally diverse employees and employees with disabilities. Different cultures utilize language nuances and interpret colloquialisms differently. Beliefs and cultures may have exposed persons to different situations considered more or less commonplace in a work environment, but less common in certain cultures. Organizational environments accommodate individual disabilities in different manners and engage a vast variety of inclusionary practices. Importantly, training must be considerate of the varied cultural characteristics of each target audience and be designed with respect for the present abilities of different groups of workers.

10.1.2 Current Abilities

Current abilities of employee learners lie in present knowledge, skills, and attitudes particular to the job. It is important to understand these abilities, or competencies, in knowledge, skills, and attitudes so that all learners can benefit from the instruction offered.

Knowledge about the job or work to be performed includes understanding of terms, logic, facts, and thinking processes used to execute tasks in a specific workplace. Knowledge regarding retail store management, for example, may or may not equate to knowledge about retail store budgets or utilizing numbers in retail business budgeting exercises. Likewise, knowledge about the documents used for underwriting insurance policies may or may not equate to knowledge needed about the documents to bind the insurance.

Skills refer to behavioral abilities—specifically abilities to use, operate, manipulate, or move in a physical manner. Work skills refer to the abilities of persons to function physically and to execute required job tasks and procedures. Skill levels may refer to manual dexterity, eye-hand coordination, speed of movement, or multi-tasking. Differing levels of manual dexterity are often depicted as skill levels required for heavy equipment operation or complicated computer processing. Likewise, eye-hand coordination may be required at differing levels of competency for jobs in manufacturing, processing, or quality control (where defects need to be identified and removed). Important to skill level depiction is specifying behavioral descriptions that adequately indicate higher or lower levels of physical precision or task execution.

Attitude refers to a person's predisposition toward work and conducting work. Attitude can be positive, neutral, or negative. Attitude, or predisposition, relates to liking or disliking work, in general. At certain organizations, attitudes of workers may refer to a range of feelings about the business generally conducted by the organization, such as its community contributions, its environmental impact, or its social citizenship endeavors. Workers in jobs may possess appropriate knowledge to understand the work, may have adequate skills to execute the job tasks, but may be impeded in performance because of a negative attitude about certain aspects of the work to the organization.

All three areas of current abilities (knowledge, skills, and attitudes) combine to collectively represent the capacity of the employees within a unit, region, or department of an organization. Diagnosing these abilities helps to differentiate the employees within your organization from others of similar skills and abilities. As an example, 45-year-old welders working on a railroad will have different knowledge, skills, and attitudes from 30-year-old welders in an automotive assembly plant—even though the basic job of 'welder' is considered similar. Describing the abilities of your employees in each of these three ability areas, as well as in general/demographic terms, enables you to fully empathize with the characteristics and capabilities of the persons who comprise your target audience. Your learning and development team can then train them as the persons they are, rather than train them as job categories.

10.1.3 Work Environment

Work environment, or context, is important because embedding training within a familiar environment enhances the likelihood of learner success on the job. There are three types of environments to be considered when designing training: the development environment, the delivery environment, and the application environment.

The development environment refers to the general orientation of workers toward the idea of on-the-job training and education at work. It is important to determine the orientation of workers toward training before sessions or workshops are offered, in order to know beforehand whether instruction is perceived as useful or beneficial for the workers themselves. At some organizations, training is perceived as useless or a waste of time by employees. At other organizations, training is highly valued by employees in order to keep skills honed and information current. This perception of the usefulness of learning and development will change as the topics or content changes. For example, a program on cell phone operating skills, which the employees already possess or already use outside of the workplace, would be perceived of little value when offered as formal training. Conversely, a program on managing cell phones for business email might be perceived as keenly useful and therefore valuable as formal training. Perceived usefulness and need for continued learning will also increase if employees are held accountable for topic mastery after the training. If employees will be held accountable for a change in behavior or for new knowledge offered in the course, its perceived value will be heightened in the learner audience. High levels of both employee perceived utility and employee accountability will heighten interest in training programs offered and improve the development environment.

The delivery environment refers to the place and manner of the instruction itself. Not every organization has facilities and conference rooms adequate for good instruction. Common factors to consider for delivery include lighting, noise, temperature, seating, equipment, and transportation. Each factor requires careful consideration because comfort and control of the place where training occurs have a significant impact upon the absorption of information offered during the instruction. Uncomfortable employees do not learn well or retain information. If learners are distracted by interference within the training place, or they are worried about access or commuting to the training location, attention will drop, and the training will have little impact (see Chapter 4, "Establish the Learning Environment").

The application environment refers to the on-the-job situation where learning from training is applied in practice. One clear purpose for conducting training is application of the knowledge, skills, and attitudes to the job. Employees are much more likely to apply the information gained during training to their jobs if the home environment is amenable to their new behavior. The home job environment includes not only the location, but also the time and resources needed for application. Resources might be equipment upgrades, computers, Web site access, or software. Time resources include allowances for practice or trial and error time. The application environment is critical for training transfer. As noted earlier, if the tools needed for application are not supported at the job site, or if line managers do not support practice and use of new skills, transfer of learning to the job will be severely hampered.

10.2 Setting Instructional Objectives

As in all project endeavors—establishing a goal and setting objectives to meet that goal are two different procedures. A training goal is a general statement about the intended overall change that the training will accomplish (see Chapter 7, "Intended Learning Outcomes"). As a learning and development manager, you will most likely be directly involved in goal setting or in framing a training goal based on the finalized needs assessment and identified performance gap. You may not be as directly involved in setting objectives. However, instructional designers on the learning and development team need objectives in order to guide what to include within the training instruction. Instructional objectives (sometimes called learning objectives) are well-articulated descriptions of the behavior which will be expressed by workers in the future—after the training. Instructional objectives are detailed in action and specific to learning topics. Objectives help to clearly distinguish between topics that need to be covered within the training and topics which can be excluded from the training. Specific instructional objectives create a highly focused unit of learning for learners—keeping your target audience focused. Additionally, instructional objectives provide a guide for designing evaluation techniques to measure the impact of your training (on the worker/in the workplace). This section focuses upon writing effective instructional objectives for designing training content.

> *If your course descriptions don't have bonafide learning objectives, you now need to go back and retrofit all your course descriptions with real learning objectives - that is the real heavy lifting (for accreditation).*
>
> ***–Dr. J. Kevin Perry***
> *Society of Automotive Engineers (SAE) International*
> *Director, Professional Development*

10.3 Write Conditions, Action Verbs, and Criteria in Instructional Objectives

Instructional objectives set for any training endeavor need to be active, specific, and measurable, as written. Documented objectives, which articulate the behavior to be mastered and exhibited upon completion of the training, need to detail the learner's action and the learner's situation. Active post-training behavior needs to be clearly described in as few words as possible and be measurable. High-quality performance objectives contain three features: an action, a condition, and a criterion. Developed by Robert Mager, all three components, together, accurately describe the performance expected of an employee in order to consider that person competent (Mager 1984).

10.3.1 Condition

Condition of performance is the first feature for writing a high-quality instructional objective. Condition depicts the circumstances under which the behavior is to be performed. It indicates the relevant conditions under which the employee will act in exhibiting job competence. Conditions also indicate tools or equipment needed, access to information needed, resources needed, or references allowed or time constraints. Conditions are written as phrases into the objective, usually as a preamble to the action to be performed. Sample conditions used in instructional objectives are:

- Using a printed map as a guide,
- With the production belt running at moderate speed,
- Without using the owner's manual,
- Based on available software tools,
- Within 30 seconds after red indicator light begins flashing,
- While driving the company truck.

10.3.2 Action Verbs

Action represents the behavior expected by the employee after training, and quality instructional objectives should use specific action verbs to express this behavior. Action verbs depict an observable behavior to a detailed degree and as such are useful in depicting the hierarchies of the learning domains explained in Chapter 7, "Intended Learning Outcomes". Action verbs will specifically apply to what the employee will know (cognitive domain), be able to do (psychomotor domain), or appreciate (affective domain). Action verbs associated with the cognitive domain need to be precise and accurate, and matched to the level of comprehension expected. A summary for action verbs useful for cognitive domain objectives at each level of cognitive mastery is presented in Fig. 10.1.

A list of action verbs useful for the psychomotor domain objectives at each level is presented in Fig. 10.1. The specific action verb used for physical action should relate to the physical dexterity level needed and the precision of the task to be performed. Certain professions use job-specific terms, such as auger, ratchet, drill, score, hit, input, plow, saw, and laser (Fig 10.2).

In every profession, specific physical terms should be chosen to represent psychomotor actions for skills particular to that job. As examples, action verbs associated with two jobs utilizing the psychomotor domain—driving a car and baking bread—are listed in Table 10.1.

Note, the actions are described in terms which are physically descriptive for the job—terms in these examples such as drives, kneads, bakes, and combines.

Actions in the affective domain are indicated by verbs which describe specific feelings that depict levels of appreciation. These feelings are generally depicted

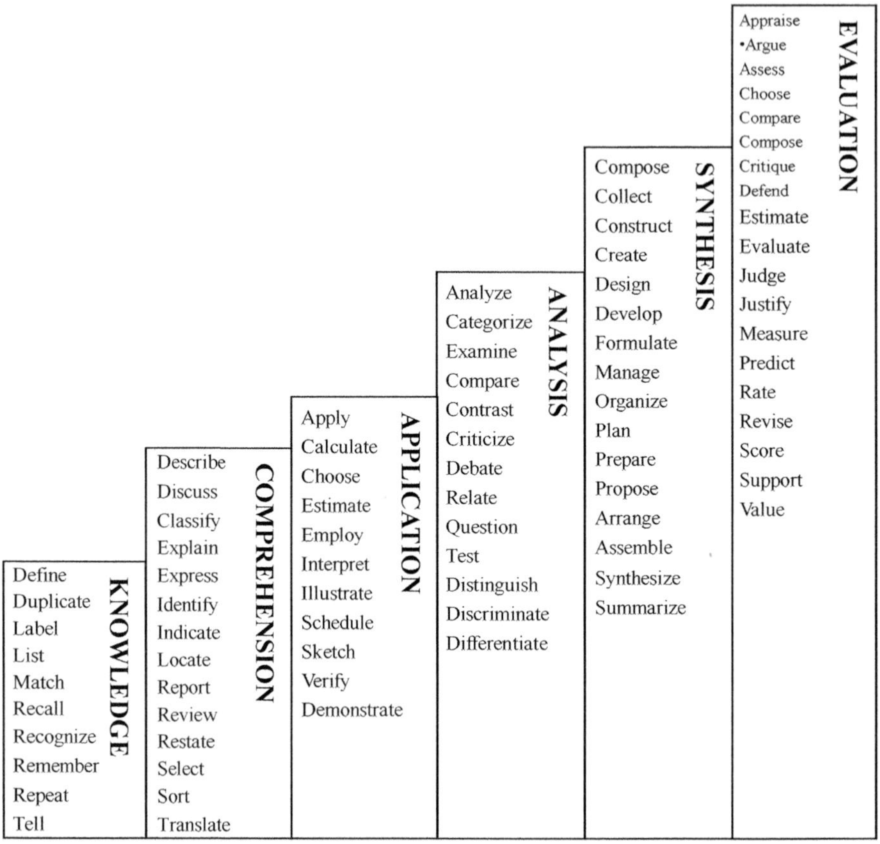

Fig. 10.1 Action verbs for cognitive domain levels (Adapted from Brown and Green [2016]; Morrison et al. [2012])

as personal behaviors, which are observable, by others. A summary of action verbs for each affective domain level is presented in Fig. 10.3.

Using specific action verbs associated with each of the domains helps the objective to be specific and therefore clear to the learner.

> *Setting instructional objectives/outcomes within the domains helps learners establish a simple base of information, and then develop more complex skills by impacting how they think about what they are learning, what they know, and how they are going to use the new knowledge.*
>
> **–Dr. Karen LaMarsh**
> *Continuing Education and Training Consultant*

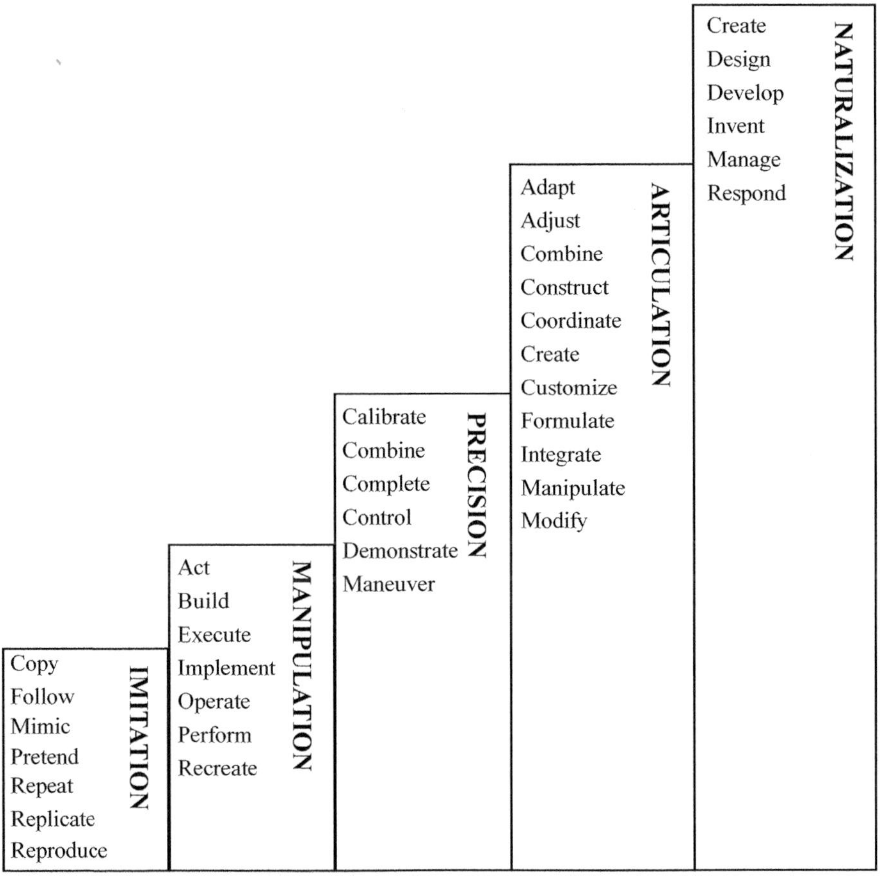

Fig. 10.2 Action verbs for psychomotor domain levels (Adapted from Dave [1975])

10.3.3 Criteria

Criteria in instructional objectives represent the standard by which the action is to be completed. Criteria in a written instructional objective usually represent the minimum level of accepted performance for the employee to be deemed competent. Basic competence in application of skills on the job is always a purpose of training, and this expectation is set forth in the criteria of the training objective. Levels of achievement, or criteria, can indicate accuracy, completeness, compliance, errors, or time periods. These phrases usually close the objective, describing the degree to which performance will be measured. Sample criteria used in performance objectives are:

Table 10.1 Sample psychomotor action verbs

Example	Imitation	Manipulation	Precision	Articulation	Naturalization
Operating a Car	Pretends to drive using simulator.	Operates vehicle by self under the supervision of a driving instructor.	Maneuvers a car into a tight parallel parking spot during the state licensure driving exam.	Manipulates car temperature, adjusts volume controls, and talk to passengers while driving.	Responds safely and effectively driving through a heavy rainstorm.
Baking Bread	Mimics instructional video on kneading techniques for baking bread.	Recreates the same bread following step by step guidance on instructional video.	Combines all ingredients, kneads correctly, and bakes bread in oven at correct temperature without instructional video.	Modifies the ingredients to bake different variations of the bread.	Creates breads and other dough-based pastries using the limited ingredients provided.

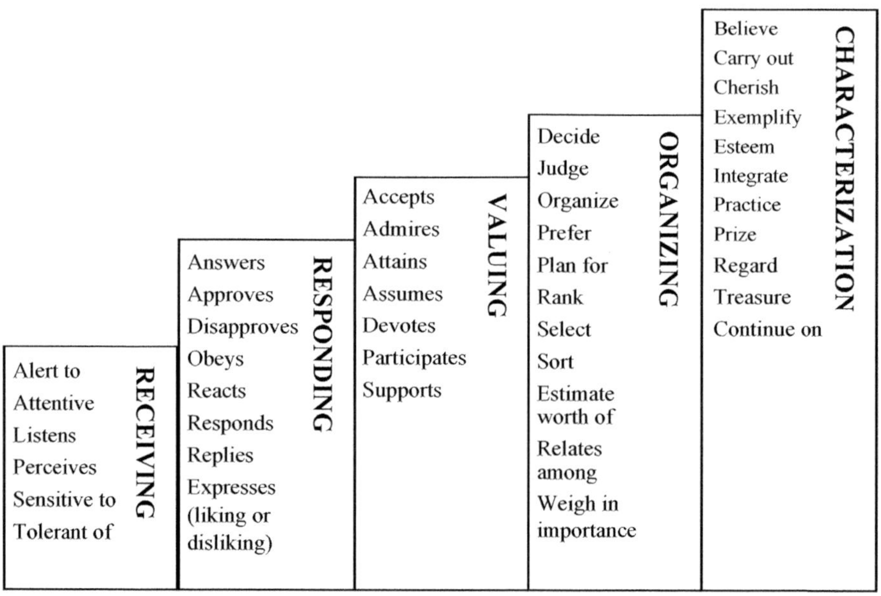

Fig. 10.3 Action verbs for affective domain levels (Adapted from Krathwohl et al. [1964])

...with 100% accuracy,
...successfully in 7 out of 10 instances,
...within 2 inches of the terminus,
...showing no smudges or streaks,
...meeting the criteria set by XYW industry standard.

By incorporating all three parts—conditions, action verbs, and criteria—your instructional objectives can be of high quality and accreditation worthy. Writing high-quality instructional objectives supports the goal of the training and adds to the professionalism of your learning organization. High-quality training objectives that are domain-focused, relative to the job(s), specific in action expected, conditioned to the application context, and depicting measurable levels of completion, create learning outcomes that are valuable to employees and to line managers.

High-quality instructional objectives are excellent estimates of what accredited training will accomplish. Additionally, good instructional objectives also help communicate training's mission to others in the organization. When written succinctly, and including all three features discussed above, instructional objectives provide clear descriptions to executives and other managers about the expected outcomes of the training that is produced. This both sets expectations for what training can accomplish and adds value to the entire organization. Further, employees obtain clarity about job performance levels and understand the rationale for participating in additional talent-based learning. Learning and development personnel can work together to produce instruction that is specific, concise, and useful in your organization. Thus, your subsequently produced training will meet the organization's goals and positively change employee outcomes.

We documented and we established goals and objectives, and that helped ensure success. When we're looking to harmonize programs, then we don't have to go back and re-establish objectives.

–Jessica Burnett
Senior Product Manager
ISACA

In this chapter, Supplemental Tool 10A—*Instructional Objectives Worksheet* is offered for practice in writing all three parts of high-quality instructional objectives.

10.4 Conclusion

Accreditation worthy learning and development programs carefully plan learning events to be uniquely appropriate for the organization's learners. Training offerings are focused upon the specific characteristics of the organization's employees—recognizing both the unique characteristics and the skill levels needed by the existing employees. Further, accredited learning and development departments adjust training to the environments within their organizations in order to assist learners in transferring newly learned skills to their specific jobs. Instruction is planned to accomplish objectives which are actionable, conditioned to the situation, and detailed in levels of competence. Specific instructional objectives are used to both guide designers and communicate to leaders because clear descriptions of the training to be produced are the result.

Manager Tips

A. Design training for the needs of the people employed within your organization. Know the characteristics and current abilities of employees in affected areas.
B. Document employee knowledge, skills, and abilities via domain category, level of competency, and specificity.
C. Write about what the learners, your target audience, will be capable of accomplishing after training.
D. Train workers in settings and conditions which closely resemble the environment where the work will be performed. Make sure the learning environment helps your target audience to apply new skills when on the job.
E. Set instructional objectives that are outcome focused and which are clear, concise, and measurable.
F. Know and utilize the three domains for changing behavior and developing talent: cognitive, psychomotor, and affective.
G. Make sure every instructional objective includes a condition, an action verb, and criteria.

Supplement

Supplement Tool 10A: Instructional Objectives Worksheet

Directions: Use this worksheet to write initial instructional objectives. For each phrase listed in the left column, the center column identifies the related component segment, or phrase, of an objective—condition, action, or criteria. Use the third column to identify similar needs for your job(s). Second, prepare basic objectives, using your phrases from the top section. Using all three components is more important than the form of the objective. Later, you can fine-tune your objectives to be more exact.

Performance Information	Component (Part of the Objective)	Your Job Needs for Performance
1. Without help from supervisor or others	Condition	
2. Using certain tools...	Condition	
3. Using certain references...	Condition	
4. Execute ____________	Action	
5. Prepare ________ orders	Action	
6. Identify parts of _________	Action	
7. To minimum specifications	Criteria	
8. Using the correct _______ templates.	Criteria	
Draft Your Instructional Objectives *At the end of the training, workers in the job of _________ should be able to:*		

Condition	**Action Verb** (Behavior)	Criteria
1.		
2.		
3.		

References and Additional Resources

Bloom, B. S. (Ed.), Engelhart, M. D., Furst, E. J., Hill, W. H., & Krathwohl, D. R. (1956). *Taxonomy of educational objectives, Handbook I: The cognitive domain*. New York: David McKay Co. www.cft.vanderbilt.edu/guides-sub-pages/blooms-taxonomy/.

Brown, A., & Green, T. D. (2016). *The essentials of instructional design: Connecting fundamental principles with process and practice* (3rd ed.). New York: Routledge.

Dave, R. H. (1975). Psychomotor levels. In R. J. Armstrong (Ed). *Developing and Writing Behavioural Objectives* (pp. 33–34). Tucson, AZ: Educational Innovators Press.

Krathwohl, D. R., Bloom, B. S., & Masia, B. B. (1964). *Taxonomy of educational objectives, the classification of educational goals. Handbook II: Affective domain*. New York: David McKay Co. ISBN 0-679-30210-7, 0-582-32385, 1.

Krathwohl, D. R., Bloom, B. S., & Masia, B. B. (1973). *Taxonomy of educational objectives, the classification of educational goals. Handbook II: Affective domain*. New York: David McKay Co. www.nwlink.com/~donclark/hrd/Bloom/affective_domain.html.

Mager, R. F. (1984). *Preparing instructional objectives* (2nd ed.). Belmont, CA: Lake Publishing.

Morrison, G. R., Ross, S. M., Kalman, H. K., & Kemp, J. E. (2012). *Designing effective instruction*. Hoboken: Wiley.

11

Methods to Achieve Consistency

Every accredited training session, workshop, or course must be delivered to employees with an intent to solve a performance problem in the workplace. After the training course, employees must be competent in their new skills, knowledge, or attitude in order to perform at a high level of proficiency when back on the job. Importantly, the experience of learners during the training sessions must assure that a performance change is achievable. Designing training content of interest, selecting appropriate methods, creating interesting activities, and determining appropriate media all play an integral part in excellent learner experiences and ultimate learner performance change. Accredited training programs deliberately plan all the key parts—content, methods, interaction, and media. This deliberate planning around the content and methods serves to both define successful learner completion and achieve lasting change.

> *The accreditation process is a way to look critically at what you're doing. For me, I was thinking about the different modalities of our different program and what is the consistency between some of these things? Where do you see some uniformity or are the courses and the contents scattershot? How are they being developed? How are they being delivered? What level of consistency do we have? So, it's kind of looking at this as … a process of reflection.*
>
> –***Peter Finn***
> *Society of Women Engineers*
> *Deputy Executive Director and*
> *Chief Learning Officer*

W. J. Rothwell et al., *Increasing Learning & Development's Impact through Accreditation*,
https://doi.org/10.1007/978-3-030-14004-5_11

11.1 Design Content

Before creating anything for delivery to an audience—it is useful for instructional designers to "imagine the intended learners," and what they will experience during training. Encourage instructional designers to first "imagine what the program will feel like to the learners." Will it feel routine and repetitive, or will it feel interesting, or even fun? Imagining what the program will feel like will remove a natural focus on the content and help designers to focus on the organization's employees as adult learners.

11.1.1 Workers as Learners

We know quite a bit about adults as learners, thanks to Malcolm Knowles (1990). Knowles delineated four key characteristics of all adults when they approach learning or are faced with a training situation. Adults are influenced by their prior learning experiences, which cause them to have fixed habits and ideas about training. Adults tend toward closed-mindedness about training and new ideas at work. Conversely, adults are rich sources of experience, rich sources of information for others, and have much to contribute to the learning of their colleagues. In today's workplace, the multiple generations of persons working together have tilted adult learners toward self-examination of whether training moves them toward an idealized self-concept. Participation in training today is influenced by the extent to which learning the topics will support the learners' own self-concept. Today's learners ask: "What will I gain, personally, from attending the training?" and "Will I become a more interesting person through training?" Adults gain the most if they can perceive of themselves during training as beneficiaries first and workers second. To effectively create this perception, we must view the relationship between worker/learners and instructors as a partnership in education. In this manner, designers can utilize the adult workers' own knowledge and experiences as a resource in planning the training for all the learners.

11.1.2 Sequencing the Content

Sequencing the content is a logical planning process where both learning and development practitioners and worker-learners can partner. Sequencing is a process for adults to engage in their own learning—both on their own and with co-workers. During sequencing, instructional designers create a logical order or a guideline for organizing the content that fits the intended learners. Guides for sequencing can follow the order of the physical world, the logic of a new concept, or be ordered according to the interests of the learners.

Physical world sequencing means structuring content according to how things occur in the real world. Real-world sequencing can be spatial, temporal, or physically kinesthetic. Spatial sequencing is ordering directionally, such as north-to-south, left-to-right, on-the-ground, or in-the-water. Temporal sequencing is ordering by history (timeline or date), ordering by speed (fast-to-slow or slow-to-fast), or ordering by procedure (step-by-step). Physically kinesthetic sequencing relates to how matter is experienced by humans (hardness, roundness, loudness, smell, or taste).

Sequencing according to the logic of a concept means a pre-determined sorting or grouping as the order. Here, information can be grouped by subject as in academic classes (English, welding, nursing, etc.), or information can be organized to make abstract notions more concrete (e.g., ordering the concept of time first by notions of sunrise/sunset, then by daylight/nightlight, then by clock measurement of hours).

Sequencing according to the interests of the learners means that a key part of the content is first related to a topic known to be of interest to the audience, such as favorite foods, popular games, or entertainment events. Connecting content to the interests of the adult learners gains attention quickly because the interest is felt as a fun or an enjoyable notion (interests might be sports, music, visual arts, service, nature, etc.). Seeking out the interests of your employees, as learners, and sequencing, accordingly, can help a designer to partner with prospective learners.

Basically, good sequencing means ordering your instructional objectives (see Chapter 10, "Deciding What to Include") into a flow which is logical for adults. Ordering content means listing which instructional objectives will be taught first, second, third, etc. for the entire course. Good sequencing places all the instructional objectives into a logical order, per a sequencing scheme such as those above. Regardless of the sequencing order utilized, one key is to apply a logical sequence that creates a pathway for the audience's learning—a pathway by which the adult learners can relate to the content personally. In this way, sequencing orders the individual thinking, the doing or expressing such that the adult learners can be successful during the training; adults can move through the information easily.

11.2 Select Methods

In learning and development, methods are techniques used to present the material for instruction. Methods are selected by the designers to facilitate learning during the training in order to achieve each of the established instructional objectives. Put simply, methods are the different manners by which learning is facilitated by the instructors during training. When selected and applied correctly, methods enable learners to both develop knowledge and skills during training and apply new knowledge and skills in the real world.

> *Reviewing instructional methods for effectiveness and efficiency helps training departments reach more participants and ensure more application to real world issues.*
>
> **–Dr. Karen LaMarsh**
> *Continuing Education and Training Consultant*

11.2.1 Methods Are Categorized

Methods are categorized according to the activity demanded of the learner target audience, as participants. Method categories include direct instruction (lecture, speech), indirect instruction (demonstrations, exercises, writing activities), experiential learning (projects, simulations), application (practice, problem solving, internships), independent study (reading, mental imagery, videos), and interactive instruction (games, role-plays, modeling, group case study). Each method demands a different degree of preparation by the instructor, different levels of facilitation skill to direct, different amounts of time to execute, and different amounts of effort on the part of the learners. An overview of several instructional methods, along with the learner impact and considerations for use, is presented at the end of this chapter. Important for managing accredited training programs is the proper selection of methods appropriate to the training goal and appropriate to each of the instructional objectives.

11.2.2 Select Methods According to Objectives

Adults need to be doing something in order to learn. Adults will not absorb information as a child does, soaking up new facts or data as "told" by a teacher. Adults must be engaged in their own learning—partnering with the facilitator and actively in control of their environments. Accredited training programs focus on adult activity and seek methods which promote active adult learners.

When selecting methods, start with the performance objectives established in planning the training (see Chapter 7, "Intended Learning Outcomes"). Recall that the performance objectives describe what workers will be able to know, do, or assimilate differently into their jobs after training. Recall that performance objectives for after training are called instructional objectives during training. Each instructional objective includes a condition, an action verb, and a criterion (see Chapter 10, "Deciding What to Include"). The action verb in the instructional objective is the critical hint to your choice of method. The method you select must relate directly to the level of knowledge or skill depicted by the action verb. For example, if the action verb indicates workers will "differentiate," then a method must be used to teach the skill of differentiation. This might be a method of a compare/contrast discussion, a distinguishing writing exercise, or a participant debate.

Just as each objective denotes different levels of knowledge, skill, or affective competency—different methods are linked as effective instructional techniques to develop competency at a specific level of expertise within one of the domains of cognitive, psychomotor or affective learning. A depiction of methods aligned with the action verbs for levels of competency in the cognitive domain is shown in Fig. 11.1.

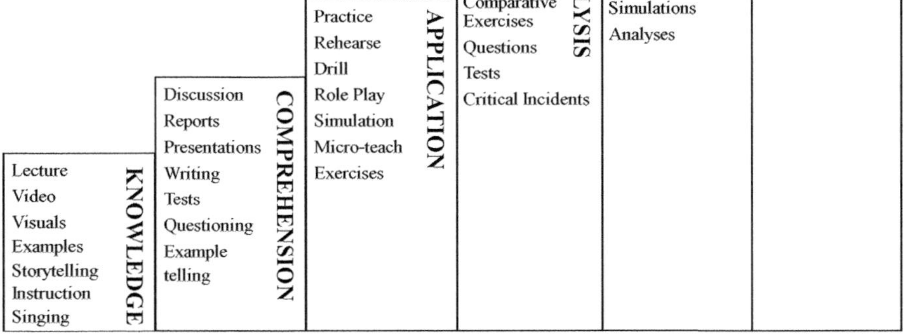

Fig. 11.1 Available methods per action verbs in objectives (cognitive domain) (Adapted from Brown and Green [2016]; Morrison et al. [2012])

Table 11.1 Participant activities for different domains

Cognitive – Acquire Knowledge:	Listening to lecture; question/answer; report of independent reading; panel discussion; video clips;' observe demonstration; recall writing; listening to stories; fill-in-the blank exercises; sentence completion; debate; dialogue with SME; create new work
Psychomotor – Develop Skill:	Mimic; assist a demonstration; try out; trial & error; copy a model; metal imagery; drill & practice; physical games; staging; simulation; execute under observation; execute trial run; obtain n ovice license
Affective – Change Attitude:	Discussion; self-assessment; role- play; dramatic reading; storytelling; improvisation; reflective writing; self- contracting; story interpretation; journaling; personal goal setting; mind-watching

11.2.3 Create Activities to Match Methods and Domains

Effective training course designs include activities for the lively engagement of adult learners. Each method naturally promotes some level of activity to be executed by the learners—from passive activity such as listening to a lecture, to extremely lively activity as in drill, practice, or playing games. Again, the method selected, and the learner activity associated with that particular method should be driven by the type of application needed on the job. Application will fall into one of the domains: cognitive; psychomotor; and affective. Designers should create activities for the learners that fall within a particular domain of learning and which align with the chosen method. A review of a few activities associated with each domain is presented in Table 11.1.

11.3 Promote Interaction

People learn best through active engagement. Therefore, the activities designed for participant engagement are important. Excellent training programs work to balance the methods and activities to help all adult learners to be engaged in learning.

> *The courses that are the most popular and the most well supported are the ones that have a significant hands-on component to them, because experiential learning tends to be the learning style that resonates.*
>
> ***–Dr. J. Kevin Perry***
> *Society of Automotive Engineers*
> *(SAE) International*
> *Director, Professional Development*

Learners do not only engage or react to the instructor, they engage with the content, with the instructor, and importantly, with each other as they learn. This means that selecting methods and activities which promote interaction with the content, and interaction with the other learners, is key.

11.3.1 Interaction with Content

Interaction with content occurs as learners are actively concentrating (thinking), practicing (doing), or emoting (feeling). Adults do not all learn in the same manner, and they engage with information, with content, and with different styles or preferences using different energies. Some people prefer to listen and concentrate on the reasoning behind topics. Others prefer to understand parts in order to understand information in dissected pieces. Still others prefer to sense the importance of information and its use in application. For instructional designers, it is always tempting to create activities that are considered "fun" to experience or "innovative" to design. However, courses and facilitators cannot adjust to the preferences of each and every learner, nor create activities which suit the interests of instructional designers. Importantly, developing training courseware around just one learning style or using only standardized activities will actually reduce the effectiveness of learning by all participants.

11.3.2 Interaction with Others

Interaction with others occurs as people are actively discussing (thinking), modeling/mimicking (doing), or mentoring/coaching (feeling). Engagement with others promotes joint learning, accomplishment and cooperative skill development. Interactive learner activities keep people stimulated and serve as both partnered practice and peer reinforcement. Practice is important in order for employees to accomplish the knowledge and/or skill to the degree of proficiency needed in their jobs. Reinforcement during training helps learners to gain confidence for personal application when back on the job. Interactive experiences with others during the training also increase a person's ability to transfer new knowledge, skills, and attitudes to their jobs.

Activities should be created to promote interaction, such as participant-to-content interaction, facilitator-to-participant interaction, and participant-to-participant interaction. These types of mixed activities, which are challenging, engage learners in the training process. Varied interactions with the content and with others further help learners to achieve the instructional objectives more readily.

11.4 Selecting Instructional Media—Training Delivery

One software that I love is Adobe Connect®. We can put people into different e-learning rooms where they can interact, and instructors can pop into the different rooms and also engage in the discussion.

–Reg Bonfoco
Canadian Financial
Securities Company
Continuing Education Specialist

Media selection means choosing the most cost-effective approach to facilitate learning and achieve important instructional objectives. While much has been written about instructional media—and research continues because instructors and learning and development managers alike are obsessed with finding approaches to deliver instruction that is least costly and effective—the reality is that research generally does not support the notion that one medium is always superior to others.

Our online platform has more modularization - one or two hours of virtual delivery. It's very bite-sized, trying to capture just-in-time learning.

–Anonymous
Multi-National Energy Corporation
Technical Learning &
Development Manager

Today, more employers focus attention on the so-called 70-20-10 rule. This idea suggests that about 70 percent of learning should occur in ways integrated to the job; 20 percent should occur through peer learning or social media; and only 10 percent of learning should occur through planned learning events such as online or onsite courses. Once instructional objectives have been identified, it is best to ask the question: "What is the most cost-effective and practical way to meet the objectives?"

Most instructors and line managers know how to plan for the 10 percent, which relates to planned course instruction or planned onsite training. Unfortunately, far fewer are familiar with ways to plan or implement the 70 percent (integrated within job) or the 20 percent (learning with peers or through social media).

11.4.1 Planning for Onsite Learning

Planning for onsite learning (the 10 percent) involves familiarity with the purpose of the method/activity, assessing available resources, content relevance, and instructor qualifications. The purpose of the method/activity should relate directly to the action in the instructional objective, as noted above. Plans must be realistic about available resources, including set-up time, assistance needed, props, and the real constraints of the physical space available. Good activities are those which are relevant to what the learners actually do on the job such that transfer is enabled.

> *Using different instructional methods and media which simulate the work environment makes the training more relevant and encourages growth.*
>
> ***–Dr. Karen LaMarsh***
> *Continuing Education and Training Consultant*

For certain activities, learning facilitators might need to be certified in a specific technique (such as Myers Briggs Type Indicator and Prezi software). Planning for onsite learning must also consider the availability of certified instructors, as resources for such activities. Expert facilitators in key methods must be available during the time(s) you are planning to offer onsite training.

11.4.2 Planning for Job-Integrated Training

Planning for job-integrated training (the 70 percent) is more difficult. The challenge comes in working with other managers to identify and support integrated job methods, such as coaching, delegation by the boss, or guided projects. Line managers must be both available and involved in employee learning, and this is not always a priority for line managers given existing business demands. Further, line managers may not be professionally rewarded for assisting employees in their learning and therefore might be reluctant to pursue job-integrated training. Line managers must be foresighted to weigh today's output from employees against tomorrow's application of new skills and potential output from employees. Planning for the 70 percent can be made easier if the organization has identified what kind of future work assignments will best build specific skills.

As an example, carrying out the budgeting process for one department's annual report will help learners to master general budgeting skills. The skills acquired through this work assignment can then be applied to other department's budgeting processes.

11.4.3 Planning for Peer Learning and Social Media Learning

Planning for peer learning and social media learning (the 20 percent) presents a separate set of difficulties. The challenge of planning for the 20 percent revolves around managing the peer resources to enable social learning to take place through role-modeling, job rotation, or deputizing methods. Again, this involves dedication and commitment from line managers to the social learning experiences. Line managers must see direct benefits from social and peer learning, and this has been difficult to correlate and quantify. Social learning also involves the availability and interest of peers, yet even within like generations, peers are not always amenable. Planning for the 20 percent can be made easier if line managers and workers identify social media (such as Facebook, LinkedIn, Snapchat, and others) where employees can pose questions, as learners, to peers or mentors who have been pre-identified as partners in the process. Of course, the timing of peer interactions and actual use by the identified parties on social media platforms cannot be controlled or measured. This lack of control can hamper organization support.

11.5 Implement a Course Planner

Learning and development departments, and therefore training managers, are called upon to ensure that the content selected, and training techniques used can logically support the learning which workers need. Many people rely upon this assurance from the learning and development department. Course learners, instructional designers, facilitators, and even other line managers must recognize the intent of the planned learning and understand how the learning will be achieved. Thus, each training course and program must be carefully designed to assure that employees actually gain the knowledge, skills, or attitudes needed to perform jobs at the levels of competency needed in your organization.

Because intended future competent performance on the job is described in performance objectives (see Chapter 7, "Intended Learning Outcomes"), these same performance objectives are used as the foundation for creating each training course. Content sequencing, method selection, and chosen learning activities are each based upon the bedrock of the established performance objectives, which course designers refer to as instructional objectives. The process of doing each of these tasks was described earlier in this chapter. In order to effectively manage the process of coordinating these tasks, the use of a course planning instrument is recommended. A course planning instrument demonstrates that all the content is primarily organized around the established performance objectives.

11.5.1 Using a Course Planning Instrument

The course planning instrument can be a matrix, a template, or a document. When completed, the course planner demonstrates how content will be ordered, which methods support the content, and which activities will be used to engage the learning process. A sample course planning instrument is shown in Table 11.2.

Use and completion of a course planning instrument are preferred by accredited training programs to demonstrate a consistent and professional approach to course purpose, design, and logic. Whether or not you use the sample instrument (Table 11.2) as a planner, your course planning document should include each of the following sections:

- Course name and description
- Instructional objectives
- Instructional method(s) per objective
- Activities per method
- Assessment of participant learning (evaluation or test method)*

**Note*—Assessment techniques for evaluating learners is discussed in Chapter 12, "Learner Feedback and Job Application".

Table 11.2 Sample course planner

COURSE PLANNING DOCUMENT	
Course Name:	
Instructor/Instructor Credentials:	
Target Audience:	
Need (Why this topic?)	
Course Description:	

Performance Objectives	
1.	
2.	
3.	
4.	

(continued)

Table 11.2 (continued)

Instructor Method		Activities / Interactions	
1.		1.	
2.		2.	
3.		3.	
4.		4.	

Participant Feedback Measures (Learner Evaluations)	
Near Transfer:	
Far Transfer	

11.6 Conclusion

Designing content, selecting appropriate methods, and creating interesting activities all impact how well adults will learn your content. Design a flow to your courses which is logical for adults, and design for adult interaction to help learners' understanding. Select media that supports learning, not just media which is inexpensive, or "fun" for designers to use. For accreditation, a detailed plan for each training course is needed. That plan should be realistic about resources and focus upon three-four key objectives per course. Always bear in mind that adult learning is most effective when the content is integrated with the activities done on the job. Thus, course content is more readily transferred to the job when line managers value and support immediate use of newly acquired skills.

Manager Tips

A. Establish your course plan from your learners' perspective, not from the instructional designer's perspective or the facilitator's perspective.
B. Consider the characteristics of adults as learners when designing training and adjust to the interests of your employees.
C. Use instructional objectives as the foundation for all content.
D. Sequence the content based upon a logical order for building knowledge or developing skills.
E. Select methods that match the domains and the action verb expressed in your objectives.
F. Keep learners active; create activities that support the action needed and which help learners to interact with each other and the content.
G. Promote peer learning and peer interaction within sessions.
H. Design course elements (objectives, methods, and activities) with a course planning instrument.
I. Recruit organization line managers to support job integration and to reinforce peer learning.

Supplement

Supplement Tool 11A: Methods Overview

TYPE OF METHOD	DIRECTION/USE	LEARNER IMPACT	CONSIDERATIONS
Lecture	Instructor-to-learner only. One-way method. Best if instructor has no notes.	Learner typically passive. Good for pure facts. Learner only listens. Retention unknown.	Need to give learner notes, or exercises to reinforce. Maybe offer paper for learner to take notes. Instr. may use power point slides. Handout of facts helpful for learner.
Lecture/ Discussion	Instructor—to—learner, but learner can talk. Discussion to be prompted by speaker.	Learner can discuss. Understanding revealed in learner Q's. Learner use of handouts unknown	Uses power point slides or visuals. Instructor's 'speaking points' can be on power point 'notes' pages. Prompt discussion with prepared Qs for Instructor. Needs discussion prompts. Handout of slides helpful for learner.
Demonstration	Showing method – good for manual skills	Learner can see end result. Still Instr. centered. Learner only experience is as 'helper 'or 'aide'.	Needs large space. Must include everyone–all must be able to 'see'. Requires much preparation. Mistake prone for Instr. Takes time. Not good for lots of learners.
Simulation	Pretend practice. Used when real practice is expensive or dangerous.	Learner completely engaged, but in 'set-up' situation. Good for safety training. Do not want learner to make mistakes on 'real' equipment.	Make sure learner not just 'having fun'. Instructor must emphasize seriousness of actual situation. Need some reinforcement 'test'. Validity is unclear.
Writing Activities	Good for learner expression. Used in F2F environments.	Very learner-centered. Learners can work independently or in pairs. Facilitator also involved as coach. Can keep learner records for evaluation.	Requires session time (20-30mins.) to conduct. Requires prep time to create exercises. Instructions must be very clear for learners to work independently. If requires 'hard' thinking-can take time for learners to finish. Learners need to feel accomplishment at end.

TYPE OF METHOD	DIRECTION/USE	LEARNER IMPACT	CONSIDERATIONS
Video Clips types: film electronic tape digital video can be silent or with sound	Immediate and visual Can be used to show motor skills – both good and bad examples.	Good for visual learners – no time for note taking or writing. Not good for thoughtful, cognitive learners. Impact upon learners not immediately clear. Good for cognitive reinforcing -topic or subject matter.	Time consuming to create. Needs multiple people to create – ISD designer usually not film maker. Portable display. Portable storage. Needs post-video discussion, which needs to be facilitated by instructor. Not appropriate for "watch –and –go". Easy for learner to draw wrong conclusion or make physical mistakes.
Mental Imagery	Used for visioning specific tasks. Used for 'seeing' strategies or game plans.	Good for learner 'thinking out' before action. Learner is mentally very active – imagining own psychomotor behavior. Learner will not recognize passage of time.	Best if no pre-handout. Some learners will resist closing eyes to 'imagine.' Some learners will 'watch' others. Need mature learner group to do effectively. Application environment usually sports or military. Reinforce with reflection writing by learners.
Modeling	Specific steps to copy and 'model' in skills, knowledge, and social actions. Good for skill building in social work setting (retail, restaurant). Excellent if model can explain thought processes while doing	Learners can do in social groups – open environment. Model acts as SME. Model is not coach. Still needs facilitator who acts as coach. Model not always verbal, which can hamper learner understanding.	Learner will not master skills in one modeling session. Training session can be on-the-job, with model. Learner will need practice to combine psychomotor, cognitive and social/affective skills. Must allow for mistakes on-the-job. Need trainer/manager to provide reinforcement, positive environment. Expensive method for employees to learn on-the job, needs time and manager support. Transfer of skills to job is excellent.

TYPE OF METHOD	DIRECTION/USE	LEARNER IMPACT	CONSIDERATIONS
Drill & Practice	Used for psychomotor skill building and artistry. ISD must understand previous skill levels of learners. Learner must be able to self-direct.	Can be learner paced. Builds confidence in learner. Learner very active physically and mentally. Instructor can be SME or model/coach.	Practice requires both organization and personal time. Some practice requires situation-specific conditions. Multiple situations must be set up almost identically for practice to re-occur. Job aid helpful as practice reminder.
Problem Solving: Purpose is to solve an issue or make a decision during session. Tools: Brainstorming Force field Fish bone Flowcharts Pareto charts Decision matrix Root cause analysis	Tools used in smaller groups of 5-8 persons. Larger groups need to be split into smaller subsets.	Active – learners usually in groups. Includes everyone. Requires knowledgeable facilitator. Learners enabled to explain reasons for decisions at end. Best for Job Transfer– individuals remember and remind others of decisions and reasons.	Requires advanced organization of subgroups. Learners need to meet in separate groups, later re convene in larger group to share decisions, even when using same tool. Requires time to analyze AND time to report back to larger group. Needs recorder and summarizer of decisions. Needs summaries distributed to all participants after session.
Case Study	Constructive approach Can be used for exploring issues with no exact answer. Good for manager training.	Learners very active. Can be very realistic. Participants can learn collaboration. Instr. Must be excellently skilled in leading discussion without providing ' answers.	Requires significant research for applicable Case. Requires much facilitator preparation–case facts and case options. Case may be distributed early as prereading. Needs 100% learner participation. Appropriate for medium to small sized groups only. Case story needs to be made available to each individual
Games Types: physical games verbal games video games written games Games situations can simulate real, or be 'fake'	Useful for building creativity. Excellent for "Openers" or "Introduction" Can also use when 'scoring' or 'wining' is important	Learners can build rapport. Learner is self-directed in actions. Problem–based games good for adult learners.	Requires much feedback of steps and reactions. Instr. Must be skilled at remarking on key moves and results. Needs 3+ people. Allow ample feedback and de-brief time. Games with no feedback = no learning.

TYPE OF METHOD	DIRECTION/USE	LEARNER IMPACT	CONSIDERATIONS
Role Play /Staging Role Play situation can be structured with script, or unstructured/unscri-pted Dramatic readings also possible.	Used for exploring emotions. Good for developing Affective skills, empathy, appreciat-ion,inquiry, listening.	Learners can be active "players', or passive observers. Instr. is in charge of the situation–creates situation. Creates roles. Active 'players' is better learning situation. Can be done F2F, online, or on audio phone.	Purpose and instructions must be explained to trainees. Requires much time (hours) for both Instructor and learners. Needs separate role play observer or videotaping for learns to 'see themselves' in action. Learner reflection on actions and results is good reinforcement technique.
Projects–long term 4 Types: Constructive "making" Aesthetic "appreciation" Problematic "solving" Drill "mastery"	Used for trainee application of skills. Skills to apply can be cognitive, psychomotor, affective, or combination. Practicums good for trainee trial and error at real situation pre-job. Also aids in learner social development in organizational settings.	Learner is independent and self–directed. May use coach on-site, separate from Instr. Instr. Is facilitator only. Does not control environment. Timing driven by learner or organization /sponsor.	Requires weeks for effective result. Costly - ($) and time. Requires resources from nonacademic sources. Syllabus has to be adjustable for different situations. Instr. must be comfortable with no control. Additional communication with practicum situation /setting is required – among facilitator/sponsor/trainee. Stages of progress emphasized with learner. Stages should be reported. Stages broken into tasks & subtasks. Learner needs to write own plan or project management design and report self-progress.

References and Additional Resources

Brown, A., & Green, T. D. (2016). *The essentials of instructional design: Connecting fundamental principles with process and practice* (3rd ed.). New York: Routledge.

Chan, J. F. (2011). *Designing and developing training programs*. San Francisco, CA: Pfeiffer.

Knowles, M. (1990). *The adult learner* (4th ed.). Houston, TX: Gulf Publishing.

Morrison, G. R., Ross, S. M., Kalman, H. K., & Kemp, J. E. (2012). *Designing effective instruction*. Hoboken: Wiley.

Rothwell, W. (2008). *Adult learning basics*. Alexandria, VA: ASTD.

Part V

Assessing Outcomes, Maintaining Records, and Program Evaluation

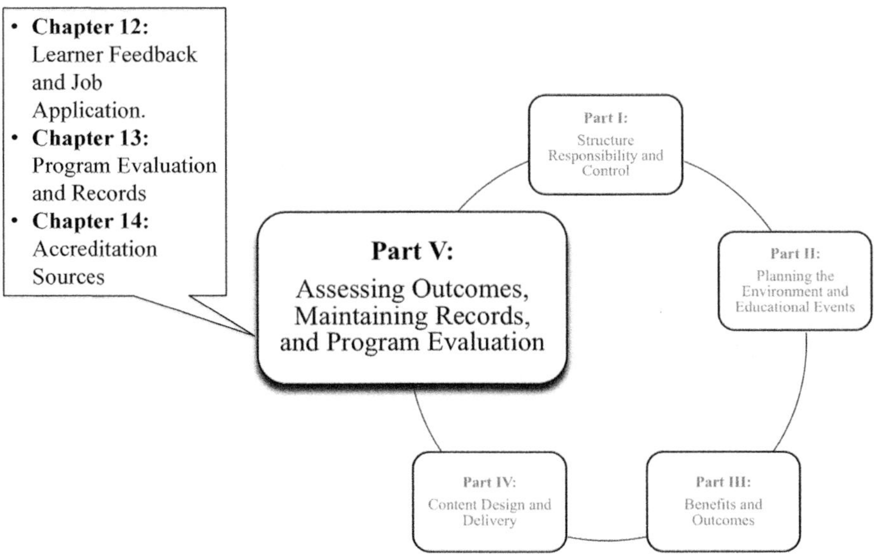

Fig. 1 Chapter organizer

For learning and development programs to gain and maintain credibility with stakeholders such as management, workers, and accrediting bodies, it is important for the learning and development function to assess outcomes, maintain records, and ensure that learning experiences are regularly and effectively evaluated. Learners must be evaluated in some way to ensure that they meet learning requirements and meet organization learning needs. Furthermore, learners must be given feedback on how well they have mastered course content in line with an established organizational policy. Organizations should also have ways to gather and record evidence to demonstrate that learners have attained mastery. Evidence of learning includes testing systems and records of how well learners have performed.

While feedback systems for learners and instructors are important, they are not enough. Organizations should also establish and sustain systems by which to evaluate full training programs. Full training program evaluations help to perpetuate continuing improvement efforts within learning and development departments. Evaluations can be established to test out programs (formative), examine results of programs (summative), or confirm the long-term effects of training (confirmative). All forms of evaluations are usually needed, though care should be taken in creating them because evaluation can be costly.

Finally, accreditation provides an external check on the overall quality of learning and development departments. Accrediting bodies look at, and evaluate, whether a learning and development department or institution meets generally accepted standards for learning program quality. Many groups exist to accredit training, and they should be explored based on how they can add value to your employee learning efforts.

The chapters in this part will focus on: providing feedback to learners and others (Chapter 12, "Learner Feedback and Job Application"); maintaining learner records and evaluating programs (Chapter 13, "Program Evaluation and Records"); and examining sources of accreditation and various bodies that accredit learning programs (Chapter 14, "Accreditation Sources").

12

Learner Feedback and Job Application

It is commonly cited in writings on training that only 8 percent of off-the-job training transfers back to the job as a changed behavior. That means, for every US dollar invested in training, an organization realizes only eight cents of impact. That seems like an abysmally poor investment. And indeed, some claim that training should be the solution of last, not first, resort because it is more expensive to do well than using performance improvement alternatives such as changing recruiting procedures, updating tools and equipment, or modifying rewards given to workers (see Rothwell et al. 2018). This chapter focuses on learner feedback and job application. It examines learner evaluation, the learner's assessment of his or her progress, and learner application of skills. Additionally, learners should be provided with feedback on their mastery of course content, and the organization should have an organizational policy to support providing feedback. Organizations should also retain evidence to verify that feedback on learner mastery is occurring. Retaining evidence includes safe ways to record and store learner results and to return those results to participants and instructors.

12.1 Providing Learners with Feedback

There is a logic to learner feedback and evaluation as demonstrated by the well-known Instructional Systems Design (ISD) model. First, worker needs are identified based on individual needs, organizational needs, and job needs (the needs assessment process). Second, performance/instructional objectives are written to ensure that training is designed to achieve on-the-job

W. J. Rothwell et al., *Increasing Learning & Development's Impact through Accreditation*,
https://doi.org/10.1007/978-3-030-14004-5_12

change and thereby meet the new performance need. Third, ways to evaluate learner performance in training—and performance back on the job—are prepared. Those learner performance evaluations are linked to the instructional/ performance objectives and are thereby also linked to the organization's needs.

Most organizations have ways to measure how well learners liked the training they attended. That is called participant evaluation, and it is related to the popular end-of-course forms that ask participants to rate the quality of instruction, the quality of the trainer, and sometimes the quality of refreshments and the physical space. Few organizations take steps to measure how well learners mastered the learning content through performance tests. Even fewer organizations take steps to follow learners back on the job to see how well they can apply in the workplace what was learned in training.

When learners are subjected to testing, they will naturally wonder who will see the test results, how those test results will be used (e.g., will failure in training lead to corrective action or to job loss?), and how long the test results might be kept before being purged from employee records. Those issues should be communicated to learners by the organization and should be part of a learning and development department's evaluation policies and procedures.

> *If we really want people to do better and to understand the information to improve themselves… then you have to give them feedback. I have been more thoughtful about evaluation for my own courses. I now ask myself, 'how could I be more communicative with my students?' and so my feedback has tripled. They get written feedback and feedback from their peers. Our learning management system gives us tools where I can video my feedback. I can audiotape my feedback. I can translate voice to text, or I can write it.*
>
> ***–Dr. Maureen C. Jones***
> *The Pennsylvania State University*
> *Accreditation Coordinator for the MHA Programs*

12.1.1 Training Evaluation Policy and Procedures

An excellent starting point for evaluation is a policy and procedure document that sets forth the organization's philosophy of evaluation, standards relevant to evaluation, and step-by-step methods used to evaluate. While it is possible to write a general policy that addresses all evaluation methods covering the entire organization (see, for instance, www.who.int/about/evaluation/evaluationpolicy.pdf), it is also possible to write the policy and procedures to focus specifically on learning event evaluations (see, for instance, www.jica.go.jp/project/cambodia/0601331/pdf/english/5_TrainingEvaluation.pdf).

Such a document helps focus attention on the objectives of evaluation in order to build consensus among decision makers on results from learning and development efforts. After all, any evaluation requires time, money, and effort, and that can direct attention away from other efforts—such as conducting needs assessment, designing and developing training, or delivering instruction.

Important questions to consider in learning evaluation policies and procedures include the following:

- Who should conduct the evaluation?
- How will training be evaluated?
- What evaluation methods are to be used?
- When will training be evaluated (before, during, after, or long after instruction)?
- Where will training be evaluated (during instruction, back on the job, or both)?
- Why is training being evaluated?
- How much time, money, and staff will the organization devote to training evaluation efforts?

In reality, the best results from training evaluations are obtained when the organization's leaders determine: Who wants the training evaluation information, and what decisions will be made based on the evaluation results? Evaluation is not conducted in a vacuum. People use the results to make decisions and changes. For instance, instructors might use evaluation results to improve future sessions. Managers might use evaluation results to determine whether training is helping to improve on-the-job work performance or output of training participants. Senior executives might use the collective results of all training evaluations to decide whether to conduct training internally or to seek an outsourcing agent. So, it is important to be clear who will use the evaluation results and how the results will be used.

> *We always had pretty decent evaluations. Mostly because there were regulators who were requiring it. One of the things the regulators always asked for was customer(learner) feedback detail. And so, we've been kind of used to asking, pretty good granular questions and…not just about the experience, but about clarity on the learning objectives… it wasn't just 'how many smiley faces are you giving us?' There had always been, four, five, maybe six questions about the course. Our learner surveys collected richer feedback than what you see probably with a non-accredited organization.*
>
> ***–Clyde Seepersad***
> *Linux Foundation*
> *General Manager,*
> *Training & Certification*

12.1.2 Record Keeping

One very important issue in training is what records will be kept of evaluation information. After all, not all training is conducted for the same reasons. Some training is conducted to help workers qualify to meet the minimum requirements to do their jobs (as in structured jobs); some training is conducted to help workers keep their skills current in the face of changing work requirements (as in updated technology); some training is conducted to prepare workers for different responsibilities (such as promotions or job transfers); some training is conducted to meet government laws, rules, or regulations (compliance training); and some training is conducted to meet some combination of these objectives.

Records must be kept for many learning and development activities, and this includes training evaluation results. Evaluation results of learner performance in training are important to ensure accountability of employees, their managers, and the organization. But recordkeeping can range from simple and informal document-based records for small organizations to complex, large data-based systems for large organizations. Just as policies and procedures should be established for conducting training evaluations, recordkeeping of evaluation results should also be documented in a written policy statement. The recordkeeping policy should cover:

- Whose training evaluation information will be the focus of attention?
- What training evaluation information will be kept?
- What training evaluation information must be kept in compliance with requirements for external bodies (such as regulators or accrediting bodies)?
- When will the training evaluation data be collected?
- How will the training evaluation data be collected and retained?
- How long will evaluation data be retained?
- Where will the training evaluation data be stored, and what security will be associated with storage and access?
- How much time, money and staff will be associated with the recordkeeping

Many human resource information systems (HRIS)—as well as many learning management systems (LMS)— include training recordkeeping systems. Many of these programs meet the basic requirements for security and for storage of evaluation information. For more information on evaluation records retention and maintenance, see Chapter 13, "Program Evaluation and Records".

12.2 Addressing Job Application of Training

An important issue in training evaluation is on-the-job application—the use of new skills by learners when back at work. Consider: defining on-the-job transfer; defining and ensuring near transfer of training; and defining and ensuring far transfer of training. The following sections address these issues.

> *A lot of the training that is developed actually does help enforce what it is that the advisors have to do on a day-to-day basis. So, all of the trainings we're doing is not just for somebody to sit there and go: 'Okay. I'm done'. This is a waste of the day. Our people actually get things that they can take away from training and take back to their office and to their practice to implement.*
>
> –***Reg Bonfoco***
> *Canadian Financial*
> *Securities Company*
> *Continuing Education Specialist*

12.2.1 Defining On-the-Job Transfer

On-the-job transfer means how much training is applied on the job. There are several ways to encourage on-the-job transfer. One way is to move away from using end-of-course instructional objectives (Chapter 10, "Deciding What to Include") and toward using back-on-the-job performance objectives (Chapter 7, "Intended Learning Outcomes"). Traditionally, learning and development practitioners have resisted a focus on performance objectives because performance objectives are tough to establish and measure. Consistent performance objectives are also tough to establish, because not all managers may require workers to adhere to the same performance standards on the job (see Chapter 11, "Methods to Achieve Consistency"). Performance objectives are also tough to measure because it can be time-consuming and expensive to follow workers back to the job to check how well or how often they apply new skills.

12.2.2 Defining and Ensuring Near Transfer of Training

Most organizational efforts to address transfer of training focus on the so-called near transfer. Near transfer examines, in a short time frame, how well learners apply directly to their jobs what they learned in training. For each performance objective—and remember that objectives are tied to learning needs—the organization establishes ways to quickly evaluate on-the-job application of what was learned in training. Typically, performance is not examined by written tests but rather by observed demonstrations. For instance, if workers are trained for job interviewing, a learning and development professional could measure that by observing the learner conduct a job interview and completing a checklist that indicates the behaviors expected to be used during interviewing.

Near transfer can be planned before, during, and after training. Specific actions can be taken to encourage near transfer. As just one example, near transfer may be encouraged if workers meet with their immediate supervisors before attending training to ensure that they are clear about what should be learned in training to return and apply to their jobs. Then, after the training, the workers can meet with their immediate supervisors again, to ensure that they did indeed learn something new, and they can accept responsibility to apply on the job what was they learned in training. As another example, a classroom instructor can ask learners to describe how they "plan to apply" to their jobs what was learned in training. That information can later be sent to the immediate supervisors of every training participant to evaluate near transfer.

12.2.3 Defining and Ensuring Far Transfer of Training

Few organizational efforts to ensure transfer of training focus on the so-called far transfer. Far transfer examines how well learners creatively apply new insights into their jobs that, while not directly gained in training, were encouraged by that training.

Perhaps a simple example will clarify. Suppose an individual participates in training and, in the course of doing so and in reflecting on what was learned, has an intuitive flash of insight about a new idea. That innovation was sparked by the training, but the topic was not directly covered in the instruction. This is one way to think of far transfer. Far transfer occurs when a new idea is generated as a consequence of a learning experience, but the new idea is not directly related to the content covered in the training session.

Perhaps you have experienced that yourself. You participate in a training event. What is said or done in the training (or educational experience) gives you a new idea. That idea, in turn, sparks innovation back on your job that could (or does) prove to be immensely valuable in reducing cost or generating new revenue for the organization.

The point here is that mainstream thinking about evaluating training results, or return on investment (ROI), does not typically include efforts to capture the value of far transfer. It is a hidden dimension. But, in a design economy in which innovative ideas matter most in achieving and sustaining competitive advantage for organizations (Gliddon and Rothwell 2018), the payoffs of far transfer from training and education could far outweigh traditional measures of results or ROI.

Like near transfer, far transfer can be planned before, during, and after training. Specific actions can be taken to encourage it. As just one example, far transfer may be encouraged if workers meet with their immediate supervisors before attending training to ensure the workers are clear about the most important problems, which should be solved for the organization. That can create a frame of reference for workers to think about while they participate as learners in training. This problem preview can then encourage learners to think creatively about ways to solve those problems in light of what is presented in training. Creative activities during the course can also prompt flashes of insight. As an example, trainers might invite learners to draw pictures about how they could apply what was learned. Drawing tends to spark creative thinking that may, in turn, lead to innovative ideas of commercial value to the organization. As another example, a classroom instructor can prompt a discussion among all participants to share how each person plans to creatively apply what was learned in training back on the job.

12.3 Managers Tips to Provide Learners with Feedback and Ensure On-the-Job Application of Training

How do managers ensure that learners receive feedback about their performance in training and about on-the-job application of what they learned in training? A simple answer is that it all begins with taking proactive steps regarding test scores, linkages to key performance indicators (KPIs), and one-on-one discussions about skill transfer. Operating managers should ask learners what feedback was received about their performance during training. For instance, did learners receive their scores on any pretests and posttests administered during training? Did learners receive feedback on how well they demonstrated skills performed in training relative to performance tests? If the answer is yes, then the next question is to ask whether that information is useful to the worker and whether it encourages workers to learn more. Operating managers play important roles in ensuring that the training feedback happens, is noteworthy, and is used to spark additional action. Supplement Tool 12A—*Brainstorming Guide—Encouraging Feedback* is provided to help operating managers think about different types of feedback.

Another way to encourage job transfer is to relate training evaluation information to the learners' KPIs. Many organizations today rate employee performance by measuring specific indicators of job performance, which are called KPIs. Training can be designed to impact KPIs, and employee learners' performance in training can be related to on-the-job KPIs.

Operating managers also play an important role in ensuring transfer of learning to the workplace. Managers can take the time to plan with learners what the learners are expected to gain from attending training and then ask employees themselves if there might be any additional ways the skills learned in training could be reinforced on the job. Importantly, if operating managers do not take active steps to encourage the transfer of learning, it is less likely to occur. Supplement Tool 12B—*Brainstorming Guide—Near Transfer of Learning* and Supplement Tool 12C—*Brainstorming Guide—Far Transfer of Learning* are provided to prompt manager thinking in this regard.

12.4 Conclusion

This chapter focused on learner feedback and the application of learner skills to jobs. It examined learner evaluation, the learner's assessment of progress, and learner transfer of new skills. Organizations should encourage operating managers to hold individual discussions with workers, both before and after the training, to encourage both near transfer and far transfer of learning back into the workplace. Organizations should also retain evidence to verify that feedback on learner mastery is occurring. That includes ways to record test scores and feed test scores back to learners and instructors.

Manager Tips

A. Ensure that the organization has a written policy and procedure for the evaluation of learner performance during training.
B. Ensure that the organization has a written policy and procedure on recordkeeping for training results and training feedback to learners.
C. Encourage instructors and managers to take the time to plan for on-the-job application of training, and then follow up with learners to ensure that they are held accountable for applying what they learned.
D. Take steps to go beyond near transfer to encourage creative applications on the job of what was learned during training, thereby encouraging far transfer.

Supplement

Supplement Tool 12A: *Brainstorming Guide—Encourage Giving Feedback*

Directions: Follow the steps and answer the questions in the worksheet to brainstorm on ways that the organization can encourage giving feedback to workers on how those workers performed while in training. For example, "the organization can give learners feedback on how they scored on training pretests and posttests." Remember to write any ideas that come to mind. Do not judge or discuss the ideas. Come up with as many ideas as possible.

STEP 1: What are all of the ways you can encourage giving feedback? List all ideas in this column.	**STEP 2:** What is in the way of implementing your idea?	**STEP 3:** What resources do you need to implement your idea?

Supplement Tool 12B: *Brainstorming Guide—Near Transfer of Learning*

Directions: Follow the steps and answer the questions in the worksheet to brainstorm on ways that the organization can encourage near transfer of learning. For example, "managers should meet with employees before they attend training–or participate in online learning–to discuss what skills are most important to learn in training to apply on the job." Come up with as many ideas as possible.

STEP 1: What are all of the ways you can encourage near transfer of learning ? List all ideas in this column.	**STEP 2:** What is in the way of implementing your idea?	**STEP 3:** What resources do you need to implement your idea?

Supplement Tool 12C: Brainstorming Guide—Far Transfer of Learning

Directions: Follow the steps and answer the questions in the worksheet to brainstorm on ways that the organization can encourage the far transfer of learning. For example, "trainers should ask learners, at the end of training, how they plan to apply on the job what they learned during training." Then, "trainers question learners how they can go beyond immediate applications to creative new thinking." Come up with as many ideas as possible.

STEP 1: What are all of the ways you can encourage far transfer of learning? List all ideas in this column.	**STEP 2:** What is in the way of implementing your idea?	**STEP 3:** What resources do you need to implement your idea?

References

Broad, M., & Newstrom, J. (1992). *Transfer of training: Action-packed strategies to ensure high payoff from training investment*. Reading, MA: Addison-Wesley.

Elkeles, T., & Pulliam, P. (2014). *Measuring the success of learning through technology: A guide for measuring impact and calculating ROI on e-learning, blended learning and mobile learning*. Alexandria, VA: Association for Talent Development.

Gliddon, D., & Rothwell, W. (Eds.). (2018). *Innovation leadership*. New York: Routledge.

Kirkpatrick, J., & Kirkpatrick, W. (2016). *Kirkpatrick's four levels of evaluation*. Alexandria, VA: Association for Talent Development.

Phillips, P., & Phillips, J. (2012). *Measuring ROI in learning and development*. Alexandria, VA: Association for Talent Development.

Rothwell, W., King, S., & Hohne, C. (2018). *Human performance improvement: Building practitioner competence* (3rd ed.). London: Routledge.

Stone, D., & Heen, S. (2015). *Thanks for the feedback*. New York: Penguin.

13

Program Evaluation and Records

Accredited learning and development departments must conduct self-evaluations of their programs and maintain a system of permanent learner records. The accuracy and availability of learner training records need to be policy driven to assure both accountability and the quality of learning and development programs. Applying immediate learner assessments, such as testing learners after the training session or holding discussions with learners (Chapter 12, "Learner Feedback and Job Application"), helps training professionals to make content or delivery improvements. Importantly, accredited training programs also establish continuous and comprehensive evaluations of their full programs in order to make structural and operational improvements. This chapter will discuss the processes of full training program evaluation, undertaken to support continual improvement of the learning and development effort.

13.1 Full Program Evaluation

Accreditation compels the organization to continuously improve the development and delivery of courses.

–Dr. Karen LaMarsh
Continuing Education and Training Consultant

W. J. Rothwell et al., *Increasing Learning & Development's Impact through Accreditation*,
https://doi.org/10.1007/978-3-030-14004-5_13

Full program evaluation seeks to determine if the learning and development department's products, its training curriculum and overall education offerings, are useful to the organization.

Both learning and development managers and executives want assurances of two items: (1) High-quality education is being delivered to the employees and (2) the training provided works continuously.

13.1.1 Purpose

The evaluation for the entire learning and development (L&D) program has a distinct purpose, and it is a comprehensive structured process. As a learning and development manager, you set the purpose for evaluating your full program, comprehensively, and select the processes of program evaluation you will undertake. One program evaluation process might be a practice to review each course or learning event during its design, or it might be a practice to pilot test all learning events for validation, or it might be an auditing practice used to make improvements in overall course design and delivery. Regardless of process or practice, full program evaluation has a purpose to document how the education provided to workers meets the overall needs of the organization and its employees on a broad scale. It is a different purpose than providing feedback to the learners individually, as discussed in Chapter 12, "Learner Feedback and Job Application". The purpose of full program evaluation is met by examining each of the learning and development department's offerings according to a set standard and summarizing the results against selected criteria.

13.1.2 Reluctance

Some training managers are hesitant to perform full evaluations of their learning and development departments, and some simply do not believe in evaluation efforts. Hesitancy can be due to a lack of confidence about whether the training adds value or a lack of confidence in examining full impact across the organization. Hesitancy can also result from a lack of resources (time and money) or a lack of expertise in evaluation techniques. The training of employees may be perceived by management as valuable to the organization in a general sense, but a budget to measure and quantify the actual value of learning efforts may not be available. Limited practice in evaluation can also stem from a business culture that simply does not support self-examination or reflection.

They (trainers) evaluated the session - while in the session and at the end of the session. But they didn't learn anything about the impact of the course.

–Scott A. Critchfield, CFP
Coach, Learning Professional

13.1.3 Comprehensive

Quality full program evaluations are comprehensive in scope. This does not mean that each detail of every element of instructional design, delivery, and learner result needs to be examined. Comprehensive means the elements of the training effort, which are selected to be examined, are examined fully using multiple data points.

Comprehensive data collection involves selecting key elements of the process and consistently obtaining information on those selected elements across all delivery points. Selected elements can be design related, instructor related, content related, training environment related, or focused upon customer (learner) satisfaction or learner achievement. Design-related elements stem from your Learning Blueprint and might include a review of course goals and instructional objectives, content analysis, sequencing review, method use, or design suitability. Instructor-related elements include instructor expertise and delivery skills. Content-related elements would include course plans, materials, and exercises, including any e-learning aspects. Training environment elements might include notifications, logistics, physical space, e-learning navigation, or audio/visual adequacy. Customer satisfaction elements might include learner reactions or operating unit manager satisfaction. Comprehensive in evaluation procedure means that once the elements to be examined are selected, data is collected specifically on those elements across your many workshops or over a prescribed time period.

13.1.4 Goal Oriented

One element, outcome achievement, is of keen interest to managers and executives because organization leaders need assurance that training is "working." Outcome achievement means collecting data to determine whether each training program, when executed, met the performance objectives set forth for that program. Collectively, all the performance objectives for one program comprise the goal of training for that one program. Thus, another way to describe evaluating outcome achievement is collecting data to determine whether each training program offered met its training goal.

13.1.5 Sources

Data should be gathered from multiple sources to assess the training element being examined. Data sources are chosen based upon the element of interest and the time during which data is available. Different data sources will be chosen if information is needed at several points over a long period of time or if information is needed at one point in time and it can be obtained fairly quickly.

As a manager, you want to be sure that each employee who has participated in one of your programs has learned the knowledge needed for the job, has developed the skills needed to perform the job, and has exited your program with a positive attitude about the work to be accomplished. To ascertain this, examination data is usually sought from the learners themselves, either during training, just after training, or later when performing jobs in the workplace.

Importantly, data can be obtained from a full range of sources. Other parties important to the training process such as designers, instructors, and technicians can be important sources of process data. Similarly, training managers, recruiters, human resource personnel, and operating managers can be key sources of data on skill performance or attitude improvement.

13.2 Focus: Formative, Summative, or Confirmative

For assessing full learning programs, an overall design or typology to the evaluation focus should be established. This aids in focusing the evaluation to certain periods of time and helps to execute evaluation tasks efficiently. Training program evaluation is divided into design typologies of formative, summative, and confirmative evaluation, thus naming the focus.

13.2.1 Formative

Formative evaluation is intended to provide information that can improve the design and development of the learning programs. Formative evaluation asks the question "How *are* we doing?" Formative evaluation is interested in the process of designing and developing instruction for adults. It looks to identify any weaknesses in segments of the design process, including creating content, sequencing, writing instructional materials, setting objectives, choosing methods, or techniques of facilitation. In a formative process, data can be collected from those involved in the design phases and also from individuals impacted by the design such as instructors, assistants, and the learners themselves. Designers use formative evaluations for making course improvements after missteps have been identified in the formative evaluation report. Improvements might be accommodating different worker profiles, refining instructional objectives, adjusting to available resources, or adapting to available technology, to name just a few.

13.2.2 Summative

Summative evaluation stresses the outcome of the training effort, and interest rests in the complete product of training courses produced by the department. Summative evaluation asks the question: "How *did* we do in the training we developed?" Summative evaluation is interested in the benefits of the training for both the individuals involved and the organization as a whole, after the experience has ended. For summative evaluation, data might be collected over a longer period of time following course end. Data can be collected from managers, learners, participant peers, or participant customers, to determine if the knowledge and skill learned during training are still being applied on the job.

> *You really have to look at: Did the training change any behavior?*
>
> *–**Scott A. Critchfield, CFP***
> *Coach, Learning Professional*

Summative evaluation naturally looks longer term to connect the results of the training with the organization's goals and operation; it is looking at far transfer of learning. Managers use summative evaluations to examine the ongoing need for the training by job or department and to identify training's impact on productivity, efficiency, and effectiveness. Given a well-documented, positive result, a summative evaluation can justify the annual training budget and learning investment.

13.2.3 Confirmative

Confirmative evaluation looks at the ongoing effects of training, long after the end of several sessions or workshops. Confirmative evaluation seeks to determine the long-lasting effects of training to support continued investment in talent development. Confirmative evaluation asks the question: "How *are we still* doing?" A large emphasis of confirmative evaluation is on the ongoing quality of learning and development as an effort expended across the organization. Confirmative evaluation assesses learning's support for the strategic direction of the organization, based upon its mission and goals (see Chapter 2, "Align Learning and Development with Organization Mission and Values") and its Learning Blueprint (see Chapter 5, "Plan for Quality and Strategic Learning"). Confirmative evaluation looks beyond the results of tests or employee performance back on the job. Confirmative evaluation takes the view of continuous improvement and seeks to collect data which can assess continuous improvement. Confirmative data might involve critiques of strategic outcomes, suggestions for program upgrades or system upgrades, ideas from competitors, or suggestions from outside practitioners in the adult education industry. In practice, confirmative evaluation is an extension of summative evaluation. Both types are used to judge the effectiveness of the learning offerings provided to employees—with summative examining effectiveness sometime after the training event and confirmative examining effectiveness after a longer period of time.

> *We evaluate the programs and the courses. Our process calls for courses to be evaluated, on average, every three years. We also seek online survey feedback from attendees, and we review these responses as they come in. If critical modifications are suggested, we make them at that time, if possible. Otherwise, we save the feedback and consider it during the regular course review and revision process.*
>
> ***–Anonymous***
> *Multi-National Energy Corporation*
> *Technical Learning &*
> *Development Manager*

13.3 Evaluation Procedures/Methods

There are many different models for conducting evaluations, and different procedures attached to each model. There are also technicians and experts in the field of evaluation who utilize various evaluative methods.

13.3.1 Kirkpatrick and Phillips Levels of Evaluation

Kirkpatrick and Phillips Levels of Evaluation is a combination of a methodology created by Donald Kirkpatrick (1998), which was later expanded by Jack Phillips (1996, 2003). The original methodology outlined four levels of evaluation ranging from satisfaction by the learners to impact upon the organization. These four levels were later amended to include a fifth level—a cost/benefit analysis or return on investment (ROI) for the organization. A review of the five levels of evaluation follows:

- Level 1—Satisfaction. Level 1 seeks a reaction of satisfaction from the learners and questions their immediate response to the training. A short survey or a brief written statement is used to seek feedback on meeting the goals of the training, the effectiveness of the instructor, and the comfort of the physical environment. Questions are usually asked immediately following the training event, but maybe sought up to one month after the training event. Level 1 evaluations measure how the content and the instructor were generally received and the credibility of the learning event in general, as experienced by the learners.
- Level 2—Learning. Level 2 evaluations seek an indication of whether learning (be it new knowledge, skill building, or attitude change) took place for the learners. A level 2 evaluation might seek recall of content, an assessment of physical dexterity, or a measure of confidence in the durability of an attitude. A level 2 (learning) evaluation might take the form of a written test, an observation of participant performance, an interview, or a focus group discussion. These types of evaluations can be administered immediately following the training event or up to 3–9 months following the training event. During a level 2 procedure, evaluators seek to understand whether the training had some immediate effect on employees. Evaluators seek to validate changes in knowledge, skill, or attitude by the learners. Level 2 evaluation reports can be used to alter or make changes in the content of the training.
- Level 3—Behavior. Level 3 evaluations seek information to assess whether learners have applied what was presented in training to their job performance. Level 3 looks for direct action changes on the job as a result of the training, usually near-term transfer. Behavior change can be self-reported by the learners, observed by others, or reported in appraisals made by those impacted by the learner's job performance (peers, subordinates, colleagues, customers, etc.). Level 3 evaluations can only be done after learners have had a fair chance to apply what they have learned, and application takes time and resources. Importantly, appraisals by third parties are believed to be more valid measures of the learner's behavior change and can also serve as an external validation for training in meeting performance objectives.

- Level 4—Results. Level 4 evaluations seek information about the value of the training to the learner's work unit, department, or organization. Level 4 evaluations look for how well the training met the organization need that was identified at the beginning of the project, or how well the training filled the gap. This level of evaluation focuses upon results for customers, system stakeholders, and operational processes in helping the organization move along its strategic path. To complete level 4 evaluations, broader data is needed to assess improvement across stakeholder groups and over longer periods of time. Level 4 evaluations might be administered multiple times between 3 and 13 months following the completion of a training program. Of key interest is whether the training program met the organization's strategic need identified in the need's assessment.
- Level 5—Return on investment (ROI). A level 5 evaluation seeks to understand the impact of the training economically. It asks whether the benefits of the training, measured in improved efficiency or effectiveness, outweigh the costs of conducting the training. It requires calculating the costs of learning management, design, and delivery and calculating the benefits to the organization in reduced mistakes, quicker production, improved quality, customer retention, or reduced turnover. These numbers can be difficult to obtain and time frames for measurement can be indistinct, making accurate calculations difficult. Further, attributing organizational benefits such as those listed above directly to the result of completed training is problematic. Line managers and others within the organization will reasonably attribute a portion of improved performance to other factors and resist attributing improvement directly to training.

Because of the effort and investment required to conduct evaluations at high levels (3, 4, and 5), most learning and development organizations procedurally conduct only level 1 or level 2 evaluations.

> *If the training evaluation uses Kirkpatrick Level 2, 3, or 4, the evaluation will also reveal how the training is directly impacting the overall organization.*
>
> ***–Dr. Karen LaMarsh***
> *Continuing Education and*
> *Training Consultant*

However, evaluations using results methods (level 4) or return on investment methods (level 5) are seldom conducted because collecting the data needed, analyzing the data into useful evaluative information, and comparing that information to a known baseline is a difficult and time-consuming process. Importantly, conducting evaluations at the higher levels maybe be beyond the capabilities of the organization's learning and development professionals.

13.3.2 Other Program Evaluation Methods

Other program evaluation methods are available, and several methods are associated with each of the three categories of evaluation focus—formative, summative, and confirmative.

For formative evaluation, or evaluation of the planning of training, evaluation methods include pre-testing of materials for comprehension or pilot testing of course parts when in development. Several formative evaluation methods involve setting out key questions about content or courseware parts, followed by evidence gathering and analysis based upon the elements in question (exercises, links, chat rooms, etc.). Other types of formative evaluations involve hiring consultants or subject matter experts to opine on the content of a program while it is being developed. The ultimate approach used in formative evaluations will vary based upon the stage of design, the availability of persons needed to critique, and the measures used to obtain appraisal data (interviews, observations, site reviews, etc.).

> *I would follow-up with the participant themselves a week later and ask for one take-away from the session that you implemented at work. Without continual follow-up after your training event, at the end of 30 days/45 days/or even 60 days, you can't say the training really had any impact.*
>
> ***–Scott A. Critchfield, CFP***
> *Coach, Learning Professional*

Summative evaluation methods focus more clearly on results of training efforts, specifically the meeting of training goals and instructional objectives. Methods for summative review generally focus upon results of the program in improving effectiveness, efficiency, or cost. Effectiveness methods might evaluate a program by comparing it to a standard or conventional offering or by using a formal research framework. Efficiency methods evaluate training programs according to the program's demand on time (the learner's), instructor and staff effort (time devoted to the project), and use of existing facilities (need for more space or numbers served in existing space). Program cost analysis includes calculating developmental costs (design, material, and equipment expenses), operational costs (recurring salaries, rent, maintenance, overhead, etc.), and instructional costs (cost of facilitator, cost of cyberspace, or cost per learner for a program).

Confirmative evaluation methods, which look at training results on an ongoing basis, are continual improvement methods. These methods examine, overtime, the impact upon all the learners or the organizational context. Within business and industry, confirmative evaluations are a series of post-program reviews, all compared against pre-set program criteria. Training programs in business or commercial enterprises usually have clearly defined program criteria that emphasize more than learner attendance or program completion records. Program criteria will relate to the appropriateness of training, competency development of employees, costs of ongoing delivery, and benefits to the organization. Any one or all of these criteria areas can be the focus of a post-program review. Post-program reviews might compare the organization's results to the criteria initially established or might re-examine the criteria against updated training practices, current competitor criteria, or criteria recommended within the adult education community.

The selection of which evaluation method to use will depend upon the type of evaluation needed, the timeframe available, and factors unique to your organization.

13.4 Report Writing and Audience

> *Full program evaluation reveals what the department's strengths and areas of improvement are in training. The organization uses this rating to determine the value of the learning department at both the learner and management level.*
>
> ***–Dr. Karen LaMarsh***
> *Continuing Education and*
> *Training Consultant*

Careful attention should be given to the summarizing and writing of the report of evaluations. It is important for others to be able to easily read and understand evaluation reports. Importantly, future support of training from line managers, as well as future financial allocations for training, will likely be influenced by the manner in which the evaluation report is written.

13.4.1 Results

Evaluation results must be carefully transformed from data, to information, to findings. Data collected from the methods and instruments used during the evaluation process will constitute a boatload of mere facts. The facts might be numerical or quantitative, as from a survey. Or, the data might be verbal and qualitative, as from interviews or focus group comments. In both instances, the initial result is only a group of data points. Through analysis of the quantitative data, descriptive information can be gained about frequency, averages, or most-often cited responses. Through analysis of the qualitative data, common themes and common values emerge which represent deeper thoughts or reasons for reactions. At this point, good information has been obtained, but only information has been gained. Findings result only after the summarized information is compared in some manner. Information can be compared to prior findings, historical information, or external information, such as industry standards or industry averages. The sharing of findings from evaluation efforts should be carefully managed in order to avoid preliminary or incorrect interpretations to be drawn by others.

13.4.2 Conclusions and Recommendations

Conclusions are drawn after comparison of evaluation findings with the standards or criteria set by the learning and development department. Conclusions can be based upon comparison of quantitative data to criteria, comparison of qualitative data to standards, or mixing both quantitative and qualitative data. Conclusions should be directed toward the original questions sought at the outset of the evaluation effort—questions about participant reaction, learning, application, or questions about achieving performance objectives, meeting business objectives, or meeting training goals. The conclusions drawn should answer the original question posed by the focus of the evaluation, be it formative (How *well* are we doing?), summative (How *did* we do?), or confirmative (How *are we still* doing?).

Recommendations are offered in response to conclusions reached and are often depicted as next steps. If one conclusion discovered discrepancies or inconsistencies, then the recommendation should offer ideas for resolution of the discrepancies or steps to assure consistency. If another conclusion drawn indicated progress being made, then the recommendation should address what type of work needs to continue to further that progress. If the conclusions are primarily supportive and indicate problem resolution, the recommendation should address whether or not training should be continued. It is important that the recommendations made be documented and specifically address current practices, so that improvements can be made to the training produced.

13.4.3 Evaluation Reports

Preparing the evaluation report needs careful attention in order to be of interest to readers and useful for decision makers. Care should be taken to present the focus of the evaluation, and thus, the applicability of conclusions reached, to the future of your program. For example—conclusions drawn from data in a formative evaluation should not be used to make decisions about program continuance but should be used to make decisions about planning upgrades, alterations, or re-design. Similarly, conclusions drawn from summative evaluations should not be used to make decisions about content additions or instructor changes. Summative evaluation results should be used to help make decisions about program effectiveness or efficiency. The presentation format of the report, itself, is also worth considering. Evaluation reports can be offered in a person-to-person conversational format, in a group presentation format with visuals, or in a written format as a document prepared for reading. You should format the report in a manner appropriate for your audience—to gain senior leader attention and to garner agreement with conclusions drawn. Table 13.1 illustrates a written evaluation report format.

Reports for executives are usually prepared in a written synopsis, while reports for managers are typically a verbal presentation of results, supported by a written document. The written report structure should be logically organized, with conclusions and recommendations highlighted first, and detailed data, data analyses, and findings presented in the body of the report. Sample responses or detailed analytics should be offered as addendum material.

Whichever evaluation focus and method(s) are utilized, accurate reporting of the evaluation process and careful recording of the results of evaluation studies are important professional learning and development practices.

It was easy to make the accreditation case to push forward for more uniformity in actually conducting real evaluations. I was able to generate some reports to give people a better insight into the outcomes of our programs and this is important for our funding. We have a few National Science Foundation grants, some private foundation grants, and corporate foundation grants. By having these evaluation strategies in place and being able to report on the outcomes was huge for us. We've been able to generate more grant funding as a result of meeting the requirements of the accreditation standards.

–Peter Finn
Society of Women Engineers
Deputy Executive Director and
Chief Learning Officer

Table 13.1 Evaluation report structure

EVALUATIVE REPORT	**Executive Summary**	**Brief Overview**	*Program Description*
			Evaluation Method
		Summarize Findings	*Key Findings*
		Next Steps	*Recommended Action Steps*
	Purpose of the Evaluation	**Scope– Program Description**	*Training Course*
			Timeframe
		Intention of Evaluation	*Formative, Summative or Confirmative*
		Accessibility	*Who will have access?*
			How report will be used
	Methodology of Evaluation	**Data Collection**	*Key Questions*
			Objective
			Participants
			Methodology
	Results		*Analysis*
			Findings
	Conclusions and Recommendations		*Meaningful Interpretations*
			Action Steps

13.5 Training Policy and Records

Accredited training programs carefully adhere to organizational policies which specifically address: the purpose and plan for learning and development within the organization; the execution of learning management within the organization; and the evaluation of training. Policies need to be established, maintained structurally, and results from evaluations recorded formally. Accurate records of learning activities need to be compiled and retained, along with documentation of learner privacy.

13.5.1 Policy

Learning and development policies that direct the training organization, its structure, purpose, and periodic evaluation, along with policies ensuring learner privacy, should be written and recorded.

13.5.1.1 Evaluation Policies

Evaluation policies should address expected evaluation activities, including purpose, frequency, and expected rigor. Some organizations elect to evaluate each training session offered to obtain learners' reaction, or to document participant learning (see Chapter 12, "Learner Feedback and Job Application"). Other times, organizations will set forth a policy standard for evaluation that directs rigor by type (formative, summative, or confirmative), breadth, and frequency. Regardless of the specific rigor dictated, accredited training programs assure that evaluation policies are documented which require a process and a reporting of evaluation results. Those policies need to be established, followed, and retained in order to formally evidence the continual improvement intent of the organization. When grounded in policy, program evaluation can be used for improvement in training management, improvement in the training experience, and improvement in the educational programs created.

13.5.1.2 Learner Privacy Policies

Learner privacy policies must also be documented and directed. This means a written policy, which assures the privacy and security of learner records, is established and followed. Learning experiences and educational success differ for each individual participating in workplace sponsored training. Individual workers are sensitive to personal training results because results can be used as a measure for their professional development and advancement or for job change. Supervisors are sensitive to training results in order to successfully guide the production efforts of employees on the job. As noted in Chapter 12, "Learner Feedback and Job Application", worker experiences during training sessions do not always translate to an immediate change in job action. The experience in any one course may not have a lasting impact (job transfer) on a learner's ultimate work performance. Thus, the recorded experience of individuals during single training sessions is a sensitive and private matter. A learner privacy policy must assure that privacy is maintained by all learning and development staff in the establishment, maintenance, and release of individual training records. Individual records should be released only with the consent of the individual and notification to the individual. Further, the written copy of the organization's learner privacy policy should be made available to all individuals who participate in training.

13.5.2 Results and Record Maintenance

Results of training events, learner participation, and evaluations conducted should be maintained and classified in an orderly document retention system. Maintenance of both training occurrence records and evaluation results provides a baseline for measuring future program improvements. Good records also enable retrieval for longitudinal program review and multi-year reporting.

13.5.2.1 Training Event Records

Training event records should document the execution of each training session or course and should include the following items:

- Course description—include any code for linking events with other courses or programs,
- Dates—both offering date(s) and completion date(s),
- Length—hours of time in training or professional development,
- Number of CEUs—approved per course.

13.5.2.2 Learner Documentation

Learner documentation is the file or record documenting each individual's participation in continuing education offered by your organization. Learner records need to be an official file retained on a learning management system (LMS) or human resource information system (HRIS). Learner records need to be secured from manipulation and should include the following items:

- Learner name and unique identifier (PIN, employee ID number, etc.)
- Programs completed—titles, dates, and codes for all programs attended, with attendance differentiated from completion
- Number of CEUs awarded—related per completed course
- Additional information (progress toward certification, licensure, or series)
- Confirmation of informing individual—successful completion notice or certificate.

13.5.3 Record Maintenance

All records of training efforts and learner participation should be carefully maintained. Permanent record keeping means an official file is maintained and a back-up system is in place to replace employee learning records in case of loss, breach (hacking), or theft. These records may need to be available for an indefinite amount of time, both for management access and for worker access even beyond the tenure of any single employee.

> *We had a learning data base. Most of it was digital. We would keep every single agenda, program outline, calendar, PowerPoint, and video tape of instructors. We'd be able to compare and contrast implementation every six months or so. If we hired new trainers or coaches to our staff, we had recorded content there to help them come up to speed. I found it very useful; we did not have to depend upon an oral tradition. Retaining all the elements helped to make our accreditation easier, too.*
>
> ***–Scott A. Critchfield, CFP***
> *Coach, Learning Professional*

Conducting quality evaluations of training programs requires a willingness to self-examine all aspects of a learning and development department. This should lead to critical reviews of which aspects of the training effort are strong and which are weaker in both design and execution. The evaluation process can be lengthy with accurate findings and conclusions requiring diligence. With management patience throughout the process, high-quality program evaluations can be specific in offering a good critical appraisal of the learning and development department's efforts and results. A secure recordkeeping system which documents the evaluation effort can not only help to defend the critical review process conducted by the learning and development department but can also justify the expense and expertise needed for upgrades to the learning system within the organization.

13.6 Conclusion

Self-evaluations of learning and development department programs are critical to obtaining accreditation. Accredited training programs establish comprehensive evaluations in order to make continual structural and operational improvements. Carefully documented evaluation findings can assist in making pinpointed recommendations for quality improvement and continuity—and this is a great help to managers of learning and development departments. Full program evaluations have a defined purpose, a focus (formative, summative, or confirmative), and are comprehensive in scope. Importantly, well-kept records of evaluation reports can both evidence areas for improvement and document continued successes.

Manager Tips

A. Seek to self-examine your full learning and development program in accordance with the culture or your organization.
B. Decide upon a focus and approach to evaluation that can identify both strengths and weaknesses in order to both document successes and make improvements in your learning programs.
C. Commit to the professional development of your learning and development staff in order to build technical skills in formative, summative and confirmative evaluation work.
D. Match evaluation methods and procedures to the formative, summative or confirmative answers sought.
E. Try for more than Level 1 or Level 2 evaluations.
F. Carefully consider the audience for evaluation reports and prepare reports accordingly.
G. Distinguish clearly among data, information, findings, conclusions, and recommendations.
H. Help executives and leaders understand evaluation results by presenting conclusions, and recommendations first, and analysis data second.
I. Maintain policies on both conducting evaluations and learner privacy.
J. Assure accurate retention of training information on a secure record keeping system.

Supplement

Supplement Tool 13A: Level 1 Sample Evaluation Form

Title of Training Course: ______________________________

Date of Session: ______________________________

Learning and Development Program		Little Value ← → Highest Value				
		1	**2**	**3**	**4**	**5**
1	The learning program met my expectations	1	2	3	4	5
2	The learning program objectives were met	1	2	3	4	5
3	The materials distributed were appropriate and useful	1	2	3	4	5
4	The topics covered were relevant to the program objectives	1	2	3	4	5
5	The training activities were useful	1	2	3	4	5
6	The time allotted for training was sufficient.	1	2	3	4	5
7	This learning experience was beneficial	1	2	3	4	5
8	The venue met my expectations	1	2	3	4	5
9	The service by support staff met my expectations	1	2	3	4	5
10	Overall rating of the program met my expectations	1	2	3	4	5

Trainer/Instructor		Little Value ← → Highest Value				
1	Knowledgeable in content areas	1	2	3	4	5
2	Clarified content in response to questions	1	2	3	4	5
3	Visual aids, hand outs, and oral presentations clarified content	1	2	3	4	5
4	Teaching methods were appropriate for subject matter	1	2	3	4	5
5	Overall rating of the trainer/instructor	1	2	3	4	5

Additional Comments:

Recommendations for Improvement:

References

Brinkerhoff, R. O. (1987). *Achieving results from training.* San Francisco, CA: Jossey-Bass.

Kirkpatrick, D. L. (1998). *Evaluating training programs* (2nd ed.). San Francisco, CA: Berrett-Koehler.

Phillips, J. J. (1996, April). Measuring ROI: The fifth level of evaluation. *Technical Skills Training, 7*(3), 10–13.

Phillips, J. J. (2003). *Return on investment in training performance improvement programs* (2nd ed.). Burlington, MA: Butterworth-Heinemann.

14

Accreditation Sources

"Accreditation is both a process and a status" (CHEA 2012). Accredited or accreditation status is granted to programs that meet or exceed the established standard of educational quality for training and education. It ensures quality assurance, as discussed in Chapter 1, "Introduction". Accreditation presents a strong value proposition; however, as a process, it can be a daunting endeavor. The process involves the content, policies, and practices of a learning and development program to be measured against a set of established standards and then scrutinized by representatives of an outside agency. Moreover, the process can be time-consuming, expensive and requires budgeting for the allocation of resources. Some of the most common challenges in accreditation are budget, workload, and uncertainty. Frustration and even anxiety have been equated to the accreditation process (Cerqueira 2006; Hasbun and Rudolph 2016). In this final chapter, the authors aim to minimize the apprehension toward accreditation. First, the preliminary steps to the accreditation process will be introduced; standards for meeting accreditation requirements will be reviewed; considerations for selecting an accrediting body will be discussed; and finally, resources and tips for success in the accreditation process will be shared.

14.1 Pre-steps to Achieve Accreditation

According to both practitioners and educators who were interviewed for this book, the challenge to accreditation is not the actual accreditation process, but the lack of preparation to begin the process. Therefore, provisional

W. J. Rothwell et al., *Increasing Learning & Development's Impact through Accreditation*,
https://doi.org/10.1007/978-3-030-14004-5_14

preparatory steps are recommended. Figure 14.1 was developed as a result of practitioner recommendations. Their direct experience reflects how various organizations from different industries encountered similar difficulties as they navigated through a practical accreditation journey.

14.2 Clarify Purpose

You have to understand that accreditation is not a requirement… so the argument has to be more than a 'nice-to-have'. It has to be how it impacts the client directly. You've got to understand, who is going to be more effective, or how is it going to direct more business… and then be able to articulate it to leadership.

*–**Clyde Seepersad***
Linux Foundation
General Manager,
Training & Certification

There are a number of benefits associated with accreditation, but the main purpose should be tied directly to the learning and development mission and vision statements, as well as to the organization's strategic objectives, as discussed in Chapter 2, "Align Learning with Organization Mission and Values". One suggestion is to conduct a Strengths, Weaknesses/Areas for improvement, Opportunities, Threats (SWOT) analysis to provide a comprehensive view of whether accreditation should be pursued. The SWOT can help specify the main purpose of pursuing accreditation and can assist in the development of a value proposition. A value proposition:

- explains how accreditation will resolve or improve the conditions for learning and development,
- clarifies specific value to the organization from being accredited,
- markets the idea of becoming accredited.

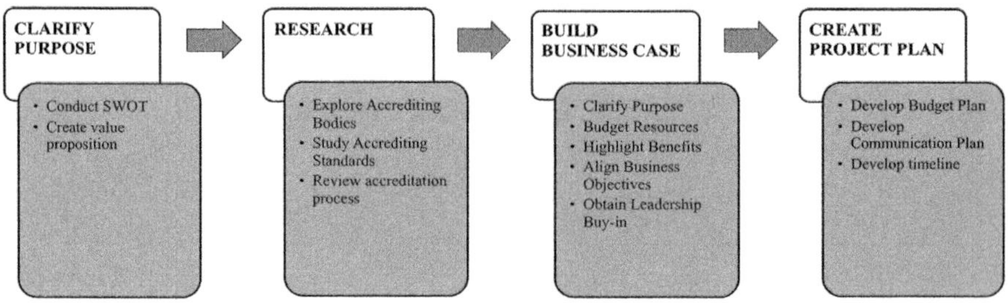

Fig. 14.1 Pre-steps to achieve accreditation

14.3 Research

An accrediting body examines and evaluates a program or institution to ensure that it meets published standards. Experts in each field typically establish these standards. Several bodies exist which accredit training programs. Some are associated with specific industries, such as the Society for Engineering Standards, the Society of Corporate Compliance and Ethics, the Society of Human Resources Management (SHRM), and the Bankers Associations (i.e., American Bankers Association). Many of these bodies offer training, themselves, to member companies or member organizations. Accreditation is also offered via professional membership dedicated to a specific field of practice, such as the American Institute of CPAs, the Council of Engineering and Scientific Society Executives, or Robert Morris Associates. Still, other organizations promote accreditation as part of an organizational mission, offering accreditation to training providers based upon learning processes rather than content. These independent accrediting bodies include such names as Accrediting Council for Continuing Education and Training (ACCET) or the International Association of Continuing Education and Training (IACET). To determine the best fit, it is important to research the accrediting bodies to comprehend the learning and training standards required.

14.3.1 Accrediting Bodies

Accreditors are private, non-profit membership organizations that abide by specific quality standards, policies, and processes to review programs. The role of accrediting bodies focuses on the issues of quality assurance. Generally, accreditors utilize two forms of review, the self-review process whereby a program examines its own operation based on the standards of the accreditor, and the peer-review process where external professionals examine the program based on the standards. Accredited status is awarded for a specific time period, typically 3–10 years, and requires learning programs to undertake a secondary review for reaccreditation.

Accrediting bodies differ in several ways: the nature of the criteria used; the way standards are developed; and how compliance with standards is measured. There are several types of accrediting bodies including voluntary associations based on membership, government or government-commissioned organizations, industry, and professional organizations. Table 14.1 lists those that accredit institutes, universities, colleges, schools, and vocational training entities.

Table 14.1 Accrediting Bodies

ACCREDITING AGENCY	BACKGROUND	WEBSITE
Accreditation Council for Continuing Medical Education (ACCME)	Accredits institutions and organizations that offer continuing medical education (CME) programs that support healthcare professionals maintain competence and learn about new and developing areas of their field.	www.accme.org
Accrediting Council for Continuing Education and Training (ACCET)	Accredits programs throughout the United States of institutions of higher education that offer continuing education and vocational programs that confer certificates or occupational associate degrees, including those programs offered via distance education. These continuing education and training programs are private career schools, corporate learning and development departments, intensive English teaching programs, trade associations, labor union training programs, religious organizations, public affairs societies, and volunteer organizations. ACCET is officially recognized by the US Department of Education and the International Organization for Standardization.	www.accet.org
American Nurses Credentialing Center (ANCC)	Accredits programs that provide high-quality continuing nursing education (CNE) and skills-based competency programs. A key factor to increasing organizational competitiveness, are the development and acquisition of relevant knowledge, skills and abilities to effectively perform in the workplace. Accreditation of training programs will ensure that quality of learning are not compromised but are measured against a set of external standards. Training standards have been developed as a tool and resource to help organizations continually improve their learning interventions.	www.nursingworld.org
Council on Occupational Education	A regional accrediting association for postsecondary occupational education institutions. They represents regional institutions in the public, private, Job Corps, Army, Navy, Department of Defense, and private industry sectors. Recognized by the US Department of Education, COE oversees more than 430 associate degree-and non-degree granting education institutions.	www.council.org

(continued)

Table 14.1 (continued)

Distance Education &Training Council	A national accrediting agency that promotes and develops distance learning as a viable alternative to traditional learning systems. DETC accredits schools and colleges that encompass over 500 online degrees, correspondence programs, and other forms of distance education that range from very small, local educational institutions, to large multinational operations. The commission accredits schools and colleges by examining their educational, ethical, and business practices, approving only those who meet its strict criteria. DETC is recognized by the US Department of Education and the Council on Higher Education Accreditation.	www.deac.org
Distance Education Accrediting Commission (DEAC)	Accredits postsecondary institutions in the United States that offer degree and/or non-degree programs primarily by the distance or correspondence education methods. w	www.deac.org
International Association for Continuing Education and Training (IACET)	A non-profit association dedicated to quality continuing education and training programs. IACET is the only standard-setting organization accredited by the American National Standards Institute (ANSI) for continuing education and training. The ASNI/IACET Standard is the core of thousands of educational programs worldwide.	www.iacet.org
National Association of State Boards of Accountancy (NASBA)	A non-profit devoted to enhancing the effectiveness of the country's 55 state boards of accountancy. NASBA accredits training providers to issue Continuing Professional Education (CPE) units for Certified Public Accountants.	www.nasba.org

14.3.2 Standards

"Standards show clear benefits on certain issues, such as efficiency, employees, systematization, customers and other stakeholders, which indicates that, in general terms, certified firms improve people, operational and stakeholder performance" (see p. 307 in Tarí et al. 2012). Standards of practice for training and development professionals promotes the quality and accountability of learning interventions.

Specific professions, such as nursing or engineering, generally have their own profession-specific national standards that adhere to an accreditation process to ensure professional competencies. Most often the accreditation standards are incorporated in the license-to-practice requirements. Professional standards are crossing national borders through collaborative interactions between accrediting bodies and international professional associations (Stanley 2012). Many standards cross-reference each other, and some are more specific to a domain or industry.

14.3.2.1 American National Standards Institute (ANSI)

The American National Standards Institute (ANSI) is the US standards and conformity assessment system. "The Institute oversees the creation, promulgation and use of thousands of norms and guidelines that directly impact businesses in nearly every sector: from acoustical devices to construction equipment, from dairy and livestock production to energy distribution, and many more. ANSI is also actively engaged in accreditation - assessing the competence of organizations determining conformance to standards." ANSI is the official US representative to the International Organization for Standardization (ISO) (www.ansi.org/about).

14.3.2.2 International Organization for Standardization (ISO)

The International Organization for Standardization (ISO) is a non-governmental organization that brings experts together to establish a consensus-based standard for "products, services and systems, to ensure quality, safety and efficiency" (www.iso.org). ISO is a worldwide federation of national standard bodies from more than 145 countries, one from each country, whose mission is to promote the development of standardization and related activities in the world, with a view to facilitating the international exchange of goods and services and to developing cooperation in the spheres of intellectual, scientific, technological, and economic activity. ISO's work results in international agreements that are published as International Standards and other types of ISO documents (www.ansi.org/standards_activities/ iso_programs/overview). The international advantage of the standards means that an organization in the USA can be assessed or tested to the same standards as an organization in the UK, to provide quality assurance in the comparability of accreditation across international borders.

14.3.2.3 Learning and Development Standards

A key factor to increasing organizational competitiveness is the development and acquisition by organizational workers of relevant knowledge, skills, and abilities to effectively perform in the workplace. Training standards have been developed as a tool and resource to help organizations continually improve their learning programs, events, and interventions (Table 14.2).

Table 14.2 Accreditation standards for learning and development

Standards	Background	Website
ISO Quality Management System Standard for Education and Training	ISO 29990:2010 is a quality management system standard for education and training that concentrates on learning and the improvement of the learning process. It provides a generic model for quality professional practice and performance, and a common reference for learning service providers (LSPs) and their clients in the design, development and delivery of non-formal education, training and development.	www.iso.org/standard/53392.html
Accrediting Council for Continuing Education & Training (ACCET) Standards for Accreditation	The ACCET standards represents good practice against which continuing education and training institutions and programs can be evaluated and improved; guides on-site reviews and relevant reports, and enables governmental agencies, employers, participants, and the general public to know the criteria by which an accredited institution or program has been evaluated.	www.docs.accet.org/downloads/docs/doc2.pdf
ANSI/IACET Standard for CEU	The ANSI/IACET Standard for Continuing Education and Training is a universal model for learning process excellence. It defines a proven model for developing effective and valuable continuing education and training (CE/T) programs by measuring a CE/T provider's training program from procedure to process to result.	www.iacet.org/standards
International Board of Standards for Training, Performance and Instruction (IBSTPI)	The International Board of Standards for Training, Performance and Instruction (ibstpi®) is a not-for-profit corporation that provides leadership to the community by setting the standards.	www.ibstpi.org/

14.4 Build Business Case

A business case is first developed during the initial research and is the justification to apply for accreditation. It outlines *why*, *how*, and *how much* is necessary. You should prepare your business case for acceptance or approval by the senior leaders within your organization. The business case for accreditation can play a significant role in the decision to support, plan, and allocate resources. You will need those resources in order to execute the accreditation process and to formally achieve accreditation. It will provide practical guidance for managing the accreditation project and can reveal critical success factors, competitor positions, and contingencies to consider. Preparing the business case involves an assessment of a business problem or opportunity and then outlines the benefits, risks, and business impact of accreditation, and most importantly, the business case compares the resource cost of accreditation to the quality cost of non-accreditation.

14.5 Create Project Plan

The goal of creating a project plan is to help facilitate the accreditation process. The Accreditation Project Plan outlines the persons responsible, critical tasks, and key due dates. The plan outline will also help communicate to executives and to other key stakeholders about every step and milestone toward accreditation status. Milestones can be helpful in organizing each step of the accreditation process (Table 14.3).

Table 14.3 Project plan for accreditation (Template)

PROJECT TITLE:				
		PROJECT TEAM		
	NAME	AREA OF EXPERTISE	DEPARTMENT	EMAIL
PROJECT LEAD				
EXECUTIVE SPONSOR				
ACCREDITATION COORDINATOR				
TEAM MEMBERS				
TEAM MEMBERS				
TEAM MEMBERS				
ACCREDITATION BENEFITS:	Accreditation will result in the following outcomes: • • •			
PROJECT OBJECTIVES: **S**pecific **M**easurable **A**chievable **R**elevant **T**imely	The overarching project objectives are: • • • •			

(continued)

Table 14.3 (continued)

PROJECT MILESTONES	**MILESTONE**	**EXPECTED DATE**	**DELIVERABLE**
	Verify Eligibility		
	Review Standards		
	Self-Audit		
	Modify Polices and Processes		
	Examine Needs Analysis		
	Modify Design Documents		
	Submit Application		
	Prepare of Site Visit		

RISK PLAN	
ASSUMPTIONS	CONSTRAINTS

COMMUNICATION PLAN				
SUBJECT	METHOD	FREQUENCY	GOAL	AUDIENCE

(continued)

Table 14.3 (continued)

BUDGET PLAN		
	Estimated Cost	Actual Cost
Accreditation Fee		

14.6 Accreditation Process

The accreditation process is a voluntary review designed to be supportive and objective. It allows organizations to demonstrate their ability to meet standard requirements established by a recognized accrediting body (see Table 14.1). A generalized accreditation process is presented in Fig. 14.2.

Initially, organizations must meet the minimum requirements in order to submit an application. It is essential to become familiar with the accrediting body's specific process and the application cost. Organizations are recommended to conduct a self-audit to make sure their current policies, procedures, and practices adhere to the standards. Compliance is determined by evaluation of written documents provided by the organization and by on-site inspection. Accreditation is awarded upon successful documentation of compliance with the current standards.

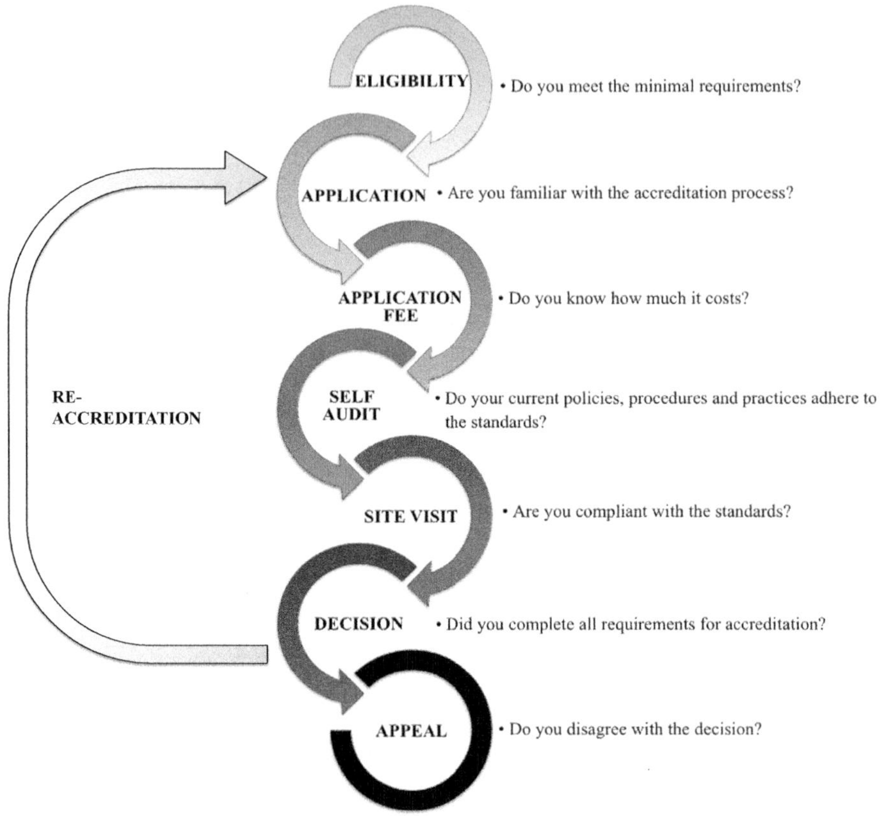

Fig. 14.2 Accreditation process

14.7 Recommendation and Tips

The work needed for accreditation is arduous, regardless of the size of the program. Lots of paperwork will be required in a strict timeline. Contents of learning programs will be scrutinized. Learning and development standards will be strictly required. However, depending on the accrediting body selected, a self-assessment and resources will be provided to assist in the process.

> *One of the first thing you do is try to allay the fears of the organizations that you're going to see. If you have a welcome call with them, then you try to put them at ease and allow them to ask any question they want to ask and remind them that we are there to help them and that the whole point of this is to give them support and answer their questions.*
>
> ***–Dr. Maureen C. Jones***
> *The Pennsylvania State University*
> *Accreditation Coordinator for the MHA Programs*

Practitioners, educators, and accrediting reviewers were interviewed to help identify best practices for success during the accreditation process (see Table 14.4). Based upon both literature research and practitioner information, the following is a list of tips and recommendations:

- Identify who will be in charge of overseeing the accreditation process,
- Develop a business case with a value proposition,
- Create a project plan,
- Allot ample amount of resources (time, money, and people),
- Research organizations and standards prior to beginning the accreditation process,
- Attend workshops and get involved with the accreditation process,
- Begin reading these materials well in advance,
- Be organized and document all steps,
- Talk with those who have been successful,
- Conduct a thorough self-assessment/audit of your organization.

Table 14.4 Recommendation and tips for accreditation: Quotes from practitioners and educators

RECOMMENDATION/ TIPS	QUOTE	PRACTITIONER / EDUCATOR	ORGANIZATION/ POSITION
Attend Workshops	*Go to the accrediting body's workshop at the outset and get an understanding of the standard and what their expectations are.*	**Dr. J. Kevin Perry**	**Society of Automotive Engineers (SAE) International** Director, Professional Development
Be organized	*Be organized. The accreditation process can take upwards of two years to complete.*	**Reg Bonfoco**	Canadian Financial Securities Company Continuing Education Specialist
Budget for the accreditation process	*Make sure you speak with the 'powers that be' within your organization to have a budget set up for this. Because a lot of organizations don't have the budget and then when it comes to the actual accreditation payment, that's where a lot of organizations will go, 'Oh my God, how are going to pay for all of this'. And it's not just the application fee–have the proper budget in place for the entire process*	**Reg Bonfoco**	Canadian Financial Securities Company Continuing Education Specialist
Build rapport with the accrediting body	*In a positive visit there was openness of dialogue and discussion and wanting to know more. In a negative one it seemed that the visitor had kind of a preconceived notion about who we are.*	**Dr. Kyle Schiefelbein-Guerrero**	**Graduate Theological Union** Director of Digital Learning
Build the business case	*Build that business case. It is really important to make the case to the C suite or to the CEO. The business case is huge, because without it, you're not going to have a chance.*	**Peter Finn**	**Society of Women Engineers (SWE)** Deputy Executive Director and Chief Learning Officer
Conduct a high-level audit	*Conduct a high-level audit to have a baseline information as you're beginning to think about the accreditation process.*	**Peter Finn**	**Society of Women Engineers (SWE)** Deputy Executive Director and Chief Learning Officer

(continued)

Table 14.4 (continued)

RECOMMENDATION/ TIPS	QUOTE	PRACTITIONER / EDUCATOR	ORGANIZATION/ POSITION
Consult with Education Specialist	*Our learning solutions manager is an adult education specialist with a different perspective from the rest of the team, who are from technical fields with a technical orientation focused on content. (This technical leaning seems to be common in corporate universities.) Our education specialist clarified what was being asked for in the accreditation process.*	Anonymous	Multi-National Energy Corporation Technical Learning & Development Manager
Create a project Management	*Have a project charter and if the organization has a project management group, get them involved right away. The project manager could actually help guide the entire process.*	**Reg Bonfoco**	Canadian Financial Securities Company Continuing Education Specialist
Do little by little every day	*Best way to prepare for accreditation is to just be aware of it all the time and do little by little every day.*	**Dr. Arthur Holder**	**Graduate Theological Union** Accreditation Liaison Officer (ALO)
Document and communicate with senior leaders	*Have clear and constant communication with the senior leaders, especially whoever will be signing-off on the final documents to be submitted.*	**Reg Bonfoco**	Canadian Financial Securities Company Continuing Education Specialist
Document your process	*Have a process in place and document every step as you go. Make notes of level or by a course level, you know exactly the process you have to take. These accreditations can last anywhere from three to five years. By the time you come up for renewal, the person who completed the process, may not necessarily be in that seat when it comes up for renewal. Have everything completely documented. And everything that you went through.*	**Reg Bonfoco**	Canadian Financial Securities Company Continuing Education Specialist

(continued)

Table 14.4 (continued)

RECOMMENDATION/ TIPS	QUOTE	PRACTITIONER / EDUCATOR	ORGANIZATION/ POSITION
Document you process	*Sometimes, even if you don't have any type of written process, like for instance, we had the swim charts and the graphs and that was easy for me to turn into a word document and make it the official process with the swim chart as an attachment. But I would imagine if someone didn't have anything documented, bet it's in someone's head. And that's a really good reason to get it out of their head and onto paper. Because people change positions. They moved to other departments. They moved to other companies. They retire. So, it really is a good opportunity for knowledge transfer and knowledge capture. Make sure you get it and have it documented.*	Anonymous	Multi-National Energy Corporation Technical Learning & Development Manager
Find the best-fit.	*Well, one of the first things that I always look at is organization -of-best- fit. Let's just say for example, there's five accrediting bodies. Once you do your research on each of those five, which organization closer matches your organization's culture, the mission and the vision so that way it makes it feel like they're part of the team. It's almost like another department.*	**Reg Bonfoco**	Canadian Financial Securities Company Continuing Education Specialist
Get involved	*Get involved! Go to the meetings ... talk to the people. Don't just go to the raining sessions .... volunteer to be an evaluator or to be on a visiting team ... because that's the way you really see 'how the sausage is made'–from the inside. Get involved on the inside ...so you can, shift away from 'the accreditor is THEM' to 'the accrediting process involves all of us and we're a part of This'. That shift ... both demystifies and gives a more self reflective position about accreditation.*	**Dr. Arthur Holder**	**Graduate Theological Union** Accreditation Liaison Officer (ALO)
Have the right people on your team	*Definitely have a team of all the right people. You want the right people on your team. Look at what are the different processes that are required and identify who owns those processes or those activities. Even if you don't have a formal process in place, someone is responsible for those activities and be sure you have them on board and aware of what's going on.*	Anonymous	Multi-National Energy Corporation Technical Learning & Development Manager

(continued)

Table 14.4 (continued)

RECOMMENDATION/ TIPS	QUOTE	PRACTITIONER / EDUCATOR	ORGANIZATION/ POSITION
Know the language of the standards	*Although it can seem very boring, it is important to read through the standards and to have them handy …and acquire the language.*	**Dr. Kyle Schiefelbein-Guerrero**	**Graduate Theological Union** Director of Digital Learning
Lean into the process	*There is a lot to gain from the process. So, don't approach it as just as set of things to check the box … really lean into it. You will find some things that may surprise you to make your operations better. I think there is a tendency to treat it like process and all you want is to be done with it … So that's the one piece of advice I give to people, I understand the temptation, I have been there. But if you really step into it… you will find surprising ways to make your company better … to make your product better.*	**Clyde Seepersad**	**Linux Foundation** General Manager, Training & Certification
Learn from the process	*It was a process of reflection. I learned a lot going through the accreditation process. So, it was just a great learning experience all the way around. As I went through the standard, just really thinking hard about what we're not doing and what we need to be doing better, I was able to evolve of our program. That was a huge takeaway for me. I mean, it was challenging but positive. I think as a result, the organization is better for it, because it's now, the fundamentals of the standards are kind of baked into our culture and in our strategy, it is really part of the fabric of the organization now.*	**Peter Finn**	**Society of Women Engineers (SWE)** Deputy Executive Director and Chief Learning Officer
Look critically at what you are doing	*Just start looking critically at some of what you're doing. Although it may be difficult, because you don't know what you don't know. But you should be able to do a critical audit of what you have, what your strengths are, and where you need some consistencies. So, I think you should take a critical look at what it is you're doing and the processes that you have in place.*	**Peter Finn**	**Society of Women Engineers (SWE)** Deputy Executive Director and Chief Learning Officer

(continued)

Table 14.4 (continued)

RECOMMENDATION/ TIPS	QUOTE	PRACTITIONER / EDUCATOR	ORGANIZATION/ POSITION
Talk to others who have completed the process	*Find another similar organization that's already gone through it and ... look for an opportunity to talk with that project manager about their experience.*	**Dr. J. Kevin Perry**	**Society of Automotive Engineers (SAE)** International Director, Professional Development
Use available resources	*There are ample resources available before you start putting money down and start the process. There are some resources available to just get you started or at least get you doing a high-level audit. There are enough resources so people don't feel too intimidated when they're starting their journey and they can kind of start checking on some things internally.*	**Peter Finn**	**Society of Women Engineers (SWE)** Deputy Executive Director and Chief Learning Officer
Utilize accreditor's resources (commissioner, workshops, tools, publications)	*The closer the organization works with the commissioner the smoother the matter, logging on to the website and listening, and reading all the different information that's on their website about the accreditation process. If you don't take advantage of that, you're going to be in a real humdinger when it comes to submitting. So, not only work with the commissioner, but also, read all the information on the accrediting body's website. The information is there. People need to truly take advantage of it and try to wrap their heads around the entire process because yes, it is very cumbersome.*	**Reg Bonfoco**	Canadian Financial Securities Company Continuing Education Specialist
Utilize your team	*Accreditation is a team effort because have to consult with other people who work in your department or with a constituency that you're serving.*	**Dr. Arthur Holder**	**Graduate Theological Union** Accreditation Liaison Officer (ALO)

14.8 Conclusions

Research has indicated that accreditation contributes to improvements in training quality, increases in learning productivity, and superior educational products. Accreditation standards that are aligned with professional competencies and which include evaluation and review rigor can ensure learning quality improvement practices. Accredited learning programs establish reputational advantage and organizational credibility because the education provided to employees really does transfer to practice and job application. Further, the coveted seal of approval offered through accreditation can help learning and development programs attract both expert instructors and learning-focused workers.

Looking forward, it is important to consider the constant evolution of work and the continuous changes needed to deliver timely and focused learning events. The trend toward a gig-economy is in full force. However, it is difficult to predict how fast the world of work will move toward a fully automated workplace. According to PwC's report *Workforce of the Future: The competing forces shaping 2030*, by 2030 "the number of US workers in full-time 'permanent' employment drops to 9% of the workforce, an all-time low" (2017, p. 12). The skills needed for the future are still unknown, but one thing is for certain, organizational changes will drive the need to adapt. Employability will require job mobility, workplace agility, and the continuous acquisition of new skills. The learning responsibility will shift toward the individual and drive a greater need for high-quality ongoing education and training from a variety of sources.

Implementing continuously improved learning and establishing standards for training development are needed to meet future demands of the global workforce and serve these flextime workers. Importantly, accountability of learning and development will also increase in the foreseeable future. Program accreditation as an insignia of high-quality work-related training and education will remain. As education evolves to address future talent needs, these factors place great demand on learning and development departments to seek and retain accreditation.

Manager Tips

A. Do your homework and learn everything you can about the process and the standards.
B. Attend accreditation training sessions.
C. Talk to colleagues at accredited organization who serve as peer reviewers about any recommended tips or suggestions about the process.
D. Talk with other accredited providers who completed the process and inquire about their experience and lessons learned.
E. Build a business case for engaging in the pursuit of accreditation in order to run a world class learning function at your organization.

Supplement

Supplement Tool 14A: Accreditation Readiness Checklist

Directions: Use this readiness checklist to determine if you are ready for accreditation.

Questions:

Pre-Accreditation Process	*YES*	*NO*
Conducted a SWOT of Learning and Development Program to determine if accreditation is appropriate.		
Established a value proposition for accreditation.		
Selected the "best-fit" accrediting body.		
Met eligibility requirements.		
Reviewed accreditation process.		
Obtained key stakeholders buy-in.		
Aligned learning and development with the organization's mission and value.		
Structured learning and development in the organization to ensure accountability.		
Managed the learning and development function effectively.		
Developed a strategic plan for learning and development.		
Assessed the needs of the learner to determine the best solution.		
Clarified the desired outcomes for learning and development programs.		
Clarified who is qualified to be involved in delivering learning interventions.		
Established standards for effective instructional delivery.		
Decided what is essential to address in learning and development programs.		
Ensured consistency across learning and development programs so that learners in one program receive treatment comparable to learners in other, similar programs.		
Took steps to ensure that learning transfers effectively back to the job and improves job performance.		
Have complete and required records and ways to ensure effective program evaluation.		
Referenced resources to become accredited.		

References

Braun, B. (2005). Building global institutions: The diffusion of management standards in the world economy—An institutional perspective. In C. G. Alvstam & E. W. Schamp (Eds.), *Linking industries across the world* (pp. 3–27). London: Ashgate.

Cerqueira, M. (2006). *A literature review on the benefits, challenges and trends in accreditation as a quality assurance system.*

Council for Higher Education Accreditation (CHEA). (2012). *The value of accreditation.* Washington DC: Council for Higher Education Accreditation.

Hasbun, T. C., & Rudolph, A. (2016). Navigating the waters of accreditation: Best practices, challenges, and lessons learned from one institution. *SAGE Open, 6*(2), 2158244016656719.

PwC. (2017). *Workforce of the future: The competing forces shaping 2030.* www.pwc.com/gx/en/services/people-organisation/workforce-of-the-future/workforce-of-the-future-the-competing-forces-shaping-2030-pwc.pdf.

Stanley, G. (2012). Challenges in the quest to create global qualifications and standards are driving change in education systems. In W. Bienkowski, J. C. Brada & G. Stanley (Eds.), *The university in the age of globalization* (pp. 3–25). London: Palgrave Macmillan.

Tarí, J. J., Molina-Azorín, J. F., & Heras, I. (2012). Benefits of the ISO 9001 and ISO 14001 standards: A literature review. *Journal of Industrial Engineering and Management, 5*(2), 297–322. https://doi.org/10.3926/jiem.488.

Index

W. J. Rothwell et al., *Increasing Learning & Development's Impact through Accreditation*, https://doi.org/10.1007/978-3-030-14004-5

D

E

Printed by Printforce, the Netherlands